Uneasy Transiti

Education and Alienation Series

Series Editor: Neville Jones, Principal Educational Psychologist, Oxfordshire

Special Educational Needs Review Volume 1
Edited by Neville Jones, Oxfordshire County Council

Disaffection from School? The Early Years
Edited by Gill Barrett, Bristol Polytechnic

School Management and Pupil Behaviour
Edited by Neville Jones, Oxfordshire County Council

Consultancy in the United Kingdom
Edited by Carol Aubrey, University of Durham

Education and Alienation in the Junior School
Edited by Jim Docking, Roehampton Institute, London

Special Educational Needs Review Volume 2
Edited by Neville Jones, Oxfordshire County Council

Exploring the Roots of Disaffection
Patricia Potts, The Open University

Needs, Rights and Opportunities
Caroline Roaf, Peers School, Oxford, and Hazel Bines, Oxford Polytechnic

Refocusing Educational Psychology
Edited by Neville Jones, Oxfordshire County Council, and Norah Frederickson, Buckinghamshire County Council and London University

Uneasy Transitions: Disaffection in Post-compulsory Education and Training
Edited by Jenny Corbett, Polytechnic of East London

Uneasy Transitions

Disaffection in post-compulsory
education and training

Edited by
Jenny Corbett

The Falmer Press

(A Member of the Taylor & Francis Group)
London · New York · Philadelphia

UK   The Falmer Press, Rankine Road, Basingstoke, Hampshire,
            RG24 OPR

USA   The Falmer Press, Taylor & Francis Inc., 1900 Frost Road,
            Suite 101, Bristol, PA 19007

First published 1990

British Library Cataloguing in Publication Data
Uneasy transitions: disaffection in post-compulsory
    education and training. — (Education and alienation
    series).
    1. England. Schools. Students. Disaffection
    I. Corbett, Jenny   II. Series
    372.181

ISBN 1-85000-795-0
ISBN 1-85000-796-9   pbk

**Library of Congress Cataloging-in-Publication Data is available on
request**

Jacket design by Caroline Archer

Typeset in 11/13 Garamond by
Chapterhouse, The Cloisters, Formby L37 3PX

*Printed in Great Britain by Burgess Science Press, Basingstoke
on paper which has a specified pH value on final paper
manufacture of not less than 7.5 and is therefore 'acid free'.*

Contents

To Felix and Ben

Introduction:
Uneasy Transitions and the Challenge of Change

Jenny Corbett

This book is one of a series being published as part of the work being carried out on the Disaffected Pupil Programme in Oxfordshire (DPP). Each of the books in the series examines factors which prevent positive learning taking place, evaluates practice which enhances learning and describes the multi-dimensional phenomenon of disaffection. It is in the nature of a programme related to the 'Disaffected Pupil' that it should be concerned with learning and personal development during primary and secondary education with a consequent focus upon the society and culture of schools. This book moves into a broader social and political context. *Uneasy Transitions* introduces the more open, diverse and complex arena of post-compulsory education and training.

The distinction between education and training, already widening within curricular divisions from 14+ in secondary schooling, is a potent source of disaffection. Taking either the 'education' or the 'training' path will define individual status ('student' or 'trainee'), career prospects and working conditions in adult life, for:

> It is only the fictional environment of training that allows us to abstract job content from job context: in reality, they are inter-mixed. Work is best defined not as a particular kind of activity but as a particular socio-economic relationship.
>
> (Squires, 1987, pp. 66–67)

It is at transition to the world of adult autonomy, employment, training or continued education that a marginalized status becomes uncomfortably evident. Gleeson (1984) emphasizes the force of this devaluing process, which he terms society's 'cultural ambivalence about the educational requirements of so-called "less able" young people' — referred to here as 'someone else's children' (pp. 110–111). It is 'someone else's children' who are the recipients of poor quality training schemes into unskilled work. The

1

different career prospects of 18-year-olds entering higher education and those leaving Youth Training (YT) will be long-term and profound. The quality of post-compulsory provision for 'someone else's children' can be disregarded as it is outside the mainstream interest: witness the public outcry against parents paying full fees for higher education, yet minimal attention paid to the inequities in training programmes for the 'less able'.

Both the recipients and the providers of training for transition are caught up in the conflicts of changes beyond their control. Barton and Walker (1984) indicated that, already in the early 1980s, teachers were being confronted with a bewildering and constant array of reforms. This process of remorseless and relentless change has escalated throughout the 1980s. By 1990, practitioners in further education are having to cope with the impact of curriculum reform, new methods of administration, new training initiatives, tighter social security rulings and a move towards 'care in the community' as health and social services visibly decline. Individual expressions of disaffection have to be set in this turbulent context, in which opportunities for negotiation are negligible.

Feelings of discomfort, distrust and rejection can arise from the need of individuals to initiate change in and for themselves as well as from the impact of external forces. In both instances, overcoming disaffection demands the assumption of new responsibilities with their corresponding pressures. As I perceive the personal and social struggle which this challenge entails as one of conflict and difficulty, I have termed these various experiences of disaffection as 'uneasy transitions'.

At the micro-level, they describe personal transitions to a stage of increased autonomy or uncomfortable compromise. At the macro-level, they examine transitions in national, local and institutional policies with their often cumbersome growth and progress, yet undeniable power to enhance or suffocate initiative. As the examples to be discussed will illustrate, personal transitions cannot be divorced from the wider context in which they operate. The latter will dictate the level to which individual autonomy can aspire.

Disaffection and Change

The term 'disaffection' can be abused by association with violence, delinquency and vandalism, giving it a 'mindless' status. Whilst this might be a convenient analogy for the popular press, it fails to illuminate the sources which foster anger and disillusionment. Individual deficit models of disaffection support corporate complacency. Rather than being apparently unreasonable reactions, expressions of disaffection can be recognized as justifiable rationales of reasoned anger. Disaffection can reflect thoughtful resistance to perceived injustice or uneasiness towards the challenge of imposed change, which is a far from mindless response.

'Transition' implies change. Whether this change is forced from without or grows from within, it can often be threatening and frightening. Change is also fraught with contradictions. Barton and Walker (1984) suggest that 'the whole network of contradictions in which teachers operate, contradictions related to the difficulties of reconciling the needs of individuals with the interests of society, has been exposed in a most painful manner' (p. 6). In many instances, external pressures on practitioners actively obstruct ways in which they can support individual needs.

If it involves a shift in status through minority groups or subordinates asserting their rights, this change is generally accompanied by conflict. Sometimes it is necessary for individuals stereotyped into a passive role (the disabled, mentally handicapped, dependent women) to resist the oppression of apparent kindness:

> Just as young, gifted and black people have to face up to the reality of prejudice in society so — in their own way — do disabled people. This prejudice is perhaps not so overt as that which confronts black people but it is real nevertheless. It often manifests itself as kindness and concern, such that provision is made for us because we are not apparently capable of looking after ourselves, or because we should not be expected to do things that other people do.
>
> (Brisenden, 1989, p. 218)

One of the uncomfortable realities which is reinforced in the examples discussed in *Uneasy Transitions* is that it is invariably easier to sit back and accept the passive, submissive role than to challenge it. Challenging the stereotype and forcing a transition necessitates the renegotiating of former relationships with dominant protagonists. This uneasy process is often delayed until late in adult life (if it occurs at all) in the case of particularly dependent individuals. It might require a dramatic alteration in life roles and learning to play a more active part is undeniably a strain. The process of transition is uneasy because it demands involvement and initiative.

In relation to disabled students, for example, if they can become 'more aware of the ways in which society depowers people with disabilities, they can put their personal experiences into a wider political context' but this 'raises a major conflict between education as an ''opening out'' process and education as a process to maintain the status quo' (Fenton and Hughes, 1989, p. 81). A change in status for depowered individuals and minority groups threatens the status quo and is, therefore, dangerous.

The complex relationship between disaffection and the process of change is examined in relation to:

1. Individuals labelled as social inadequates and educational failures, influenced by political and economic factors beyond their control.
2. Difficulties of initiating changes in social status for marginalized groups, unused to political participacion.
3. Changes for formerly dependent individuals, which involve the rejection of values presented by carers.
4. Frustrations created for practitioners by becoming passive recipients of changes in their own practice.

What emerges in all the diverse aspects of disaffection which are described is the peripheral and powerless status of the individuals and groups involved. They experience feelings of frustration and disappointment in their inability to influence the hierarchical structure which has relegated them to this lowly position.

The stratification into different work and educational experiences, whilst often disguised under various rhetorical descriptions, can produce angry disaffection in the most astute members of the group being marginalized. It is noticeable that such perceptive individuals are generally ill-rewarded for their observations, the deficit model returning to comfort complacency.

No Real Choice

A realization of the real limitations behind the rhetoric of freedom of choice can promote disaffection. This applies to both students and staff in post-compulsory education. External factors can severely impede scope to exercise choice in decision-making.

Over the last decade, young people who find themselves unable to find accommodation or employment have been punished by poverty:

> Not only have such individuals failed to step on the ladder of personal development (i.e. "failing themselves"), but they have also failed to gain access to the merry-go-round of employment, (i.e. "failing society" by failing to contribute to productive capacity). This double "failure" is punishable by economic and social dispossession (i.e. poverty).
>
> (Jeffcutt, 1987, p. 17)

Pollitt, Booth and Kay (1989), in a recent Shelter report, illustrate how 'the safety net of welfare has collapsed since the introduction of compulsory

Youth Training for unemployed under-18-year-olds' (p. 4). Government rhetoric implies that young people on YT will inevitably be living at home, with the financial and emotional support of parents (as part of the myth of the nuclear family). Many young people, however, are unable to live at home. The 1989 Shelter report found that, of thirty-one cases examined, '10 young people left home after family disputes or breakdowns; 10 left home after "abuse" or violence; 11 were thrown out' (p. 7). In theory, compulsory YTS (as it was then called) was supposed to foster individual initiative. In practice, it has restricted choice and created youthful vagrancy:

> If the government youth training scheme was conceived as weaning young people off dependency on the state, it has failed. Together with the clampdown on benefit — no YTS, no pay — and the drastic shortage of affordable accommodation, it has reduced young people's scope to show their initiative, forcing them into often impossible home-lives, and from there into a hopelessly precarious "independence" without the resources to make a reasonable go of adult life.
>
> (Pollitt, Booth and Kay, 1989, p. 17)

Recent press coverage indicates that prosecution of homeless youngsters, under the 1824 Vagrancy Act, has increased significantly, as their daily begging on the London streets becomes a social embarrassment (Carvel, 1990).

Whilst some young people have been made poor through their estrangement with families, others have experienced long-standing labelling as both socially inadequate and educationally backward. The relationship between poverty throughout adult life and childhood classification of having 'moderate learning difficulties' is reinforced in Hamilton's (1989) report. This is a follow-up study of 1157 people labelled with 'moderate learning difficulties' as children. Now aged 23, they have had continued experiences of financial hardship:

> Our findings highlight the fact that this is a low income group and although it is a group with special needs, it is a group that is largely without special entitlements. Nearly one third of the group received unemployment or other supplementary benefits while the remaining two-thirds were self-supporting. Linked with this, the findings also show these people to be particularly vulnerable in the housing market, with few options of accommodation outside of their parental home.
>
> (Hamilton, 1989, p. 23)

A substantial proportion of the trainees in YT are classified as experiencing 'moderate learning difficulties' (Stowell, 1987). This number is likely to be replicated in the Employment Training (ET) Scheme, another compulsory training initiative, targeted at the long-term unemployed:

> It becomes not a question of statistics, of numbers in "deprived" areas, but one of emotions, feelings of depression, of being trapped, hopelessness and for most, making the best of what is available so that "life" does not pass them by. Priorities have to be decided upon, but there are certain luxuries of decision making if a person already has a sufficient income and home that they can call their own. Many young people are lacking one, and many are lacking both. For them employment training formally offers hope, but there is also no real choice.
>
> (West, 1989, p. 36)

Such individuals, caught within an uncomfortable transition in which they have no real choice, are likely to develop disaffection.

It is not only young people who feel dispossessed but those who are involved in their teaching and training find themselves robbed of the little control they had. Lawn and Ozga (1988) refer to the 'proletarianization' of teaching, whereby teachers lose autonomy, enjoy fewer opportunities for creativity and become increasingly tied to external pressures, forcing them into confining and narrowly specified roles. This process of devaluing professional skills has led to disaffection from experienced and dedicated long-serving teachers. Mike Gatford, writing in the *Times Educational Supplement* of 29th December 1989, says that his reasons for resigning from a senior secondary post, after seventeen years teaching in one borough, 'all stem from "initiatives" introduced by the Conservative Party since 1979, and in particular Mr. Baker's ill-thought-out and badly-timed Education Act. These "initiatives" are resulting in an unbearable and unreasonable extra workload' (p. 12). This unbearable workload is felt also in further education, where initiatives from government and the Training Agency have promoted constant demands on staff, introduced new and sometimes difficult students and entailed complex curriculum developments, all alongside an erosion of working conditions and status.

A Degrading Rite of Passage

The process of transition to adult/worker/citizen status is made more difficult and frustrating for those marginalized through gender, race, class or disability. Ostensibly, the post-compulsory education sector is responsive to minority needs, demographic trends indicating that young people from ethnic minorities will enter higher education in the 1990s in a larger proportion than ever before (Windsor Fellowship, 1989). Yet, the dominant white, male ethos is still shown to predominate in adult and further education classes (FEU, 1989). In a creative writing evening class, for example, male, white writers were the sole form of stimulus for a group which included black and women students. Such an emphasis unavoidably suggests that 'Black or women writers have nothing of consequence to offer in discussions about styles of writing' (FEU, 1989 (a), p. 38).

It is well documented that black trainees are disadvantaged within YT:

> Black YTS trainees were less likely to get jobs because they tended to get taken on in Mode B (non employment-based schemes). As continued experience of unemployment will typically impel people to seek skilled employment it points to an overall downward social mobility among black young people regardless of qualifications.
>
> (Bynner, 1988, p. 5)

The low status of workshop-based (formerly Mode B) YT demoralizes both staff and trainees. It can foster cynicism and discourage the promotion of good training, as this member of staff indicates:

> In general there is no doubt in my mind that YTS has been used to massage unemployment figures. However, that does not mean that it need not be good training . . . I am still aware of some of the basic problems of low status, poor pay, poor outcomes, especially three months after the young person has left the scheme.
>
> (FEU, 1989 (b), p. 234)

Where I suggested there were distinct divisions between the 'education' and 'training' routes, there are now marked distinctions between the quality of training offered to different groups:

> At the upscale end of the market, private arrangements now dominate. Low cost and low content schemes are aggressively targeted at the more marginal segments of society.
>
> (Worcester, 1989, p. 33)

That marginalized groups are expected to passively accept oppression and discrimination in post-compulsory education and training reflects a general public assumption about social worth and citizen status for 'someone else's children'.

Where evident needs are ignored, it is because they are the requirements of second-class citizens and, as such, of little consequence. This applies to people with disabilities which require them to use wheelchairs for mobility. Their choice of transport, access and spontaneous social life is severely restricted, unless they are financially independent. To use the London underground they must:

> be accompanied by an able-bodied escort, and are required to give 24 hours notice before your intended journey.
>
> (Department of Transport, 1989, 8.1)

Against this apparent indifference, the goal of USA disability civil rights is to provide for individual disabled people 'accessible public transportation, community-based independent living support services, sign language interpreters, mobility aids and skills training, adequate housing, appropriate medical care, communications access and aids, and appropriate and adequate employment' (Funk, 1987, p. 24). This accords with the Council of Europe (1988) commitment to 'provide a normal place in society for disabled people' (p. 2), yet Oliver (1988) suggests that in Britain this implies no more than that disabled people will be expected to 'compete with other groups for available scarce resources' (p. 22). In the context of finding appropriate and adequate employment, Griffiths (1989) demonstrates, through numerous individual examples, the need for long-term support, empowerment and employer-training.

If this uneasy transition is not to become a degrading rite of passage, the needs of minority groups have to be addressed. Positive discrimination has to be applied to combat the complacency of covert oppression in post-compulsory education and training, employment, housing, access and social status. The individuals are not to blame for failure promoted by prejudice and sustained by economic inequalities.

Controlled Independence

For many young people with congenital disabilities, the transition into adulthood is complicated by emotional insecurity and a heightened level of passive dependency (Anderson and Clarke, 1982; Hutchinson and Tennyson, 1986). Habitual caring for a dependent child, now adolescent, appears to encourage some parents to promote a 'sort of controlled independence' in which 'the person with disabilities was "allowed" to be independent in some spheres but not in others: for example, employment was sometimes considered to be acceptable but moving from the parental home was not on the agenda' (Wertheimer, 1989, p. 19). Professionals might unintentionally exert a control over the quality of 'independence', such that the individuals concerned are exposed to further stress and anxiety rather than experiencing genuine choice and dignity (Corbett, 1989).

The level of independence which it is possible to achieve is actually controlled by the level of available services. As these are still chronically under-resourced and often inappropriately organized, they leave the consumer with minimal control over their life choices but with maximum frustration at unrealized expectations (Brisenden, 1989; Clarke and Hirst, 1989).

Young people and adults with 'severe learning difficulties' are now attending post-compulsory education in increasing numbers (Stowell, 1987). Teaching approaches and curricular developments in further and adult education have fostered the skills required for autonomy, self-advocacy and independence. Dee (1988) recognizes that this entails 'allowing the students the dignity of risk' (p. 29). This need to permit risk-taking can create conflict between those professionals promoting initiative and the parents who prefer a 'controlled independence'.

Listening to what the individuals concerned say and feel is essential, yet has often been ignored in the past. When students are marginalized by communication difficulties and a child-like status, they need particular sensitivity in assessing just what they are wanting to do or say. A reversal of roles is required, in that carers — be they parents or staff — have to place the student's values above their own. A reasonable level of care and support has to be measured against the assumption of 'knowing what is best'. If services for formerly dependent people are genuinely consumer-led, this has to involve a redistribution of power. This can lead to the rejection or dismissal of carers who refuse to adapt to a changing pattern adopted by their clients; it can lead to vulnerable individuals being allowed to cope with difficulties and failures, without their usual cushion of paternalistic protection (Brown and Ringma, 1989). Either way, it involves a marked shift in responsibility.

Even in the innovative area of computer technology and technical aids, mistakes have been made through professionals anticipating what disabled people will need, rather than asking them for feedback and adapting equipment accordingly. Recent research into the use of new technology for students with disabilities indicates that consumer power has now assumed its rightful status and that the students' views are taken seriously (Training Agency, 1989; Vincent, 1989).

Conclusion

The contributors to this volume offer a wide range of perspectives on the issues of disaffection and the challenge of change. This divergence results inevitably from the particular roles which they play and from their specific experiences of practice. We hear the views of college lecturers, counsellors and YTS/YT instructors, themselves trapped in the influences of external changes beyond their control. As practitioners, they offer a range of strategies and teaching approaches to cope with daily situations. We share the experiences and perceptions of students in higher education, further and adult education and in YTS (now YT). Whilst these reflect disparate backgrounds, they have in common the frustrations of coping with the degradation of marginalized status.

The 'outsider' impressions of a commercial manager, engaged in commerce/education links, offer a refreshing candour to that peculiar insularity found within the educational world. These school compacts, in which employers guarantee jobs in return for agreed goals, have proved to encourage more pupils to stay on beyond the minimum leaving age, and to have caused GCSE passes to rise (Jackson, 1989). Broadening out still further, we have a regional focus on how administrators plan to cope with the challenge of change and a national perspective on developments of National Vocational Qualifications (NVQs) and their possible impact on individuals in the process of transition from school to employment.

Despite the range of perspectives, the view of disaffection which emerges shares the following unifying features:

1. Disaffection arises from a particular historical, social, economic and political context.
2. The experience of disaffection is not confined to students but can be shared by practitioners.
3. The realization that disaffection can result from individual awareness of powerlessness and marginalization fosters commitment to empowering minority groups.
4. Practitioners need support to cope with that level of disaffection which can arise from the discomfort and challenge of change.

Disaffection is not context-free. For those people perceived to have 'special needs' of one kind or another, disaffected behaviour is rarely a part of their deviant condition but more likely to be a response to unreasonable demands and expectations. I agree with Barton (1988) that consideration of political issues is central 'if we are to achieve an adequate understanding and explanation of developments surrounding special education, or to provide a basis from which change can be attempted' (p. 6). The message spoken throughout this book is not one of blaming individuals for inadequacies and ineptitudes but of alerting them to the inequalities they will need to fight.

Although I have emphasized the complexities and difficulties inherent in these issues, the attitude of contributors is ultimately constructive. In recognizing ambiguities and frustrations, they display a welcome humility. Barton (1989) calls for critical self-awareness among professionals which means we have 'a genuine acknowledgment of our limitations and a recognition of the fragile basis on which many of our assessments and decisions are based' (p. 19). When those practitioners are working in adverse circumstances in which they play only supporting roles, this awareness can be both a comfort and strength, as well as disturbing and challenging. Perhaps the most positive and potentially productive source of disaffection is the anger among the professionals themselves. They are concerned with empowering the people whose needs they serve. This they do within the context of their own limitations and disaffections.

The political context of catering appropriately for minority groups in post-compulsory education and training is clearly illustrated in the case of Birmingham. In this city, a massive industrial recession and dramatic population shifts demanded that further education colleges adapted to suit changing economic needs and a new clientele (Hall, 1988). This responsiveness included a more innovative and flexible approach to continuing education than the traditional 'take it or leave it' inertia. For some potential students, particularly those in inner-city deprived areas with no history of further education, services had to come out to meet them on their own ground. A project based at Handsworth Technical College, for example, initiated a guidance unit within the local community which offered outreach work to adults, was receptive to their views and developed similar provision across the city (FEU, 1989 (c)). The way in which Birmingham's further education services responded to the challenge of change is the subject of a chapter in this volume.

This recognition of the need for services to change has implications for those practitioners who are expected to adapt. This is often uncomfortable because it entails subjecting habitual practice to critical analysis. When educational administrators from Birmingham Continuing Education Division were engaged in planning major changes in further education services, they provided the relevant practitioners with a support network and an active participation in evaluating needs. They were thus empowering potentially disaffected individuals.

This book begins with the perceptions and daily experiences of grassroot college lecturers, trying to cope. It ends with reflections on regional and national strategies to support and ease the challenges of change. This circle unites the needs of uneasy individuals with the possibilities available to them. In the political arena of change, what emerges forcefully is the importance of networking and group support, given the complex and demanding nature of the struggle involved.

References

ANDERSON, E. and CLARKE, L. (1982) *Disability in Adolescence*, London, Methuen.

BARTON, L. and WALKER, S. (1984) *Social Crisis and Educational Research*, London, Croom Helm.

BARTON, L. (1988) *The Politics of Special Educational Needs*, Lewes, Falmer Press.

BARTON, L. (1990) 'The Necessity of a Self Critical Perspective', in, MITCHELL, D. and BROWN, R. (eds) *Early Intervention for Young Children with Special Needs*, London, Chapman & Hall.

BRISENDEN, S. (1989) 'Young, Gifted and Disabled: entering the employment market', *Disability, Handicap and Society*, 4, 3, pp. 217–220.

BROWN, C. and RINGMA, C. (1989) 'New Disability Services: the critical role of staff in a consumer-directed empowerment model of service for physically disabled people', *Disability, Handicap and Society*, 4, 3, pp. 241–258.

BYNNER, J. (1988) 'Young People: Employment, Culture and Identity', Economic and Social Research Council Research Briefing.

CARVEL, J. (1990) 'Destitute teenagers face jail penalty', *The Guardian*, January 3rd.

CLARKE, A. and HIRST, M. (1989) 'Disability in Adulthood: ten-year follow-up of young people with disabilities', *Disability, Handicap and Society*, 4, 3, pp. 271–284.

CORBETT, J. (1989) 'The Quality of Life in the "Independence" Curriculum', *Disability, Handicap and Society*, 4, 2, pp. 145–163.

COUNCIL OF EUROPE (1988) *Legislation on the rehabilitation of disabled people*, Strasbourg, Council of Europe.

DEE, L. (1988) *New Directions*, London, FEU/NFER.

DEPARTMENT OF TRANSPORT (1989) *Door to Door: A Guide to Transport for People with Disabilities*, London, Department of Transport.

FENTON, M. and HUGHES, P. (1989) *Passivity to Empowerment*, London, Royal Association for Disability and Rehabilitation.

FURTHER EDUCATION UNIT (1989a) *Black Perspectives on Adult Education*, London, FEU.

FURTHER EDUCATION UNIT (1989b) *Two-Year YTS Evaluation: Final Report*, London, FEU.

FURTHER EDUCATION UNIT (1989c) *Educational Guidance: new responses for inner cities*, London, FEU/REPLAN.

FUNK, F. (1987) 'Disability Rights: From Caste to Class in the Context of Civil Rights', in, GARTNER, A. and JOE, T. *Images of the Disabled, Disabling Images*, New York, Praeger.

GATFORD, M. (1989) 'Reasons to resign', *Times Educational Supplement*, 29th December.

GLEESON, D. (1984) 'Someone Else's Children: The New Vocationalism in Further Education and Training', in, BARTON, L. and WALKER, S. *Social Crisis and Educational Research*, London, Croom Helm.

GRIFFITHS, M. (1989) *Enabled to Work: Support into Employment for Young People with Disabilities*, London, FEU.

HALL, G. (1988) 'NAFE into the nineties: the emergent Birmingham FE system', in, PARKES, D. (ed) *Managing a Changing FE*, London, Longman/FEU.

HAMILTON, M. (1989) *Learning for Life: The experience and needs of young adults with moderate learning difficulties*, Manchester, The Rathbone Society.

HUTCHINSON, D. and TENNYSON, C. (1986) *Transition to Adulthood*, London, FEU.

JACKSON, M. (1989) 'Fifth-years stay on in job-link scheme', *Times Educational Supplement*, 15th December.

JEFFCUTT, P. (1987) 'Vandal or Visionary? The MSC as an agent of change in education and training', in, JEFFCUTT, P. (ed) *The Policies of Progress? Contemporary Issues in Educational Change*, University of Southampton, Department of Education and Adult Education.

LAWN, M. and OZGA, J. (1988) 'The educational worker? A reassessment of teachers', in, OZGA, J. (ed) *Schoolwork: Approaches to the Labour Process of Teaching*, Milton Keynes, Open University Press.

OLIVER, M. (1989) 'The Social and Political Context of Educational Policy: The Case of Special Needs', in, BARTON, L. (ed) *The Politics of Special Educational Needs*, Lewes, Falmer Press.

POLLITT, N., BOOTH, A. and KAY, H. (1989) *Hard Times: Young and Homeless*, London, Shelter.

SQUIRES, G. (1987) *The Curriculum Beyond School*, London, Hodder & Stoughton.

STOWELL, R. (1987) *Catching Up?*, London, National Bureau for Handicapped Students.

TRAINING AGENCY (1989) *Open Learning and People with Disabilities: Information and Access*, Conference report.

VINCENT, T. (1989) *New Technology, Disability and Special Educational Needs*, London, FEU.

WERTHEIMER, A. (1989) *Self-Advocacy and Parents: the impact of self-advocacy on the parents of young people with disabilities*, London, FEU.

WEST, A. (1989) 'Beauty and the Beast', *Youth and Policy*, 27, pp. 36–39.

WINDSOR FELLOWSHIP (1989) *WF and 1992: demographic trends*, discussion paper.

WORCESTER, K. (1989) 'The New Politics of Training', *Youth and Policy*, 27, pp. 32–35.

PART ONE
COPING WITH DISAFFECTION

1
The Changing Further Education Structure: A Basis for Conscription?

Brendan Major

Introduction

What follows is a personal analysis by a practising lecturer into the causes, effects and consequences of some aspects of disaffection within the further education system. The aspects I shall discuss are those manifestations of disaffection which constitute challenging, aggressive, or disruptive behaviour within the classroom. Other chapters in this volume will be dealing with the constructive aspects of disaffection and with non-challenging disaffection. The decision not to deal with all aspects of disaffection is partly to avoid duplication but also to reflect the priorities of many lecturing staff in their dealing with disaffection, i.e. survival and success in the classroom or workshop. I shall be using the term disaffection throughout this chapter to mean disruptive attitudes or behaviour.

From Night School to the Modular Curriculum

It is well nigh impossible to define further education (FE). It is sometimes described as a bucket into which can be put anything related to education or training for the post-16 year old, except that provided by schools, polytechnics and universities. Thus the service is best defined by exclusion and by describing what it does not include.

In Britain, post-school education and training not undertaken at university has always been a haphazard affair. The entitlement to day release for 16–18 year olds required in the 1944 Education Act and reaffirmed in the 1959 Crowther Report was never implemented. National resources tended to be channelled into implementing the recommendations of the Robbins Report on Higher Education 1964.

The tradition of further education in Britain until the 1960s was characterized by the 'night school' ethos. Governments and ideologues before and since have sometimes dressed up this situation as being the embodiment of voluntarism and argued that the system allowed access to any who wished to better themselves.

> England never closes the door or refuses a second chance to anyone who has the persistence to continue and the ability to succeed. This system is not perfect but it is there, and it is a tradition which sometimes evokes the admiration of observers from abroad.
>
> (Lowndes, 1969, p. 317)

This short-sighted and snobbish political stance which made the individual rather than the employer responsible for training inevitably caused the skill base of Britain to diminish and various government reports in the late 1950s and early 1960s called for a more systematic approach to industrial training. The culmination of this pressure was the Industrial Training Act of 1964 which set up twenty-four Industrial Training Boards (ITBs) with power to levy employers and sponsor training. Further education featured highly in the provision of this training with ITBs purchasing training programmes from colleges of further education. The training itself was not qualitatively different from that which had gone before.

The shortcomings of the 1964 Industrial Training Act in relation to the better co-ordination of training nationally, tackling specific skill shortages and the training of sub-technician personnel were addressed in the Employment and Training Act of 1973 which set up the Manpower Services Commission (MSC). The setting up of the MSC represented a radical change of direction for central government, which for the first time was attempting to link in a systematic way training provision with employment and employee needs.

A few years later, in 1976, the Labour Government launched a pilot programme (Unified Vocational Preparation) aimed at providing training and education for those young people who had left school and entered jobs which had not previously carried an entitlement or even an expectation of further training. Many colleges launched UVP schemes and they did so with a mixture of enthusiasm and pragmatism; enthusiasm because they were well able to provide the mix of training and education required by the schemes, and pragmatism because the mounting pressure of unemployment was leaving some further education institutions thin on enrolments.

It should be emphasized that the UVP did not represent any radical rethink in terms of curricular philosophy, although the root of present curricular models is often traced back to this programme. The training and education provided under UVPs was general and work related but not work specific. However, it has this character because it was aimed at young people, generally poor school-achievers, who were at the time involved in unskilled work. The numbers involved in UVP were very small.

In 1977 the MSC introduced the Youth Opportunities Programme (YOP) which attempted to provide unemployed young people with training and work experience appropriate to their needs, with the aim of their securing employment at the earliest possible moment. Although the majority of programme sponsors were private employers (63 per cent), many used the services of further education institutions to provide the 'off the job' elements of the training. The increasing level of unemployment, reductions in number of apprenticeships and the general decline in the industrial base of the country, put great pressure on further education institutions to take on YOP groups. YOP programmes were qualitatively different from most previous further education programmes. They were roll-on/roll-off, and did not usually lead to a recognized qualification.

In October 1981 the Conservative Government, against the advice of the MSC, trade unions, educational interests and political opponents, abolished sixteen of the twenty-four ITBs, reduced the scope of a further two and began winding down funding for the remaining six.

The MSC became *de facto* the primary body responsible for co-ordinating the training needs of the nation. The replacement of the YOP programme by the Youth Training Scheme in 1983 clarified further the power base of the MSC in determining the nature of training. Over the next few years resources were transferred from local authority control to the MSC so that by 1987 the MSC, under direct central government influence, controlled a significant amount of the national training budget. Subsequent developments have seen the MSC undergo more changes and in its current form, as the Training Agency — a branch of the Department of Employment — it funds training provision which may or may not purchase elements from further education institutions.

The White Paper, 'Training for the 1990s', advocates the establishment of Training and Enterprise Councils run by local employers who will co-ordinate the purchase and delivery of training on a regional basis.

In tandem with this move away from Local Education Authority (LEA) controlled training and education provision, a new curriculum philosophy was gaining support. The long accepted inappropriateness of GCE exams for all but the top 20 per cent of school children was addressed and after a brief flirtation with the notion of a Certificate of Extended Education (advocated in the Keohane Report to Parliament in 1979) the Government endorsed the Certificate of Pre-Vocational Education (CPVE) in 1982. The remit of the CPVE had more in common with the UVP curricular model than with the subject or career specific qualifications which had previously characterized further education provision. Courses leading to a CPVE were expected to:

1. offer a broad programme of general education related to various types of employment;
2. develop effective skills such as self-motivation, adaptability, sense of responsibility;
3. help students decide on the type of job they would wish to do.

FE institutions have had a large input into the provision of CPVE either alone or in consort with schools, and the curricular philosophy underpinning CPVE was adopted by many YTS providers and employers, using YTS to fund the initial training of young employees. The attraction of this ostensibly liberal curricular model to employers and private YTS providers was obvious. An emphasis on transferable skills would hopefully make for a more malleable workforce and specific skill/task training could be ordered in much smaller blocks.

Youth Training (YT) is now effectively compulsory for all young people not remaining in full-time education, and the Employment Training Initiative (ET) extends this compulsion to all long-term unemployed adults, so for the first time the further education system is having to deal in large numbers with students who have not chosen to be there but who have effectively been conscripted into a training programme. Coupled to this is the preferred curricular model of the Training Agency with its emphasis on the disciplines of work (punctuality, deference, ambition, respect, fiscal and civic responsibility) without actually providing complete training in any specific trade.

The Training Agency remit is couched in the double speak of the new vocationalism; 'syllabus', 'assessment', and 'skilling' are ousted in favour of 'negotiated learning', 'profiling', and 'transferable skill acquisition'. The reality is that employers need no longer fund the complete training of craftspeople because the new curriculum allows them to order bespoke training to their exact needs. Why would a double glazing firm fund a three-year apprenticeship in carpentry when a one-year YT/ET scheme can teach a student how to fit windows? The short-term benefits to employers are attractive but the long-term effects of skill disintegration, poor quality work and the reduced self-image of 'operatives' as opposed to 'craftspeople' are serious. It is ironic that, in an economic climate predicated on the supposed freedom of choice, a primary element in that economy (training) is founded on the basis of conscription. The flexibility of the bespoke curriculum may represent an increase in choice for employers but it can be a tyranny on employees or those needing employment.

It is the combination of these two elements, the transfer of funding away from LEAs to the Training Agency and the adoption of a new curriculum model, which has occasioned the present rise in disaffection within the ranks of the further education student cohort. In this respect further education is now expected to police a new Poor Law of training in return for labour.

The Second Chance Reconsidered

The training and education needs of commerce and industry may well have spawned the further education system but there is also a long-standing and strong tradition within the service that it will provide a 'second chance' at qualification or self-improvement for those who, for whatever reason, did not achieve what they wished at school.

The 'academic' sector of the further education service has always attracted a very varied cohort of students: school under-achievers, adult returners and students re-taking exams, for example. Since the early 1970s the pressure from local communities on LEAs to provide a second chance curriculum was sufficient to produce large departments in most FE colleges offering GCE (now GCSEs), 'A' level and possibly a large portfolio of other qualifications. The new climate has not left this portion of the further education curriculum unaffected.

Demographic trends have resulted in a diminishing number of school leavers and this trend will continue until the turn of the century. Thus a primary source of students for this part of the further education curriculum is diminishing and, as the competition for places reduces and government pressure on lecturers to teach larger classes becomes more intense, so the calibre of students inevitably diminishes. Another pressure on student numbers comes from a more general central government policy shift which seeks to constrain the availability of the traditional second chance route; 16–18 year olds have now been denied access to a facility to study part-time and must enrol under YT, unemployed adults are 'encouraged' at RESTART interviews to get any sort of employment or enter ET, there is reduced funding for discretionary grants and there is now a threat to ACCESS courses from higher education institutions seeking to provide their own pre-entry courses. All this conspires to reduce the pool of post-16-year-old academic students.

Consequently, in FE classrooms throughout the country lecturers of academic subjects are having to teach new and demanding courses to larger bodies of less able students. This is fertile ground for disaffection and anger.

A pattern is beginning to emerge in relation to the government's preferred character of post-16 training and education in this country. A clear emphasis is being put on *work place* based training and assessment (National Council for Vocational Qualifications), a new imperative around competence based training and assessment, modularization of curriculum delivery and further inducements for employers to provide their own training (Training and Enterprise Councils). What this will mean in practice, over the next decade, is that further education will be expected to deliver only those parts of the curriculum which employers feel they cannot provide, and to deliver the whole curriculum only to those students whom employers do not wish to engage. In the light of this it seems inevitable that low motivation and disaffection will become increasingly common within the further education service.

Hard to Teach, Reluctant to Learn

Disaffection as a serious concern has only recently appeared on the agenda of further education. This is not to deny that in the past lecturers have had to deal with student aggression and discontent. Tom Sharp's insights in *Wilt* (1976) are keenly observed vignettes of some aspects of further and higher education. Certain parts of the traditional further education curriculum have historically always encountered disaffection (e.g. the General Studies component in craft and technician studies). But in recent years the perceived scale of the problem has risen so sharply that lecturing staff now see coping with disaffection as a primary element in the national education debate.

Lecturers report that the manifestation of disaffection is now more aggressive, more blatant and more challenging. They also report that a higher proportion of their students display symptoms of disaffection. This perceived increase in disaffection within further education is difficult if not impossible to quantify, but professional bodies representing teachers in schools report that the incidence of aggression and threat has increased significantly over the past ten years and this would seem to support the consensus among practising lecturers that disaffection in further education is on the increase.

While the received wisdom, even in some college staffrooms, may place the blame for this increase in discontent (or decline in motivation) on the heads of individual students, this psychological 'student as misfit' model plainly does not address the root of the problem.

More realistically, lecturing staff identify the twin demands of the new curriculum and the introduction of various forms of conscription and market-led education as the real reasons why for the first time they are having to 'teach' significant numbers of unwilling students. Many further education staff are taken aback by this challenge of disaffection. There are two principal reasons why this may be the case. Firstly, inadequate training given to lecturing staff and, secondly, resentment from students who consider college an extension of school which they ought to have left behind. In common mythology real workers have finished with all this teaching/learning business.

Why Hard to Teach?

It is significant that further education is delivered by 'lecturers' not 'teachers'. This is not a casual difference of nomenclature. The term 'teacher' carries with it a common understanding that the learning for which they are responsible is somehow interactive and that teachers can 'teach' things which the pupil may not want to learn. Put another way, it is accepted that the school teacher is at least partly responsible for cultivating motivation in his students, or failing that, able to control his charges. The Elton Report (DES, 1989) states that a teacher's ability to control pupils is 'probably the single most important factor in achieving good standards of classroom behaviour'. Lecturing, however, implies one-way traffic only with no responsibility accepted for coaching the slow, dealing with discontent, providing motivation, or moulding attitudes. This didactic model of teaching is a product of the old curricular model of further education which, as outlined above, has its somewhat eclectic roots in the traditions of higher education, adult education and industrial training.

The notion that teaching can be done in this one-way manner is still prevalent in higher education and the reason that it can survive is because of the academic 'A' level toll-gate on entrants to higher education. Only the able and the motivated gain access to higher education in Britain and this cohort of students are expected to take responsibility for their own learning or perish in the attempt. Indeed, the real world value of many non-vocational degree qualifications is based on the assumed value of this rite of passage, i.e. anyone who has a degree must be self-motivated, be able to deal with concepts, and have the ability to learn. Attendance at almost any university lecture will illustrate that staff are not only able to disregard good pedagogic practice but are indeed discouraged by the higher education culture from encouraging interaction with students in any but the most constrained circumstances.

This luxury of assumed motivation used also to apply to the further education sector. Students were there because they wanted to learn or wanted a qualification. Many staff still hanker after the days when disruptive or challenging student conduct could be dealt with by 'sending the lad (sic) back to his governor'. However, post MSC, many students have no governor (employer); they may be in School Link classes, be unemployed, or have the college itself, the training agent, as their wage master. It is noteworthy also that the threat of financial penalty implied in being sent from college is hardly punitive for a YT or ET trainee on possibly as little as £30 per week.

The changes in further education structure and its expected curriculum offer outlined above have not been matched by any coherent staff development programme. Teacher training is not a prerequisite for employment as a lecturer in further education. This anomaly is a legacy from those early days when the skills of 'teaching', if they were considered at all, were very secondary to the subject skills. Some local authorities offer in-service teacher training but many still do not and it is more by luck than judgment that the lecturing force in further education is able to undertake the pedagogic tasks presented by the demands of the new vocationalism. It is also not insignificant that many lecturers resent what they see as the de-skilling of their subject specialisms by the encroaching disintegration of the curriculum model, i.e. modularization and open learning for example.

Further education staff are thus poorly trained in dealing with the challenge of disaffection. Lecturers who in the past were only expected to be subject specialists are now, like their school teacher colleagues, required to devote massive amounts of their time to the work of classroom management, which is essentially the business of controlling and managing disaffection and dependency.

Why Reluctant to Learn?

It would be difficult for any honest observer to review the quality of the training provision provided under the aegis of many YT, ET and CPVE schemes and not reach a conclusion that it was in many respects lacking. This must reflect in the first instance shortcomings in the structure of the schemes themselves. Serious criticisms have been levelled in respect of the use of these schemes:

- accusations of job substitution;
- the de-skilling inherent in many programmes;
- poor counselling and guidance given to applicants;
- students used as cheap labour;
- complex and valueless qualification routes;
- chronic under-resourcing.

These problems were countered at national level by a typical 'carrot and stick' response. The 'carrot' was a small one: trainees were brought under the protection of the Health and Safety at Work Act, guidance and counselling has become a more integral part of Employment Training schemes, and a system of review and monitoring was introduced (YT providers now have to have Approved Training Organization Status). The 'stick' was significantly more impressive: the YTS scheme was extended to two years (without any extra funding), its initial voluntary status was removed, previous adult training programmes were subsumed under the new ET system and the necessity for educational input was reduced in relation to ET.

In the light of this, many able students were resentful of the compulsory nature of the schemes (for example, in 1984 375,000 students entered YTS but less then 238,000 completed). There were also many less able students with a history of under-achievement or rejection at school who found the college component of their training programme difficult to accept. FE colleges have sometimes been referred to as 'secondary schools with ash trays' and, where this was the case, such students resented the extension of school into their adult life.

There is no shortage of genuine grievances in relation to the new vocationalism, but the presence of legitimate grievances does not necessarily lead to disaffection. A principal reason for many students choosing dis-affection lies in the ideological framework underpinning central government training policy: namely, the myth that the victims of economic slump are culpable in their own predicament. In December 1984 the Prime Minister announced that 'young people ought not to be idle . . . and should not have the option of being unemployed'.

In this situation, where the dominant culture is both prescriptive and domineering, challenging counter-cultures flourish. Some of these counter-cultures carry their rejection of the dominant culture to a point where they invert the received logic of success and achievement. In these situations challenging behaviour carries kudos within peer groups. The danger is that, on occasions, otherwise able students will squander genuine opportunity in exchange for the immediate gratification of enhanced status within the counter-culture. Students adopting this attitude contribute to the process of policing their own oppression. This is not a blanket criticism of such behaviour since a student may be justified in rejecting an oppressive, in-effectual, de-skilling further education programme and in these situations a lecturer should not confuse diffusing disaffection with being an apologist or salesperson for substandard provision. No. The lecturer's task must be to channel this rejection into useful opposition and away from destructive behaviour.

Strategies and Tactics for Addressing Disaffection

It follows from the above that though disaffection may manifest itself in the classroom or workshop, its primary source lies elsewhere. When interviewing students who are plainly disaffected they usually focus their disaffection on the course, its content, or the institution and only rarely on the individual teacher. Their discontent is often well placed: unhappiness with the nature of their training, insufficient wages or grant, training without skilling. In short, things beyond the control of the classroom teacher. Strategies for dealing with disaffected students must be placed in the context that in many instances the 'cure' for a student's disaffection lies outside the control of the individual classroom teacher.

This premise, however apparently obvious, flies in the face of one of the strongest pieces of received wisdom in relation to the teaching profession, i.e. the myth of the charismatic teacher (James Cagney in *Angels with Dirty Faces*, Spencer Tracey in *Boys' Town*) able to empathise with their students and bring them to their full potential. While accepting that teaching has its share of charismatic personalities, it is plainly foolish to expect all staff to be so charismatic that they should be able to 'sell' education and training (particularly suspect or substandard education) to even the most reluctant student.

It is not possible to accept any of the arguments put forward above about the conscriptive nature of the new further education, the choking of resources from the further education sector, and the contradictions inherent in the recruitment and training of staff, and at the same time expect all staff to be able to deal with the often understandable disaffection of some students. However, the myth persists, and it makes staff reluctant to come forward and demand the staff development necessary to help them cope with disaffective behaviour. It also makes staff reluctant to lobby actively against the iniquitous aspects of the new further education since such activity is seen as either an admission of their own failure as teachers or as an attack on the new curriculum model which has draped itself in the trappings of liberal pedagogy.

Strategies

Strategies for coping with disaffection are necessarily complex since they may involve many different partners in the education process: central government, the Training Agency, Training and Enterprise Councils, Examining and Validating Bodies, college management, recruitment and marketing staff, employers, students, parents and schools. It is doubtful, however, if a coherent strategic plan for dealing with disaffection will ever be undertaken since some of the major players in the design and delivery of further education are unable, ideologically, to admit the coercive nature of much contemporary further education provision.

However, at an institutional level, primary elements in any strategic response to the challenge of disaffection must be:

1. *Recruitment*

   Careful attention must be given to appropriate recruitment. This is not a euphemism for excluding students with records of under/low achievement. The incidence of disaffection among able mature students may be less than among their less able peers but this is probably a consequence of their expressing dissatisfaction in less disruptive, more efficient ways. A recruitment policy driven by the need to ensure large classes will inevitably invite the misplacing of students on inappropriate courses.

2. *Liaison*

   Even the most sophisticated recruitment process must accept the reality that institutions often have to accept 'contract work' from large employers or training providers and thus have no control over the recruitment process. In this case, indeed in all cases, the need for clear liaison between institution and 'employer' is crucial. A mismatch between student and course may be resolved satisfactorily if there is co-operation between all parties.

3. *Consultation*

   Unfortunately the Training Agency has mis-appropriated the term 'counselling' and lent to it a clearly remedial/punitive function. Initial consultation with the student should have formed part of the recruitment process and continuous consultation should offer the student the opportunity to air concerns, receive tutorial advice and help fine-tune the college provision. There is clearly a role for both group and individual tutorial work.

4. *Discipline*

   There must be in place a clear, usable disciplinary procedure and the students must be made aware of how it operates from the start of the course. There must also be clear statements of expected conduct and these must be adhered to consistently and fairly.

5. *Resourcing*

   The use of inappropriate staff, accommodation, or resources must be avoided. This is not a reference to using staff who 'can't cope with difficult students' but the use, for example, of non-subject specialists to 'baby-sit' a group, recruiting over-large groups and teaching inappropriate mixes of students.

Tactics

Whilst the devising of appropriate *strategies* is undoubtedly the most important issue, for the classroom teacher the devising of *tactics* for coping with disaffection is probably more imperative. The suggestions given below are distilled from conversations with many practising lecturers.

1. Disaffection should be addressed as early as possible. The longer such behaviour is permitted to go unchallenged, the more difficult it becomes to deal with it appropriately.
2. The teaching situation should be constructed in such a way that opportunities are regularly given to students to question the rationale and/or quality of the provision. Questions raised by students in this situation must be taken seriously and if necessary staff should facilitate the pursuit of any complaint.
3. Interview students individually. Experience tells that the most abusive and aggressive student can be both reasonable and articulate when offered the opportunity to express themselves individually.
4. Never promise what cannot be delivered.
5. The power imbalance between students and staff places a duty on the staff not to abuse their intelligence to bamboozle the student with jargon, coerce with implied threat, or patronize with ideology. In the recent past, the device of the supposed 'negotiated learning agenda' has occasioned the imposition of some unreasonable 'contractual' terms on the student. In truth, the ability of a lecturer (instructed to teach a given group of students a given syllabus within prescribed resources) and a student (compelled to attend a course) to engage in meaningful negotiation is very limited. They are quite simply not the primary players in the situation.
6. Invoke the disciplinary procedure in dealing with a disciplinary offence.
7. Students should be disciplined in private.

An adequate response to disaffection should not aim to simply quell the challenge but should seek to address the root of the discontent. Consequently the ground rules suggested above attempt to respect both the student's right to express dissatisfaction and the lecturer's right to insist on orderly conduct (though not necessarily compliance).

Serious challenging behaviour strikes at the heart of the consensus relationship which must exist between teacher and student. Some lecturers meet the challenge and impose order by force of will (they have, if you like, won the battle between lecturer and student). Others capitulate and the curriculum begins to disintegrate (a victory for the alienated student?). Both are, of course, defeats.

Conclusion

The further education service is currently undergoing a radical change. New powers vested in college governing bodies will make them well nigh autonomous institutions. The old arbitrary rationale of LEA funded further education (industrial training, second chance education, evening classes, etc.) will be replaced with a much more directive policy steer: the market. The new Training and Enterprise Councils will direct increasing amounts of public funds into training which meets the short term needs of industry and commerce. The consequences for publicly funded further education are serious.

Colleges able to capitalize on their existing resource base and market themselves successfully will attract more and more prestigious work, and with it the level of disaffection among the student cohort will decline. Why? Because employers have no commitment to education or training; their concern (understandably) is with competence and production. Thus employers will act as the gate keepers to disaffection and only the compliant will gain access to employer-based training. The division of students between the old mode A and mode B in the early days of YTS reflected just this division.

Conversely, colleges unable or unwilling to sacrifice the principles of equity in relation to post–16 educational entitlement will increasingly find themselves servicing students conscripted into post school education. These will include those unable to gain access to employer-based programmes or on courses leading to minimal qualifications. Funding for such colleges will decline as more and more resources are moved from LEA control to employer networks and as the consensus that difficult teaching requires more resourcing fades. For these colleges, disaffection will become a permanent feature and the spiral of decline will become inevitable.

For the classroom or workshop lecturer, then, the strategic 'options' on addressing disaffection are largely out of their control. Only by collective action can staff ensure that the institution retains a balanced curriculum offer, that governors use their powers of financial virement to resource education on a basis of entitlement and not prestige, and that the institution constructs a coherent response to dealing with disaffection.

The simple truth about disaffection is that unless a student can be persuaded of the necessity or desirability of participating in a curriculum offer, no progress can be made. 'Teaching by stealth' or 'teaching by coercion' are methodologies inevitably doomed to failure. It is the task of the institution to offer every student the maximum opportunity to 'own' their own education.

References

DEPARTMENT OF EDUCATION AND SCIENCE (1989) *Behaviour and Discipline in Schools*, (The Elton Report) London, HMSO.

LOWNDES, G. (1969) *The Silent Social Revolution: An Account of the Expansion of Public Education in England and Wales 1895–1965*, Oxford, Oxford University Press.

SHARP, T. (1976) *Wilt*, London, Secker and Warburg.

2
Complicated Lives:
Students with Special Education Needs in the Inner
City

Anne Wilkinson

Introduction

Over the past four years I have worked in an inner city college, based at a site which was situated in one of the poorest areas of the United Kingdom. During that time, as Special Educational Needs Co-ordinator, I met a wide range of students whose needs varied enormously. Some of those needs we were able to meet but for other students their experiences at college just added to the turmoil of their already complicated lives; it is with these students that this chapter is concerned.

First of all, let us consider who we mean when we speak of students with special educational needs (SEN), a phrase which is all too easily banded about but which, in fact, has quite different definitions, varying from authority to authority and profession to profession. In this chapter SEN includes learning difficulties, physical disability, sensory impairment, specific learning difficulty and emotional and behavioural difficulties.

It is important to remember that the students or young people themselves have not read this definition and so can hardly be blamed if they fail to fall neatly into one of the categories. The majority of students will have a range of needs and so, while a ramp is helpful, it doesn't actually solve anyone's difficulties.

I have not included bilingual students within this definition. Some bilingual students do have learning difficulties, but the vast majority need some assistance in learning the language, not assistance in learning. I know that some authorities include English as a second language (ESL) within their SEN provision. The authority I worked for did not; the community was multi-ethnic and it would have been inappropriate to combine these two very different areas of work.

The definition given above gives an indication of the range of need. It does not give an indication of the range of SEN students for whom the FE college may be expected to make provision; the majority of whom will have more than one educational need. It is this multiplicity of need which creates the challenge for the colleges.

When I first took up the post of SEN co-ordinator I already had experience of SEN teaching with another authority. My own education and training had taken place predominantly in the further education sector and I had lived for many years in the inner city. Naively, I believed that this gave me a reasonable background of experience for the demands I expected from the new post. In part it did, but only in part. It gave me a starting point and I quickly discovered that I had a lot to learn. In this respect the students were extremely helpful, presenting me and the college with new and exciting problems on an almost daily basis.

Students arrived at the college via a number of routes: careers, social services, direct from the schools and through word of mouth. They also arrived with a varying amount of background information. The philosophy of the college was that it provided a fresh start for students, a philosophy which, in the main, I agree with. However, how does a college know what it needs to know until it finds out? If a student has, and possibly still is, being sexually abused in the home, that student needs to feel confident and secure in the college. The staff should be aware of the situation and positively supportive. Not all staff need to know, but key staff must be aware of the situations in which some students are living.

Domestic Factors

The overwhelming factor was the sheer level of poverty that these students lived in. They were amongst the poorest in a poor area. My first winter in post was bitterly cold with a fair amount of snow. Throughout this the students continued to attend, dressed in flimsy clothes, sandals and no socks. One day a contingent of students arrived in my office (they never did come singly) to complain that a member of the cleaning staff had commented on the inappropriateness of their clothes. They were angry, not because of the criticism as such, but because this person hadn't realized that these were the only clothes that they had. Why do I mention that it was a member of the cleaning staff? Simply because, unlike the teaching staff, she lived locally and yet was still unaware of the level of poverty that existed.

On the day that YTS giros were paid, you could guarantee that a number of parents would be present to collect the money from their son or daughter. Very few of the SEN Youth Training Scheme trainees were able to keep any real part of the allowance, which was often regarded as a major contribution to the family's income. All the families depended on benefits and income support. Many of them had more than one child with special educational needs and, perhaps most importantly, the majority of parents also had learning difficulties and/or emotional and behavioural difficulties.

I quickly discovered that many of the parents had themselves been students at the local special schools. Literacy problems tended to run right through the family, creating enormous communication difficulties between the college and the community it was trying to serve. The following example gives an indication of the depth of this problem.

The trainees were due to go out on work placement, always a difficult time. One trainee, in particular, was not only anxious about work experience but was also going through a difficult time at home. At one stage it seemed that they would withdraw her from the college. The trainee did not want to leave, nor was she ready to. I wrote what I thought to be a carefully worded letter explaining how the trainee would benefit from the work experience and how well she was doing on the course. A few days later she came into my office, sat down and rolled up her sleeves saying, 'Look what you've done'. Her arms were covered in bruises.

Apparently no-one at home was able to read the letter, but they immediately assumed that there had been trouble at the college and reacted accordingly. Eventually they asked a neighbour to read the letter, but the neighbour couldn't read very well either and so the assumption that it was bad news continued. The parents wouldn't come into the college and so I was never able to explain. The trainee however was allowed to remain on the course and go out on the work experience.

The majority of SEN students had brothers and sisters who also attended or had attended the local special schools. One family had their eldest daughter at a school for those with emotional and behavioural difficulties, the next attended a school for those with moderate learning difficulties and the youngest was at a school for the delicate. The choice of school seemed almost arbitrary. All three had learning difficulties, two were tiny and pale and all three had emotional and behavioural problems. This was an often repeated pattern.

Some of the students had previously been at boarding school. They were usually those who were believed to be at risk in the home environment or had behavioural difficulties which the home could not cope with. For them, the adjustment to college life was only part of a far greater adjustment to living at home again. The return home was very stressful for all concerned. Many of the students had been at boarding school since the age of nine or ten, only coming home for holidays. Interestingly, this group of students were often the most tenacious in terms of their determination to stay at college, regardless of what was happening at home.

I am using the word 'family' to describe whatever unit the young person was living in. It does not refer to a nuclear family. The majority of students lived with a natural parent and a step-parent and with a range of siblings who would usually keep their own family names. For example, when parents separate, one or more children may remain with the mother, whilst the others would stay with the father. The children would usually retain a relationship with both parents and when they had problems in one home would go to stay with the other parent. Full brothers and sisters may have different names whilst half and/or step brothers and sisters may share the same name. In adolescence, some students would change their name. One student, who was at the college for two years, constantly changed between his father's and his step-father's name. Other families had a more practical solution. They simply invented a new name for the new family and changed everyone's name accordingly. Inevitably, whilst many of the children thrived happily, others had difficulty in adapting to the changes.

Adolescence is a difficult time, even for young people who have a lot of support from family and friends. For youngsters who do not have that support and who, in addition, may be under pressure from a family which needs them to find a job, particularly when there is a lack of understanding of the emotional and educational difficulties the young person has, adolescence can become a nightmare. Students with SEN usually mature later and so these difficulties are arising at an age (17–20 years) when most other young people are taking their place in the adult world. Behaviour which would have been acceptable in a younger person can pose many more problems when the person concerned is nearly twenty years of age.

At a very vulnerable stage of their development, then, many of the young people I taught would often be staying with different relatives every few weeks. Housing conditions were cramped and so they would always be either sharing a room or sleeping in the living room. The flats were cold and damp and the area boasted one of the highest rates of TB in the country. Colds and flu were common but so too were asthma and bronchitis. Partly due to lack of money and partly because of a lack of understanding, the diet tended to be of a very low nutritional standard, consisting in the main of chips which did little to help either build up resistance to infection or to improve their general state of health. Some students quite clearly did not get enough food to maintain their health.

A lack of hygiene in some of the families also exacerbated the health problems. This was particularly true of chairbound students, one of whom needed constant medical attention because of infections which could have been avoided if the family had been able to implement a high standard of hygiene in the home.

Domestic factors played an enormous part, in most cases, in compounding the difficulties the students were trying to cope with and overcome. Any provision to meet their needs must recognize, take account of and attempt to counter-balance these factors.

Cultural Factors

Not surprisingly, many students having had a less than successful school career arrive at college with something less than a totally positive expectation of what they will be able to achieve there. Referred to college by teachers, careers or social services and encouraged by families who do not want them hanging around the house, it is not always the decision the young person might have made. However, their choice is limited and their chances of finding employment are low. Faced with this, college may well be seen as better than nothing, especially if they are eligible for any income, grant or trainee allowance.

Some students do arrive at college full of hope that it will lead to work experience and a job. In the main these students have moderate learning difficulties only and tend to come from a supportive home background which has given them a positive self image.

As the majority of SEN students have been at special schools they are often unaware of the differences between college and school. Link courses are very important for these students as they give them a taste of college in a very supportive atmosphere. In the schools they will have had short lessons, rarely more than forty minutes, and the whole of their day will have been structured for them and carefully supervised. At the local schools I worked with, the lunch break was also only forty minutes as it was felt that the children couldn't cope with a longer period of unstructured time. The schools tended to be very small and covered the total school age range from five upwards. College, with its three hour sessions, twenty minute tea breaks and hour-long lunches took some adapting to, as did the change in size of institution and the age range.

The demands on the teaching staff were (and still are) enormous. Students, used to a large amount of individual attention, find it difficult to adapt to working alone for part of the time. Accustomed to teachers who played a major part in their lives, they expected and demanded that same level of pastoral care. Whilst we attempted to meet their needs, they also had to learn that college was different and that they had to make their own decisions.

Essentially, the students wanted to be able to work and to be independent. Unfortunately they had no clear idea of how to achieve this. College was alternately seen as a means towards this end or as a hindrance which seemed to put up barriers and restrict the opportunities available. As was the case with many of the mainstream students, all their families had experience of schools but few had had first-hand experience of college and so there was an element of confusion about what the college was about and what level of support it was able to offer. The very range and level of courses was bewildering and it was difficult for students to find their way through the system. This problem is by no means one which is exclusive to SEN students.

Colleges have been aware of this difficulty for a while and most have made great strides in simplifying the information about courses. A gulf still exists though, particularly with the students I am discussing, between the college's view of what students' aims should be and what they actually are. It is all too easy to impose on others our own values and ideas. Part of encouraging students to make decisions is respecting those decisions and valuing them. Students are at college for a relatively short time (one, two, maybe three years), after which they must be able to return full time to their community. Colleges must therefore be aware of and sensitive to the cultural values of the communities they serve.

The College and its Role

The college I worked in took its role as a community college seriously and made every attempt to welcome all students and to try to provide courses that would meet the needs of the community. Inevitably, though, the predominant culture of the institution was that of the staff who worked there rather than that of the students. The students constantly change, whereas the staff are a relatively constant body. The college was also sited in an area which had one of the lowest staying-on rates and one of the highest truancy rates. It was not an area where education was highly sought after. Changes in circumstances, such as high levels of unemployment, were the main reasons for people turning to the college. The chief problem in the area was not so much a shortage of jobs but a mismatch of skills. Research has shown that many people travelled into the area for work, particularly for the more highly skilled or qualified jobs. The college saw its role as helping to redress the imbalance between skills and education required and that available within the community.

The SEN section tried to provide a wide range of opportunities for students. It used all the college facilities and ensured that all its students perceived themselves as having a role in the college as a whole. They were, for example, encouraged to play an active role in the students union and in one year SEN students held the posts of Social Secretary and Sports Secretary. The first encounter with the college was, for most students, the Link course which ran on two days a week, offering a wide range of options from computing to motor vehicle maintenance, brickwork to catering, woodwork to services for people and the caring professions. Students could choose one to four options. Any student experiencing difficulties could reduce the number of options or change their programme. There was always close liaison with the schools in an attempt to deal with any problems as they arose. The philosophy behind this course was that it would offer students an opportunity both to find out about the college and to try a wide range of skills in a safe and supportive environment. One of the difficulties many special schools face is that they do not have a wide range of equipment and workshops for the students so college is seen as an ideal way of broadening the curriculum.

The full-time course was designed for students who, for a variety of reasons, were not ready or able to join the SEN YTS. Students on this course were able to receive a great deal of individual attention. In addition to building on their basic skills, the aim of this course was to help the students to become more independent and confident in their own abilities. Communication, visits, travel and work experience were major components of this course.

The two year YTS course catered for those students who were ready to try work experience which was determined by their social and communication skills rather than their ability to read and write.

Both the full-time and YTS courses aimed to provide the students with experience of a wide range of practical skills and equipment including motor vehicle maintenance, building, woodwork, computing, catering and health care as integral parts of the courses.

We also ran a bridge course on two days a week during the third term for Easter and summer school leavers who were considering joining the college full time. This course was double staffed for all sessions and enabled both staff and students to consider in depth the most appropriate course and programme for each student. It was particularly helpful for students who were due to leave boarding school and start college without having attended any of the Link courses.

Through this package of provision coupled with the overall policy of the college we hoped to meet the needs of the majority of the SEN students who applied. Staff at the college were, in the main, very supportive of its community role and responsibility. Despite this a number of students had great difficulty in adapting to and coping with the demands of college life. Outlined below are the brief case histories of a cross-section of the students we were trying to cater for.

Susan

Susan initially joined the college on a Link course. She attended a local school for those with moderate learning difficulties. There were problems immediately. Susan was very insecure and reacted violently if she thought that anyone had said anything about her or given her a 'funny' look. As she was quite tall and well built, this response of hers could quite quickly get out of hand. At this stage we knew very little about her background.

Susan attended regularly but continued to have difficulties controlling her temper. At the end of the year she asked to attend college full time on the YTS course. After some discussion we decided to accept her onto the course. It was as her tutor that I began to find out more about her background. For instance, every few months she had to attend a clinic for what she described as the 'needle' and which I subsequently discovered was a regular contraceptive injection. Susan lived with her foster parents who clearly cared about her but her ambition was to return to live with her mother. She had been taken into care when she had been thought to be a prostitute in her early teens and so was fostered well away from her home area. The contraceptive injection had been agreed as she was regarded as being out of control and it was felt, by social services, that the risk of pregnancy was too great and indeed Susan did talk constantly of her desire to have a child.

Susan's parents suffered from poor health and themselves had learning difficulties. Despite the fact that Susan could not read, her mother hoped that one day she would become a teacher. Susan got on with her mother but had a very poor relationship with her father. Her relationship with her sister was variable.

Whilst with the foster parents, Susan received a lot of supervision and support. She tried hard at college and apart from difficulties in controlling her temper her progress was good. She went out on work experience, working with the elderly and coped better than we had dared hope.

In the background all the time was the move to reunite Susan with her family. Eventually she began to return for weekends and finally she moved back home permanently. Without the support she had been receiving Susan found it very difficult to cope, although for a while she continued to attend college despite the long journey. Problems at home and arguments spilled over into the college and both her attendance and behaviour became more aggressive and erratic. Eventually she ceased attending although she would still come in to visit us. The last time I spoke to her she told me she was living with someone who beat her up and that she had had a miscarriage. I have no way of knowing exactly what happened, why she left home or what she is doing now. At twenty-one she is too old for social services to take an interest.

Jane

Jane arrived at the college to enrol with a friend and joined the YTS. She was initially very quiet but soon settled in and began to play a more active part in the class. It quickly became obvious that whilst there were gaps in her education she was coping with the work very easily. I contacted her school for a reference but heard nothing for a while. In the meantime we began to suspect that Jane had not told us the whole truth in relation to her age. Her mother came in but the situation was no clearer and we insisted that a birth certificate be supplied.

We soon learned that Jane was too young to leave school and so was obviously ineligible for the YTS. We also learned that she had truanted for much of her time at school. It was decided that, as she wouldn't attend school but would attend college, she would be allowed to continue at college on a link basis until she was old enough to join the YTS. Shortly after this Jane ran away from home and we arrived at college to find the police had been out looking for her all weekend. Jane was at college as usual. Her parents were informed but Jane wouldn't see them alone and insisted that she wanted to go into care.

It was only at this stage that we really began to find out anything about Jane. A social worker arrived almost immediately. Jane had been living with her mother and step-father. The name the family used had been made up and was not the name of either parent. The whole family now used this new name. Jane had been in care in the 1970s. The reason given was the 'child's development had been avoidably prevented or neglected'. Apparently she had been found under-nourished, looking through dustbins for food. She had returned home on trial but the care order had never been revoked.

Relations with her family were very difficult and they were not told where she was staying initially. It must also be said that they didn't try very hard to find her once they knew that she was no longer receiving her training allowance. Eventually contact was made with the family but Jane never returned home.

Jane continued at college but there were increasing behavioural problems and her attendance declined. She went on work experience and whilst she had potential she never really succeeded in the way that she could have done under different circumstances. She left the YTS when all her friends had left and for a short time joined a community programme. When I last saw her she was unemployed and living in a council flat with her boyfriend.

John

John joined the YTS when it was only a one-year course. He was 18 years old and lived in a hostel. He was very enthusiastic about college as he was keen to improve his reading and writing. His brother was in the army and ideally John would have liked to join him. His parents were separated and he did not get on with his step-father, which was why he was living in the hostel.

Despite housing and financial difficulties, John persevered at college and had a very successful work placement at the local geriatric day centre. The housing problems began to take their toll and he left college before completing his YTS. From time to time I would receive requests for references. A few weeks ago he wrote to say that he was now working.

Danny

Danny arrived from boarding school, and joined the YTS. He lived at home with his father, step-mother and brothers and sisters. The family were aware of Danny's behavioural and educational difficulties and did not have an unrealistic expectation of what he would be able to achieve. At first we thought he might be autistic. He had severe communication problems and difficulty relating to others in the class. It became apparent that he wasn't — but he was extraordinarily stubborn in his desire to work by himself and in his own way.

Danny was very precise and methodical and was happiest when he had a very clear task to accomplish. This was explained when he went on work experience, but, as often happens, employers do not always appreciate the needs of their trainees. On his first day he was given a float of change for customers using the supermarket trolleys and brief instructions. Much to the horror of the employers, they discovered that within a couple of hours he had managed to give away all the change to the customers. On another occasion, he sold tomatoes for 3p a pound and nearly caused a riot. Despite these minor hiccups Danny stayed on his work experience and some employers learned to listen when we described our student's learning difficulties. Danny not only completed the YTS course but also got a full-time job at the end of it as a result of his work placement. Unfortunately, without the support of the college, he found full-time work difficult and he eventually lost the job after six months.

Conclusion

These students were typical of the majority of students on the SEN courses and, as you can see, their learning difficulties were often the least of their problems. If a college is to provide for these students then it must take these personal circumstances into consideration when designing the courses.

Perhaps the most important way in which to begin to meet these needs is by ensuring that the course work is presented in a very supportive way so that students are not placed in embarrassing situations in terms of the skills and/or knowledge that they lack. Lecturers must always be aware that many of the students will never learn to read or write and so success must be recognized in other ways. Every person is different and not all feel life would be intolerable without being able to read the newspapers or a good book. It is the students' values that count and colleges must ensure that students are able to grow and develop their own skills and talents so that they can live active, fulfilled lives.

The bridge course which I mentioned earlier was particularly successful because of the level of planning and staffing that were put into it. All sessions were double staffed which ensured that the students received a lot of individual attention and any problems which did arise could be dealt with immediately without disrupting the whole class. The staff teaching on the course had regular weekly meetings and obviously discussed progress informally as well. As a result the students felt very secure and confident about their relations with staff.

The ability range in the group was enormous, from those with three or four GCSEs to those who were totally illiterate. The double staffing enabled us, not only to give the students individual attention, but also to help teach them how to work together and in preparing strategies for dealing with their difficulties. For example, one student who could barely read at all was very upset about her inability and couldn't cope with any written work. If a member of staff wasn't with her all the time she would become disruptive and/or walk out. She learned in that group that, although she couldn't read, she had some very important skills. She was extremely articulate and imaginative and when working on a project with a small group of the students she took on the role of dictating the answers to those who could write. As she gained in confidence she began to realize that she was in fact one of the brightest in the group and then her reading began to improve.

Unfortunately that level of staffing is not always possible but the method of working is still valid. Time needs to be spent helping the students to understand what their strengths are. They have had plenty of opportunity to understand what their weaknesses are and often arrive at college with a very low self esteem.

There is much talk in further education about flexibility of approach and nowhere is that more important than on SEN courses. I have tried to give an indication of some of the range of problems SEN students in inner cities may have. It follows then that there will be times when the student is unable to cope with attending regularly. For students going through a domestic crisis, college may be the only secure part of their lives. What they do not need at such a time is a warning that they may lose their college place also.

Colleges cannot be expected to meet everyone's needs all the time but for SEN students like the ones I have described we can go a long way in helping them to achieve their true potential with time and effort. Many of the students I taught had learning difficulties as a result of their domestic situation. College is often the first time that anyone has begun to treat them as an adult. Inevitably, there will be problems. They are coming from a totally different environment from that of the lecturers and administrators whose responsibility it is to make them feel welcome. Part of our role is to show empathy for their complicated lives.

3
A Curriculum to Counteract Disaffection: Valuing Experiential Learning

Maggie Hollingsworth

Introduction

'Experiential learning' is used here to describe the skills and knowledge acquired through personal experience outside, at the margins of and occasionally within conventional educational institutions. This learning has characteristically not been recognized through any formal assessment or certification process, although in recent years movements have been made to suggest ways in which its value may be assessed against academic entry requirements in both further and higher education (Evans, 1987).

Experiential learning falls into two main categories:

Planned or sponsored experiential learning which takes place as part of the learning programme of a particular course. By definition it is based on practical activity rather than lectures or seminars, and includes not only the practical assignment but time to reflect and help with debriefing. Examples include work experience, community service, off-site visits, trips and excursions.

Prior experiential learning which describes the knowledge and skills which students carry with them from informal learning-from-life acquired outside or through the informal curriculum of schools and colleges. This category may also include learning gained from courses previously attended but for which no formal credit was gained.

Such learning is not a new phenomenon in education and training. Initial training schemes for professions and trades have included practical work to develop job related skills; the Youth Training Scheme recognized this by focusing on work-based learning throughout its training programmes. Education has, for many years, included elements of sponsored experiential learning and has seen successful programmes, particularly with very young children, develop through a focus on practical activity. The potential benefits were recognized with the growth of active learning approaches across a wider age range in the 1960s and 70s. More recently, the focus on student centred learning has encouraged more teachers to plan lessons using the experiences and interests of students as starting points. Students benefit from a more relevant and appropriate curriculum, and teachers from a better motivated and less disaffected class.

What is unusual is the move by accrediting bodies in the last few years to make experiential learning a necessary part of some courses, rather than simply one of a number of possible ways of working. Developments such as CPVE, Records of Achievement and more recently GCSE, have emphasized the central role of activity based learning in the curriculum and have under-lined the need to develop systematic reporting systems which take account of the knowledge and skills demonstrated through such activity. The require-ment is that we formally recognize and make use of that which was formerly unrecognized.

The Theoretical Framework

Experiential learning builds on the premise that individuals learn more effectively when they are actively involved in the learning process. However, participation on its own does not guarantee learning; if this were the case fewer of us who have been brought up in families would be poor parents. Individuals need to understand what it is about their experience which is sig-nificant to them, to relate this to other learning and to build 'mental maps' which will enable them to accommodate past and future learning. This implies a complex cycle of recognition, internalization and transfer which is not easily achieved but which may be facilitated by knowledge of the process and by the availability of outside help.

A useful framework for understanding how this might take place is provided by David Kolb's description of the learning cycle (Fig. 1). He suggests that the learning process is cyclical and continuous; concrete experi-ence is the basis of reflection, abstraction and conceptualization which leads to a testing of hypotheses in new situations through further concrete experi-ence.

In the case of sponsored or current experiential learning, the concrete experience is provided by activities offered during the course or period of enrolment. With prior learning, the student uses the concrete experience from any of a number of sources: as part of a family, peer or friendship group, from part-time work or involvement in sport or other activities. For those young people whose past lacks the variety of experience of those more

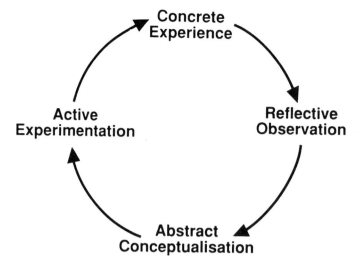

Figure 3.1 Taken from 'Learning by Doing' (Kolb, 1988) FEU, p. 10.

privileged, further education can compensate in part by offering positive learning experiences through participative projects, residential courses and visits and by offering pointers for significant sources of learning.

Following the concrete experience, support is needed to enable the students to reflect on the experience and to draw on the concepts and generalizations which might be made from it. This is an important part of the learning process during which students develop ideas about what they know and can do as a result of taking part in an activity. It is the stage at which they tend to underestimate the significance of their achievements and hence their capacity to learn. It requires sensitivity on the part of the teacher and powers of self assessment in the learner.

Once these abstractions have been made, assistance may be required to help individuals formulate hypotheses and draw conclusions about the accuracy and hence the significance of their learning. Students should be encouraged to use their existing or new found skills in different situations, and to try out ideas in a variety of contexts. Tutors can provide opportunities for the testing of theories and concepts and the development and consolidation of skills in safe, non-threatening situations. This does not imply that young people should not be challenged by difficult or unknown situations. It does mean that skilful, supportive tutoring and guidance are an essential factor in the development of self-confident, competent young learners.

New Relationships between Teacher and Learner

Didactic teaching often puts the teacher in the role of story teller, describer of events or activities and provider of second-hand abstractions and generalizations. Students are robbed of the opportunity to experience 'live' events on which to build their understanding, and rarely is recognition given to the knowledge and experience brought to lessons by participants. Instead, assumptions are made about student starting points and about the quality and value of previous learning. These assumptions undermine the individual and devalue past experience.

Using an experiential approach means recognizing that individuals learn without being taught. This means encouraging students to participate in events and activities which will provide the basis for later reflection and conceptualization, recognizing the skills they bring with them and allowing them to build on knowledge and ideas gained from past experience. It means extending the range of learners, learning contexts and methods generally accepted in educational institutions. It requires changes in the role of the teacher and in the relationship between teacher and learner. More importantly, it challenges the notion of knowledge as being something 'out there' and places it within the experience of each student.

Recording and Assessing Experiential Learning

Keeping a descriptive record of experience is not often a problem since a variety of techniques, from paper-based to video, photographic and audio, are available to assist with the process. However, although it may say a great deal about the experience, this will not tell the observer very much about the learner. The problem lies in the fact that we cannot use a picture of an event to assess the student's role in it, neither can we determine from a description what specific learning a student has internalized, except perhaps by a process of intuition. To refer back to Kolb's cycle, when the learner is still at the initial stages of experience and observation the learning outcomes remain unclear.

The issue is not with the recording of the experience but in the assessment of learning which has resulted from it. This is a more technically difficult process because it is complicated both by the context and the complexity of experiential learning. Analyzing learning derived from experience means de-contextualizing and re-using skills and knowledge which is an integral part of the learner. Recording experiential learning is also controversial because it requires learners not only to identify significant features of their own learning but also to open them to more public scrutiny. Since this may, in the case of prior experiential learning, involve revealing often sensitive and possibly damaging past experience in support of a learning claim, the student must be counselled as part of the course to ensure that the process is supportive rather than undermining.

In everyday life, assessments are often made in an informal, *ad hoc* way; for example in selecting relevant information for a letter of application or talking over events in the past with a friend or member of the family.

By formalizing the *process* of assessment of experiential learning, students can become more aware of existing and future learning opportunities and can see the relevance of learning which has already taken place. The process enables both student and teacher to reflect on experiences which are part of the course or which are brought with the student as prior learning, and to identify actual learning which has taken place. They can also identify and describe competences they have developed prior to and during the course and can produce from this a list of competence statements which define more clearly the specific learning areas. Together with examples of work and other relevant evidence, the *product*, a 'portfolio' of learning (usually in the form of a ring binder with additional supporting material), provides evidence for the learning claim. This is a formal record of learning which students may take with them when they leave the course.

Whether the product is used or not, the process if handled correctly should be illuminating and confidence building. Assessing experiential learning can:

> enable young people to understand the value of an event or a specific period of their lives;
> provide an indication of personal strengths as part of life or career planning;
> increase self confidence after a period of failure in personal life;
> provide support in job applications;
> help support an application for further course of study which would normally require qualifications for entry.

The Flexible Approach

Because it focuses on learners and builds on skills, knowledge and experience already owned by them, using experiential learning techniques with young people does not mean working in any one single way. Rather it involves a variety of approaches appropriate to individuals and groups of students each of which encourages them to capitalize on learning opportunities offered by an activity in a different way.

Two developments in further education have encouraged the growth of experiential learning: the Certificate of Pre-vocational Education (CPVE) and the Youth Training Scheme (YTS). The most obvious reason for this is the lack of formal examinations associated with each. Assessment is by means of a profile of achievement which lists areas of competence which may be addressed during the course. In both cases a framework of aims and objectives is provided by the establishing/accrediting bodies but the process and content of the college based element is largely left to colleges (and, in the case of YTS, can be negotiated with the employer or managing agent). There is, therefore, no requirement for an approved syllabus across courses, no defined or regulated subject matter and no specific academic requirements for students entering or leaving. The way is clear for imaginative and creative tutors to design courses which use practical, activity based approaches and build on both prior and sponsored experiential learning.

Some examples of the kind of work involved in these and other courses are described below. Where these are taken from actual college courses, to preserve anonymity and to protect the students and tutors concerned, names and some contextual and personal details have been changed.

Example 1   Sponsored Experiental Learning

The CPVE Experience — Developing Skills through Mini-Enterprise

Woodfield College runs a CPVE course as part of a borough consortium arrangement. It draws 16 and 17 year olds from local secondary schools in a deprived inner city area where there is a high proportion of disaffected young people and high unemployment, and where the staying on rate is very low. The college takes fifty students and offers modules in four vocational areas. The students decide, after a short induction programme, which vocational modules they want to address:

The Service Engineering cluster of the Technical Services module offered within the CPVE was developed from a BTEC module. Although in the past it had recruited well, there had been problems with students who were not always well motivated. Behaviour and attendance were often poor and the standard of work suffered. The course tutor decided that the solution could be to make the course more relevant and work related; to change the focus of the course from learning *about* engineering to learning *through* the process of engineering.

The precise nature of the mini-enterprise project adopted by the group was discussed with the students and it was decided to set up an electrical repair workshop. Students had already acquired some skill in the design and testing of circuits and the tutor felt confident that they could develop service engineering experience in a work-related setting. In addition there was a well-resourced electronics laboratory which would house the project. The process of starting up and running the enterprise moved forward quickly from initial market research through contacting suppliers, advertising, logging incoming equipment, preparing estimates and effecting the necessary repairs. As part of the enterprise, members of the group took management and supervisory roles but all participated in the actual repair work, several developing expertise in servicing specific items of equipment. Within a very short time the workshop had established a reputation for prompt, reliable and efficient service and was even showing a profit.

Throughout the course emphasis was placed on monitoring, guidance and counselling. Time was set aside for the group to meet to discuss progress and talk through problems relating to the enterprise. In addition each student was assigned a personal tutor with whom to review personal progress and discuss new learning targets. This was done at regular tutorial sessions when experiences in the workshop were discussed and competences which had been demonstrated were recorded on a progress profile. The students gained in maturity and confidence throughout the life of the workshop, taking on responsibility beyond the expectations of tutors. They developed a range of skills in core areas of communication, numeracy, problem solving and information technology as well as in practical skills and science and technology. More importantly, they recognized in themselves the skills they already possessed and had built on during the course, demonstrating an awareness of personal development which would help them decide what to do at the end of the course.

The process of recording experiential learning from a course such as this might involve tutors in the following stages:

1. listing the activities which are included as part of the course — the *learning opportunities*;
2. breaking each of these down into tasks which can be performed as individuals;
3. relating these to areas of competence or actual profile statements on the progress profile — *possible learning outcomes*;
4. during each review, negotiating with the student which of the profile statements have been achieved since the previous review, carefully considering both hard evidence (e.g., customers contacted, repairs effected) and soft evidence (pupils' self assessments, own and other tutors' assessments) — the *actual learning outcomes*;
5. checking with the student whether any additional learning

outcomes not listed in column 1 resulted from the current experience or from prior learning.

Example 2   Prior Experiential Learning

YTS — Analyzing the Learning Process by Recording Skills and Knowledge from Work Based Learning

Millbank College is situated in an inner city area in the Midlands. It takes YTS trainees from a large managing agency, most of them in retailing. Although several work in larger shops many are employed in small retail outlets dealing in a variety of household goods where they work longer hours and are given a great deal of responsibility. There is some tension between the two groups. Those who work in larger shops usually enjoy better working conditions and a good social life which is envied by the others. Those in smaller shops often have a closer relationship with their employer, enjoy more autonomy and get greater job satisfaction.

The tutor to the YTS course developed a good working relationship with the trainees although she saw them for only one day a week. She was, however, disturbed by their constant jealousy and bad feeling when they discussed their work placements. She decided to try to develop, in each trainee, knowledge of the different opportunities available in each work placement and an understanding of the common skills needed to work in the retail trade. Since the trainees themselves were more clearly able to describe the circumstances in which they worked it was decided to work from their experiences, analyzing and comparing situations in a structured way. This activity would not wholly replace the teaching and learning which were a normal part of the course but would be separate from and complementary to it.

For an hour each week the trainees were encouraged to reflect on the experiences of the workplace through small group work and paired activities. During the first sessions trainees were asked to think about good and bad experiences which they had had at work. The tutor volunteered some examples of her own which set the pattern for the kind of information expected. She also warned the group that they need not disclose sensitive information to other group members. Trainees were asked to talk through some of their experiences in pairs and to make a note of the kinds of things they may have learned as a result. These notes were written on cards and placed in a hat, and were then read out to the group anonymously. After comments from the group the list was amended and a copy provided for each group member. A similar list is shown below:

being given responsibility	can work on my own
	can show I am reliable
working long hours	physically strong
	can cope with own feelings of resentment
serving customers	cheerful
	know a lot about the stock
	can offer advice
	good communicator
being bored	able to hide feelings if necessary
making friends at work	good at relationships
	help out others
travelling to work	finding my way
	arriving on time
being poorly paid	managing on a budget
	negotiating for loans from adults

The trainees were asked to add to the list at work, if possible by discussing the sorts of activities, skills and qualities involved with their employer and/or supervisor. The tutor also contacted a number of work placements to inform employers and supervisors about the project.

As a result a more comprehensive list of work related activities was drawn up by the group and was used as a basis for discussion and comparison during subsequent sessions. Each trainee spent some time with a partner providing feedback, using the finished checklist to register the learning opportunities offered within his or her own workplace. This was a basis for a lively group discussion about how those with fewer apparent opportunities could make up the deficit. The discussion centred around the use of prior learning.

The experiment achieved its aim; it allowed the trainees to analyze and understand the process of learning through a detailed study of their own experiences. Although the checklists were not, in this case, used in any formal way to register the achievements of individual trainees, a number of trainees did begin to assess their own performance against the list. Probably more important was the fact that they had acquired knowledge and understanding of the process of learning, and would be aware of the possibilities of using prior learning and more able to make use of sponsored opportunities available in the future.

Example 3 — Prior and On-course Learning Together

Working with the Young Unemployed on Portfolio Preparation

Crosspoint College has a wide variety of full time vocationally oriented courses aimed at full time and day release students and is now developing its provision for unemployed students. The 'Moving On' course is designed for young people between 18 and 24 who are unemployed and who have no clear idea about what they might do next. Most have no formal qualifications and have dropped out of education before the statutory leaving age; some have been in care, some have suffered illness and breakdown, and some have disabilities. All have learning difficulties of one kind or another and have been rejected by or have rejected the education system.

The course is part-time, one afternoon and one evening a week for a maximum of two terms. It aims to provide an opportunity for students to meet together in a supportive atmosphere, to increase self awareness and to develop self confidence. The course is intended to open the minds of students through an eclectic mixture of literature, drama and the arts, and includes formal taught sessions as well as group work, oral work and individual writing. Students are also expected to produce a portfolio of experiential learning which can include both on-course (sponsored) and prior learning. The tutor organizes the sessions so that individuals may attend flexibly, and may participate only in the portfolio preparation classes if they wish. Group sessions focusing on prior learning are each free standing and are supported by parallel individual counselling throughout the duration of the course. Young men and women enrolled on the course come for a variety of reasons: for the company of others, for an extended form of personal or careers counselling and to review or renew learning in order to gain entry to a formal course of study.

Before joining the course, students were made aware of the nature of the activities which would take place during portfolio preparation and were given the opportunity to decide whether this would be appropriate to their personal needs and future plans. Care was taken to ensure that potential students would be given control over the process and the product of the course and examples of students' work were used to show the type of work which would be done.

Portfolio preparation here involved the following stages and strategies:

Stage 1: *Reflecting on Life Experience*

Reflection on life experience to identify past events and activities which had significance as sources of learning. This involved a variety of strategies with groups and individuals including drawing a lifeline, discussing events in the past in pairs and brainstorming outcomes, writing a detailed curriculum vitae. Carefully structured groupwork helped reduce isolation, identified commonalities and allowed students to share painful or pleasant experiences in a supportive atmosphere.

Stage 2: Going into Detail

Production of more detailed accounts of specific areas of learning in greater detail; on cassette, photo-montage and in writing — and including accounts of events in childhood, a list of tasks involved in a job/work experience/training scheme, a tape made by a band in which one student played and a set of photographs taken on a club residential. Much of this work was completed individually following discussions with the tutor. Occasionally a student would work at home with a friend or partner.

Stage 3: Identification of Actual Learning

This involved analyzing the performance of each activity for the skills and knowledge which were demonstrated therein. This was done in pairs with a checklist of generic skills which could be used in a variety of situations on taught courses and which was particularly appropriate for prior learning. The analysis could also have been done using a checklist devised by the student (but the student would need help with writing statements from scratch), or provided by a course tutor as entry requirements against which to assess students without formal qualifications.

Stage 4: Selection of Relevant Items

Those students who had decided to use their portfolio to help them gain entry to a vocational course at the college which would otherwise have required qualifications were encouraged to present learning which was appropriate and relevant to the proposed exit point, and to match the competences they had identified with the requirements of the proposed course. This meant several hours of preparatory work by the tutor who was faced with the task of establishing prerequisite knowledge, relevant skills and competences at suitable levels with the prospective admissions tutor.

Stage 5:   Providing the Evidence

During an individual counselling session students were encouraged to review the possible sources of evidence which would support the learning which they had identified. Where appropriate this was assembled in a folder with the checklist. The kind of evidence which was offered included photographs of and designs for joinery, certificates, testimonials, descriptions of visits. Essays, poetry and film and book reviews prepared as part of the taught course were also included.

Stage 6:   Assembling the Portfolio

Students spent some time re-writing, sorting and ordering items for inclusion in the portfolio. Portfolios had to have numbered pages and a list of contents for easy reference. Students who wanted entry to a further course of study and those who intended to use it to help them during a job or training interview were encouraged to write a personal statement in support of their application, based on the contents of the portfolio. They were taught how to use the portfolio at interview and given practice interviews by the tutor to increase their confidence.

Stage 7:   Using the Portfolio

The course completed, the students could now use the portfolio however they wished, as a confidence raiser, a definer of skills and talents or as a passport to future learning.

This is an example of a contents page from a portfolio (James was applying for the catering course at Crosspoint):

> List of competences demonstrated in the portfolio.
> Description of a significant event from my childhood.
> Account of learning from work in a DIY shop.
> Photographs and description of decoration of mural on camper van and decoration of bike.
> Review of 'My Beautiful Launderette'.
> My weekly budget.
> Open testimonial from my social worker.
> Account of work with local boys' club.
> Closing statement giving reasons for wanting to work in catering.

Summary and Conclusion

Young people know and can do a great deal more than they, or their tutors, imagine. When they enter further education they already have a wealth of experience and many skills on which to build. Sadly, these often go un-recognized or are subordinated to the kind of book learning which many young people have already rejected during compulsory schooling.

Using prior learning in the classroom helps young people to demon-strate their achievements to themselves and others. It enables them to recognize the worth of their own experience, to understand their own capa-bilities and even to gain formal credit within the education system for skills, aptitudes and knowledge developed through life. The experiences of YTS trainees and young unemployed people illustrate this clearly.

Setting up situations in the classroom which encourage students to take an active role in learning and involve them in greater responsibility for their learning is an excellent way of motivating disaffected young people. The experience of CPVE students running their own small business in electrical repairs is a good example of successful sponsored learning which benefited from enthusiasm, lateral thinking and a flexible approach by teaching staff.

The assessment of experiential learning requires a new approach which rests on the concept of competence unfamiliar to students and teachers used to working with a subject based syllabus. It is through this approach that students discover and record what they have done and can do, and can use the resulting profile to help plan a future career, to find a job or to secure a college place. The process of competence assessment involved in certificating experiential learning takes discussion beyond the student and into the colleges where it raises issues about traditional methods of assessment, about teaching methods, course design and course content. This wider discussion is beginning in earnest now that falling rolls threaten to take away the trad-itional supply of students from futher education colleges.

Young people today can challenge conventional notions of academic success using the skills, knowledge and experience which have in the past remained untapped, uncharted and unrecognized.

References

EVANS, N. (1987) *Assessing Experiential Learning*, London, FEU.
GIBBS, G. (1988) *Learning by Doing*, London, FEU.
KOLB, D. (1984) *Experiential Learning — Experience as the Source of Learning and Development*, New Jersey, Prentice-Hall.

4
Overcoming Passive Disaffection: Students with Severe Physical Disability

David Hutchinson

Introduction

Disaffection can take many forms and it may be considered strange to suggest that students with severe physical disability might show but the remotest symptom of it. However, if one takes the view that disaffection in education might be any behavioural factor that prevents positive learning taking place, then it can be argued that this student group can show every bit as much disaffection as can any other student group. In this case however, the disaffection is not of an aggressive nature, indeed, the opposite is very much the case. I shall call this type of disaffection *passive* and the ensuing chapter will describe approaches which have been developed by one college of further education in an attempt to overcome it.

The Manifestation of Passive Disaffection

The most appropriate way in which I can indicate the manifestation of passive disaffection is through a case-study approach. I shall describe 'Janet'. The person described is, of course, a mythical character and not a real individual. Her characteristics are, however, taken from a range of young people with severe physical disability with whom I have worked.

Janet was born with spina-bifida and hydrocephalus. In the very early days of her life she had operations to close the hole in her back and to fit a valve to control the hydrocephalus. She is paralysed from the waist down requiring her to use a wheelchair and she is incontinent of bladder and bowel. From the age of 5 Janet attended a residential special school some fifty miles away from her home. In fact, she attended this same school for all of her school life, returning home only at half terms and for longer school holidays. All her friends were from the same school though most of them lived away from Janet's town so any contact was in term time only or by letter and telephone during the holidays. All the young people who were Janet's neighbours at home attended the local schools so that Janet's relationships with them were as passing acquaintances.

At 16 years of age Janet left school and returned home to live with her mother and younger brother, her father having left home when Janet was aged 10. She appeared verbally confident, but was reported by her school to be functionally illiterate. Her levels of attainment in numeracy were also very weak especially in the use of money where Janet was very inexperienced. She was said to be independent in self-care, but was very lazy and needed constant reminders to empty her appliance. Janet's social worker reports that life in Janet's home is a struggle now that she is back home. Mum has a part-time job but money, in particular, is a problem.

Whilst Janet has a good relationship with her mother and her brother it is one based very much upon her high dependency on them for many aspects of her life. Janet's brother, especially, is beginning to resent this, though he tries hard not to show it publically, since time spent on Janet's behalf means less time for doing his own things. Janet, too, is aware of these tensions and tends to avoid asking her brother for too much. Nevertheless, she does not moderate her demands on her mother and this too arouses further stress within the family since Mum has no time to herself. Janet reminisces fondly over her friendships whilst at school but, in reality, she has seen none of these friends since leaving school and has lost contact with most of them even by letter or telephone. Janet's social life outside the home is confined to a weekly visit to the local physically handicapped and able-bodied club and she lists her main activities as watching 'soaps' on television and playing her records.

In many ways Janet is fortunate in that her local college of further education makes special provision for disabled school-leavers. On leaving school therefore Janet went straight to college. When she joined the course, staff found it very difficult to work with Janet as she did not seem to be interested in any of the activities offered to her and she was content to sit for long periods of time doing nothing. Specific assessments carried out at the time that Janet entered college revealed:

1. She was not independent financially and was not aware of the allowances which were paid to her.
2. She had difficulty in performing simple homeskills tasks such as cutting, peeling, chopping, opening tins, making tea/coffee, etc.
3. She could not accept responsibility for her own personal care needs.
4. She had poor mobility skills and was entirely reliant upon others to

move her out of her home and, since the family was poor and had no transport, this rarely happened.

5. She had a poor self-image and, whilst ostensibly happy, really lacked confidence.

6. She was very passive in almost every aspect of her life and accepted without question what was done for or to her.

Janet's description illustrates some aspects of the range of characteristics likely to be found in a similar group of young people. Some of these characteristics are not exclusive to young people with disabilities nor should they be seen as specific characteristics possessed by every young person with a severe physical disability. I would stress that such young people should not be seen as a homogeneous group but as unique individuals with many differences. Nevertheless Janet's situation does reveal many of the difficulties presented at the time of transition into the adult world, a period through which most young people pass at some time in their life which is generally accepted as a phase characterized by uncertainty, doubts and the need to establish an identity and role in life. What is difficult for the majority of young people is doubly traumatic for young people with a disability for whom the future is often a bleak and unattractive prospect. Above all, however, research (Hutchinson and Tennyson, 1986) has shown that the passivity of this group of young people is a significant issue in the development of educational programmes to meet their needs and has become a major influence on curriculum design as will be discussed later in the chapter.

The Causes of Passive Disaffection

Janet's situation and that of people like her might be seen as a criticism of her past experiences and it could be said that her disability has been turned into a handicap by environmental influences. Let us examine the truth of this statement in respect of some of those environmental influences.

Many young people with severe physical disability, especially those with spina-bifida and hydrocephalus, have spent long periods of their lives in and out of hospitals receiving treatment. Gliedman and Roth (1980) talk about the 'theft of the future' from many handicapped youths. Those who remain 'perpetual patients' because of severe disability do not develop socially — they remain stuck in time, citizens of a therapeutic state where there are only good patients and bad patients, not grown-ups and children, and where 'cradle to grave' institutions take care of them for life. Gliedman and Roth suggest that every disabled child is vulnerable not merely because of the genuine limitations imposed on them by their disability but also by the 'destructive, demeaning, and entirely unnecessary stereotypes and role expectations that are the destiny of those who grow up handicapped'.

According to Gliedman and Roth, this vulnerability is at its greatest in the young person's relationships with the specialist medical, educational and other services provided. It is generally recognized that the medical model of disability has, for a long time, been a negative force in determining the life chances of people with disability. Gliedman and Roth refer to their alarm with the way in which providers of services view their clients through a 'medical or quasi-medical lens' which transforms every issue concerning the individual into a matter of 'social pathology'. This has the effect of creating a situation where policy makers think of handicap, like other areas of disadvantage, as a social disease. At the level of the individual, Gliedman and Roth suggest that the implications of the social pathology model make it 'natural' for professionals to assume the role of 'expert' and make decisions over the life of the individual which go well beyond the parameters of their technical expertise. The implications of this for the disabled young person include being the passive receiver of help and assistance. This, in turn, engenders in the young person the inability to simply ask — they find it very difficult to shed the passive role of receiver and put on the one of being in control of their lives and of 'ordering' services.

It is true to say, therefore, that many young people with severe physical disability grow up with a socially communicated sense of stigma and doom and the socially generated expectation that disabled children have no real future as adults. Their self-image, forged from the reflections of others, is poor and has to come to terms in one way or another with the prejudices and stigmatization of non-disabled people. As Gliedman and Roth say:

> if one thing is clear from the autobiographies of the handicapped, it is that the first hazard that many face is the demoralisation that can result from having one's competence as an individual constantly challenged while one is growing up — not because one actually is incompetent but because the able-bodied think one is.

Anderson and Clarke (1982) and Bookis (1985) suggest that one of the main purposes of school is to prepare a young person for future life and to make the transition to adult life as trouble free as possible. They further suggest that schools find this a difficult task which may explain why the Warnock Report (DES, 1978) referred to gaps in services for young people with special educational needs in the transition from school to adult life. A report published in 1985 (OECD/CERI, 1985) suggested that people with disabilities tend to be less well educated, less well trained, and possibly slower, not because of their disability, but:

In this context the low standards and expectations of special schools and the lack of effective teaching in mainstream schools is equally unsatisfactory and both represent a failure to assist young people in their development and serve to limit their life chances.

The process of transition from child to adult, and the gradual acceptance of adult responsibilites, is one which culminates as a result of exposure to many different experiences and influences. Many young people with disabilities will have missed many formative experiences in their early lives: for example, being allowed to make mistakes and learn from them, being allowed to exercise choice, being expected to accept responsibility and being involved in making decisions which affect their own lives and, perhaps, those of others.

Too often in the past the provision made available to young people with disabilities has emphasized too much their special needs and this has been used as a justification for segregated provision, especially in the context of education. This has had the effect of setting such young people apart from the mainstream of society where they have become the objects of fear, pity or patronage. For too long, attention has been focused on the special needs of the young people to the detriment of their basic needs and rights as human beings; needs and rights which the rest of us take for granted. They need to have a choice and be able to exercise that choice, to have control over their life, to love and be loved, to take risks and accept the consequences of their decisions.

By every social measure disabled people are to be seen on the margins of society as dependent beings and this view, reflected by what has been provided by way of education, has led to disabled people becoming perpetual children, prepared only for a life of limited personal autonomy and certainly not for full participation in society.

Overcoming Passive Disaffection.

Many of the problems described above can only be met via political and fundamental social change. As Oliver (1987) suggests, policy makers must look at the services which they provide and identify ways in which they are currently disabling, for example, through poor physical access, negative attitudes amongst staff or an inappropriate or inaccessible curriculum. This would form the starting point towards the provision of 'enabling' services which, backed up through the development of an equal opportunities policy could facilitate the full participation of disabled people providing they have a full involvement in the drawing up of such policies and in the design and delivery of services.

In the light of what has been said thus far, it is, perhaps, the type of educational provision that has been made available to people like Janet that has played a major role in creating passive disaffection. It therefore follows that it is that service which can probably play the most powerful role in attempting to meet her needs. Oliver (1987) describes disability as an 'ascribed social status not an illness' and he suggests that 'disabled children must be made to understand that they do not have something wrong with them; rather society is unwilling or unable to organise itself so that their particular needs are taken into account'. He believes that this view should be incorporated into the curriculum and that young people with disabilities should be encouraged to understand and seek to achieve their rights.

An additional dimension to the problem is that raised by Fish (1987) who indicates the difficulty of defining adulthood as a precise legal and social status. Adulthood is defined differently in different countries and different cultures; nevertheless, what he terms the 'coming of age' might be observed in four main areas of life:

personal autonomy and independence;
productive activity;
social interaction, community participation, recreational and leisure activities;
roles within the family.

Drawing up a 'checklist' of needs which will, amongst other things, enable service providers to evaluate their provision and, in particular, its relevance to the needs of individuals is no easy task. However, the points made above do, in fact, suggest a way forward. Perhaps a way of addressing the issues might be to look at the purposes of post-school education for young people with disabilities. Bradley (1985) suggests that further education should be preparing young people to assume the 'adult' role and that this preparation might consist of:–

1. Preparation for work including paid employment — this will include transferable skills that enable young people to carry out a variety of work tasks and the social skills that enable them to function effectively in the world of work.
2. Preparation for daily living — this involves the life skills necessary for personal survival and the social skills needed for successful interaction with other people.
3. Preparation for free time — a specific input on constructive ways of spending leisure time and on coping with the possibility of unemployment will be needed here.

4. Preparation for further education and training — special provision should be seen not as an end in itself but as a means of facilitating students' progression on to other learning experiences.

I should like to suggest that the establishment of a curriculum framework based upon the transition to adulthood for young people with severe physical disability should be done in the context of mainstream curriculum development and that themes which are of relevance to all young people are just as crucial to this particular group. Stemming from this philosophy has been the emergence of the notion of a common core curriculum which is a statement of consensus about the kind of education that should be available to all young people. This is perhaps best developed in the curriculum framework published for the Certificate in Pre-vocational Education (1984). This includes ten themes in its core area:

Personal and Career Development.
Communication.
Numeracy.
Science and Technology.
Industrial, Social and Environmental Studies.
Information Technology.
Problem-Solving.
Practical Skills.
Social Skills.
Creative Development.

Bradley (1985) emphasizes the point that the curriculum framework offered within the Certificate of Pre-Vocational Education should be seen as dynamic and responsive to both local conditions and changing circumstances. Moreover, whilst each of the core areas is relevant to all students, the detailed objectives and learning experiences associated with them and incorporated into learning programmes will have to reflect the needs of particular student groups and of individuals within these groups. Additionally each area should be reflected in a balanced way across the curriculum.

It is important to stress, therefore, that the needs of young people with severe physical disability are synonymous with those of all young people in the first instance. Only when this primary set of needs has received attention should we begin to consider the special needs associated with their disabilities. This emphasis on the 'person first' is not often reflected in current practice and the evidence for this lies in the aims of educational provision which assumes that young people with disabilities need special preparation for the transition to adulthood or, worse still, is expressed in terms of 'significant living without work', an unhappy concept which appears to deny to those who do not have work such important life-style determining characteristics as: economic independence, an opportunity to develop a social life, status in society, an opportunity to participate in community affairs, dignity and independence.

A College's Response

The research project entitled 'Transition to Adulthood' commenced at the North Nottinghamshire College of Further Education in 1983 with funds made available from the Further Education Unit and the Nottinghamshire County Council. Whilst the College had been involved in developing provision for disabled students since 1969, the completion of access facilities for students with severe physical disabilities in 1978 saw an increase in applications from that particular group of students. The young people concerned had either a congenital disability or an acquired disability resulting, perhaps, from head injury sustained in some traumatic episode such as a road traffic accident. At the outset it was discovered that the primary physical disability was often accompanied by cognitive difficulties and other psychological problems such as emotional lability. Above all, passivity emerged as the major characteristic presented by the students and it became a major influence on the curriculum established to meet the needs of the students. Throughout the curriculum development work which took place, an account of which has been published (Hutchinson and Tennyson, 1986), an emphasis was placed upon devising ways in which the students could become actively involved in their own learning. As such, concern over the content of the educational programmes developed has been subordinate to the need to concentrate on identifying the most effective teaching and learning strategies. As Hutchinson and Tennyson (1986) point out

> the guiding principle underlying all the work undertaken was to instil into the students a sense of worth and value in order that they are able to develop the necessary confidence and esteem to become active in their own lives.

At the beginning of the project there was no suitable curriculum model in existence upon which to base the work. An initial response was to attempt to develop the concept outlined in the Warnock Report (1978) entitled 'significant living without work'. This involved offering individualized programmes of experience, the main rationale for which was to catch up on what the student had missed out on in their previous experiences, hence the early concentration on 'extension' studies, topped up with recreational and creative activities. However, the notion of 'significant living without work' fell into growing disrepute during the late 1970s and early 1980s as the whole idea became more and more contentious and raised problems of definition and attitudinal objections which were deeply rooted. As the population of people with disabilities became more confident in articulating their concerns, more disabled writers expressed their fears over the stereotyping and discrimination created by concepts such as 'significant living without work' which could be applied generically to the whole population of disabled people without any regard being paid to their real needs and aspirations.

Nevertheless, many of the problems of stereotyping can be overcome if the concept of living a life without paid employment can be seen to have equal relevance to all young people. The economic situation is such that finding alternatives to work has now become a reality for many young people. This fact has caused many colleges to re-assess their educational programmes and the role that they play in helping to meet the needs of this group of young people. This need for the re-assessment of provision is well expressed in the FEU publication 'Skills for Living' (FEU, 1982):

> with decreasing employment prospects ... there is a growing debate about the relative merits of preparation for work, preparation for adult life and preparation for life without paid employment ... What is needed is a curriculum which achieves the correct balance between them.

It was this desire to develop and evaluate a curriculum framework, designed to meet the needs of young people with severe physical disability, and assist them in moving towards the goals of achieving maximum personal independence and living purposeful lives, that led the staff at the North Nottinghamshire College of Further Education to secure research funding in order to facilitate their work.

At the heart of this exercise in developing a responsive curriculum framework was the philosophy of keeping the basic needs of all students, which have been described above, as first priority and, secondly, making a determined effort not to become pre-occupied with 'special needs' *per se*. At all times every attempt was made to highlight and build on the students' abilities, pushing them forward to explore the boundaries of what is and what is not possible for them as an individual.

The Curriculum

The curriculum which was established was intended to overcome the major effects of passive disaffection which have been described above and develop the students' potential for independence in all spheres of adult life. Moreover, it was designed to put the young people into a position where they were able to accept responsibility for their own lives. However, this does presuppose that there will be resources and facilities available within the community to enable this to happen.

The content of the programme, as developed, spans a potential two years of full-time college placement. For some individuals it has been possible to contract this into a one year programme whilst, for others, it has been necessary to expand it to three years. The framework is modular and consists of two types of module:

Core Modules

1. Personal Care — to enable individual students to maximize their potential in the management of their own personal care.
2. Personal Development — to develop social competence, to increase self-confidence and foster personal development.
3. Independent Living Skills — to acquire the necessary skills and confidence to cope with everyday living situations.
4. Leisure Mobility — to change dysfunction into function where possible for everyday living.
5. Social Experience — to encourage management, organizational and social skills.

Option Modules

Around the framework of Core Modules other negotiated options from across the whole college curriculum are incorporated into an individual programme, and timetable, for each student. The model indicated in Figure 4.1 summarizes the outcomes and the range of options available to students on completion of what became termed as the 'Transition to Adulthood' programme. It is anticipated that these outcomes/options would enable each individual to develop their own 'significant' lifestyle.

The model developed reflects the needs of all adults, with or without

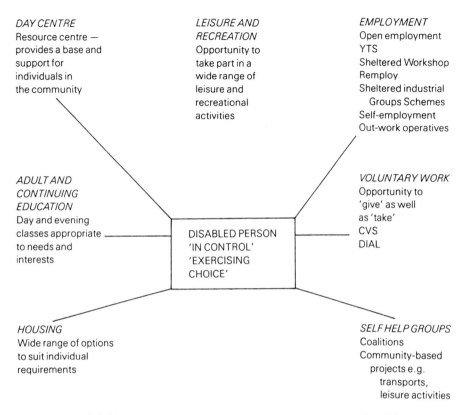

DAY CENTRE
Resource centre —
provides a base and
support for
individuals in
the community

LEISURE AND
RECREATION
Opportunity to
take part in a
wide range of
leisure and
recreational
activities

EMPLOYMENT
Open employment
YTS
Sheltered Workshop
Remploy
Sheltered industrial
    Groups Schemes
Self-employment
Out-work operatives

ADULT AND
CONTINUING
EDUCATION
Day and evening
classes appropriate
to needs and
interests

DISABLED PERSON
'IN CONTROL'
'EXERCISING
CHOICE'

VOLUNTARY WORK
Opportunity to
'give' as well
as 'take'
CVS
DIAL

HOUSING
Wide range of options
to suit individual
requirements

SELF HELP GROUPS
Coalitions
Community-based
    projects e.g.
        transports,
        leisure activities

Figure 4.1 Model based on 'Transition to Adulthood' programme, FEU, 1986

disabilities. It does not propose any radical change in provision, but does suggest a fundamental change in emphasis. The disabled person is still too often seen by many professionals as the passive recipient of their benevolence. The balance of power needs to be re-aligned with the disabled person at the centre, in control of their own life, able to expect as a right the opportunity and facilities to exercise choice over their own lifestyle. The 'Transition to Adulthood' programme as described aims to negate the effects of passive disaffection and equip the young person with the ability and confidence to carry out this role. It is then the responsibility of the community to provide the means and opportunities for this to be possible.

Since so much in overcoming passive disaffection depends upon attitudinal change, it must be seen, perhaps, as an evolutionary rather than a revolutionary matter. What could change things dramatically however, and is absolutely essential, is the establishment of a co-operative joint planning and service delivery network. The research undertaken at the North Nottinghamshire College of Further Education has shown that no matter

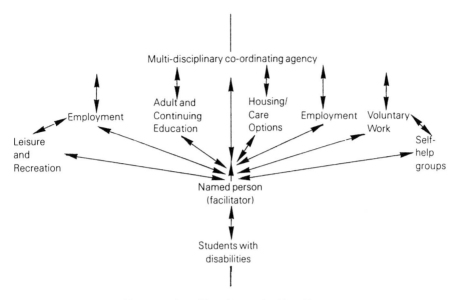

Figure 4.2 Role of facilitator from 'Transition to Adulthood' programme, FEU, 1986

how successful a curriculum is in meeting needs, any progress made in college has to be maintained and extended if the original problems it was attempting to meet are not to re-emerge at a later date. The system of service delivery post-college can be characterized by ambiguity and overlap of services with professionals motivated by self interest engaging in power politics and vying to serve the needs of clients, features which of themselves can lead to passive disaffection as identified above. The net result of this situation is disabling rather than enabling for the young person and negates the benefits which might accrue from a college programme. The only way forward, therefore, is for the many service providers to work co-operatively and in a co-ordinated way, no matter how painful a process this may be, to ensure that individual needs are met.

Finally, to return to our mythical character, if 'Janet' is not to be bewildered in her search for independence, as to which of the many service providers she should turn to for help, perhaps we should return to the notion first identified in the Warnock Report (DES, 1978) — the concept of a 'named' person to help the young person find their way through uncharted territories. Where necessary, they act as an advocate, a facilitator and a stimulator to self-reliance. A jointly funded, inter-disciplinary and multi-agency role is vital in linking together the many different professionals and resources that are available and this in turn would help fill the gaps which inevitably result from separate provision. Figure 2 illustrates how such a role might be developed in practice.

References

ANDERSON, E. and CLARKE, L. (1982) *Disability in Adolescence*, London, Methuen.

BOOKIS, J. (1983) *Beyond the School Gate — A study of disabled young people aged 13–19*. London, RADAR.

BRADLEY, J. (1985) 'Developing the Curriculum — Module Two', in *From Coping to Confidence*, London, DES/FEU.

DEPARTMENT OF EDUCATION AND SCIENCE (1978) *Special Educational Needs: Report of the Committee of Enquiry into the Education of Handicapped Children and Young People* (The Warnock Report) Cmnd 7212, London, HMSO.

FISH, J. (1987) *Transition to Adulthood — A Conceptual Framework*. Paper presented to the national launch of 'Transition to Adulthood', FEU, 1986, London.*

FURTHER EDUCATION UNIT (1982) *Skills for Living*, London, DES.

GLIEDMAN, J. and ROTH, W. (1980) *The Unexpected Minority: handicapped children in America*, New York, Harcourt, Brace and Jovanovich.

HUTCHINSON, D. and TENNYSON, C. (1986) *Transition to Adulthood — A Curriculum Framework for Students with Severe Physical Disability*, London, FEU.

JOINT BOARD FOR PRE-VOCATIONAL EDUCATION, (1984) *The Certificate of Pre-Vocational Education: Consultative Document*, London, CGLI/BTEC Joint Board.

OECD/CERI, (1985) *Handicapped Youth at Work*, Paris, OECD/CERI.

OLIVER, M. (1987) *Some Reflections on Disabling Services*, Paper presented to the national launch of 'Transition to Adulthood', FEU, 1986, London.*

(*These two papers by Fish and Oliver, presented to the national launch of 'Transition to Adulthood' (FEU, 1986) appear in Hutchinson, D. *Supporting Transition to Adulthood: A Staff Training Package*. published by the FEU in 1990).

5
Role Conflict and Role Diffusion:
The Counsellor in Further Education

Lynne Chapman

Effective counselling consists of a definitely structured permissive relationship, which allows the client to gain an understanding of himself to a degree which enables him to take new, positive steps in the light of his new orientation.

(Rogers, 1942)

The purpose of counselling is to facilitate wise choices of the sort on which a person's later development depends.

(Tyler, 1961)

Counselling is a situation in which two people, a client and a counsellor, meet together on an agreed number of occasions during which the counsellor facilitates the other's exploration, understanding and solution of a problem issue by listening, clarifying, sometimes challenging and by offering a safe environment. It is in that safe environment, in the counsellor's room, that problems arising from disaffection within the further education system may surface and either may or may not achieve some resolution. Does disaffection find its way into the counselling room? How is it dealt with there? And what is recycled back from the counselling room into the college? In order to answer these questions we need to consider the counsellor and the student separately, before looking at the possible outcomes to their encounter.

The Counsellor's Role

Whilst it is certainly the case that in some colleges of further education the counsellor's role consists of working with students on personal issues or matters relating to career choice, it is also true that in many institutions the counsellor is called upon to wear several different, sometimes conflicting 'hats'. Thus, it is not unknown for a further education counsellor to be expected to:

provide personal and careers counselling;
advise students on welfare issues such as grants, legal matters, and
accommodation;
be the adviser to overseas students;
carry out a teaching role.

If it is taken into account that, even when undertaking a purely counselling
role, the college counsellor needs to maintain links with a wide range of
outside agencies including the local social services department and the
careers service, as well as maintaining efficient links with other college staff, it
is easy to see the potential that exists for role conflict and role diffusion.

Professional counsellors are trained to maintain a relationship with a
client that has very clear boundaries, to be non-judgmental, objective and to
refrain from giving advice. It becomes apparent that many of the other roles
they are expected to play are in conflict with this training, and it is not
surprising if at times, both counsellor and student are confused about the
exact nature of the counsellor's role within the college.

The confusion is often further compounded by the conditions under
which many further education counsellors have to function. Whilst their
counterpart in higher education can usually expect to have the minimum
necessary facilities, such as a private room, a telephone and the services of a
receptionist, many counsellors in further education still do not have the
simple facility of a counselling room where they can work with students in
quiet and privacy. Rooms are sometimes shared, so that the counsellor can
only be sure of privacy at agreed times of the day or week; it is not unknown
for counsellors to be working at one end of a partitioned room, with the
other section being used as a classroom or even as a snack bar. Too often they
work in uncarpeted, uncurtained rooms, with inappropriate furniture in
surroundings that are noisy and where interruptions are possible. None of
these conditions is conducive either to concentration on the part of the
counsellor, or to openness and self-disclosure by the student. The subtle
message conveyed to both is that the work they are trying to do together is
not highly valued by the institution.

It has been suggested that the counsellor's role is sometimes unclear,
and its boundaries difficult to sustain. Where counsellors have professional
training, they will be likely to have a clear understanding of the potential
difficulties. They will, for example, recognize the possible blurring of
boundaries that can occur if they are counsellors to students they also teach
and will observe precise boundaries between the two activities, helping the
students to do likewise. However, not all counsellors in further education
will have received professional training. Whilst in higher education it is now
less and less the case that a counsellor's functions are likely to be assigned to a

member of staff who lacks the appropriate training, there still appears to be a belief extant in some further education circles that counselling is somehow an extension of 'welfare' and that no specific training is required. This assumption does a grave disservice to the professionalism and skills of the many counsellors in further education who have sought and undergone training, and who carry out their work with great dedication and integrity. It means, moreover, that untrained counsellors are constantly being expected to exhibit skills and knowledge which they have had no opportunity to acquire. If they are aware that they lack the necessary skills to do the work, they may be damaged by a persisting sense of failure and inadequacy. If unaware of it, the students who come to them for help may be damaged, or, recognizing that available support is limited, may simply not come back.

The situation is perhaps similar to that of classroom teachers whose expertise and experience are often diminished by the belief expressed by others (non-teachers!) that, because everyone has been to school, everyone is somehow an 'expert' on education. Similarly, because everyone has problems, it can sometimes be assumed that helping people with problems through counselling is just a matter of 'common sense' and that anyone can do it. This is no more true of counselling than it is of teaching, and the case for having untrained counsellors in schools and colleges is as weak as that for having untrained teachers!

We see then how the expectations made of counsellors (that they will perform a wide variety of roles which may conflict; that they will be able to work in inappropriate surroundings and sometimes without training) can make it hard to achieve a sense of role that is clearly defined, both for themselves and others. When one's role is not clear it is also difficult to evaluate one's effectiveness within that role, and then a real sense of achievement and self-worth in relation to work will be difficult to obtain. Counsellors do not, in any case, tend to receive such obvious proof of the success or failure of their endeavours as teachers do. When the students they have taught pass their examinations or complete a course successfully, there is in that some degree of feedback for teachers that will help them and indeed others, to measure their effectiveness. By contrast, the confidential nature of counsellors' work means that, very often, only they and their clients know what they have achieved together and the client's 'thank you' when the work is done is often the only feedback they will receive. Thus, much of their work may have to be self-evaluated, and we have already seen that this is difficult to do, where no clear sense of role exists.

There is a danger here that the stage is being set for the counsellor to become marginalized in relation to the institution. If they perceive themselves and are perceived by others as a kind of 'hybrid' — part teacher, part something else — carrying out a lot of rather vague tasks which 'anyone can do', then they will be seen as peripheral to the mainstream life of the college. This is especially so if their status is low in terms of grade and salary. If this occurs, they may well come to feel isolated from colleagues, alienated from and unvalued by the institution. In a word, they may feel disaffected.

The Student

What of the student? What are the pressures that may bring them to the college counsellor's room? Further education encompasses a wide range of students with a wide range of needs, but before looking a little more closely at some of that variety of need, it is important first to consider the 'standard' further education student, the 16 to 19 year old.

The 16–19 Year Old

In brief, the young person aged between 16 and 19 years is in the process of transition from childhood to adult life and may be seen as experiencing pressures of three kinds: own developmental tasks, marginal position in society and external pressures from society.

The Developmental Tasks

The 16–19 year old is inevitably engaged upon the developmental tasks of late adolescence. These have been identified by Erikson (1968) as:

the achievement of an autonomous identity,
the ability to achieve close, intimate relationships with other people.

Wall (1968) has further suggested that the achievement of a sense of autonomous identity includes the formation of:

the sexual self
the social self
the vocational self
the philosophic self.

Thus, the young person at this transitional stage has a vast number of questions to ask and to answer about himself:

What work will I do? What will I be good at? What lifestyle do I want?

What kind of man/woman will I be? What does being a man or woman really mean anyway? Will I be attractive/acceptable sexually? Do I want to become a parent eventually?

How do I get on with other people? Can I trust them? Can they trust me? How will I know?

What do I really believe about life? How do I know if what I believe is right or wrong? Does anyone really know?

In seeking the answers to these questions some students will need the support of someone else, and that 'other' may well be the counsellor.

A Marginal Position in Society

By definition 16–19 year olds are in transition. They stand on the threshold of adulthood and over the next few years will become progressively responsible, in the eyes of society, for their decisions and actions. In the meantime, they are often expected to exercise adult self-discipline, judgment and control without the corresponding power and freedom of action.

Because adolescence is prolonged in our culture, young people, though physically mature or maturing, are still dependent upon parents or guardians financially, legally and emotionally. They occupy a place on the margin of adult society, neither wholly dependent nor wholly responsible, which is experienced sometimes as a lack of personal validity, or as a deep sense of belonging nowhere. From that may spring feelings of confusion and alienation, which may bring the student to the counsellor's room.

Pressures from Society

It is commonplace for an older generation to say to a younger: 'Things were harder in our youth: you have it easy; you've "never had it so good." Yet, despite the existence in Britain in 1990 of a standard of living that is comparatively higher than that of forty years ago, with an availability of luxury goods and labour-saving technology only dreamed of in years past, and in spite of the vast range of choices offered by a consumer society, it may be argued that the 16 to 19 year old today experiences pressures that are at least as complex as those felt by preceding generations.

Unemployment amongst school leavers is still high and many young people experience pressure to attend training schemes of questionable value, in order to receive social benefit payments, whilst various changes in the benefit system itself means, in effect, that young people are more likely to be totally financially dependent upon their parents if they are unable to obtain employment.

The pressure to be sexually active from an early age is considerable, as is the pressure to experiment with a wide range of addictive substances. Add to these the pressures of a society in which casual violence would appear to be increasing and the pace of social change ever accelerating, and it is not surprising if some young people feel bewildered, uncertain of their place and perhaps disillusioned about the adult world which they are about to enter.

Confusion, marginality, disillusionment; from such experience of oneself in relation to the world, alienation and disaffection may result.

Specific Student Groups

Further education attracts many students who have very specific needs in addition to those of the average 16 to 19 year old, and each group may produce specific counselling needs.

Female Students

If the chief developmental task of late adolescence is the achievement of a sense of autonomous identity, it needs to be recognized that this may be harder for the teenage girl than for her male counterpart. Feminist analysis of social and psychological development has shown how common it has been for women to be identified in terms of their relationships to other people — as a wife, mother, daughter, secretary — rather than as individuals in their own right. It is a well-researched fact that academic performance amongst girls often declines after the onset of puberty, not through biological factors, but because girls believe they will not be perceived by boys as attractive if they are also seen to be 'brainy'. Thus, many girls fail to achieve their full potential from their early teens onward. Therefore, the girl struggling to achieve a sense of self as she moves towards adulthood can experience real conflict, since she may believe that if she is genuinely 'herself' she will not be acceptable as a woman to other people. Some of these issues can manifest themselves in the counselling room in the form of anorexia nervosa, bulimia, depression or an unwanted pregnancy.

Students Belonging to Ethnic Minority Groups.

Students from an ethnic minority background, be it Afro-Caribbean, Asian or any other, will almost certainly have encountered racism by the age of 16 to 19. They may have repeatedly received the message that the society in which they live perceives them as alien, although they were born and bred in that society. In addition, young people from ethnic minority groups, in particular those from an Afro-Caribbean background, are more likely to be perceived as failing in the educational system than average. Therefore it is possible that young people from this group may arrive in further education feeling that, on the one hand, the education system has failed them, whilst on the other hand perceiving further education as their last chance to gain a foothold in a society that increasingly places value upon qualifications and skills.

If they do not find in the college an environment that reflects their needs and aspirations, if the curriculum takes no account of what they have to contribute, if the staff who teach them offer no role models, being mostly white and middle-class, then it is likely that the students will begin to disaffiliate from the college. To what extent they will find it feasible to approach the counselling service, since the majority of counsellors also tend to be white and middle-class, is a moot point.

Students with Special Educational Needs

Twenty years ago students identified nowadays as having special educational needs would have been unlikely to participate in further education at all, in any large numbers. Since the publication of the Warnock Report (DES, 1978), the further education sector has made significant efforts to increase and improve provision for this group, and their numbers have grown considerably. Some students now participate in further education on a fully integrated basis, whilst many more, in particular students with learning difficulties, are on discrete courses. Many further education colleges now have a special needs co-ordinator in post.

Students who have special educational needs will experience the same pressures as any 16 to 19 year olds, both developmental and societal. In addition, they will almost certainly come to further education carrying a feeling of 'difference', of not quite belonging as of right to the mainstream world. In particular, those students who have hitherto attended special schools are likely to need support, in order to deal with being part of a mainstream college. Where students have attended residential special schools located outside their home areas, they may have problems in forming social relationships, since unlike the average student, they are unlikely to have a core group of peers moving with them from school to the local FE college from which to form a circle of particular friends.

If the position of the average 16 to 19 year old can be described as marginal, then that of the young person with special educational needs may be experienced as peripheral to the margin! Many young people with a disability form a minority of one within their own families and their communities, and at adolescence there can be a strong desire to identify solely with the able-bodied world, whilst rejecting any identification with other people with disabilities, often perceived as a stigmatized group. That rejection means that the mutual support and solidarity that can be experienced by other minority groups is not available. They may feel that they can neither identify whole-heartedly with others who have disabilities, nor yet belong entirely to the able-bodied world; affiliation becomes problematic.

Paradoxically, separation may be equally problematic for the student who has special educational needs. It can be much more difficult to begin the necessary separation from parents which is such a normal feature of the transition to adulthood. The sheer fact of physical dependence upon a parent for the most intimate personal care needs can mean that the bid for independence is so much harder to make. Where parents find it hard to let go of their role as parents, where they have an emotional need for their son or daughter to remain a child, then the fact that their 'child' has a disability may feel like a justification of their prolonged parenting. Both student and parent may need the benefit of the counselling room in order for the process of separation and the achieving of a separate identity to begin.

Overseas Students

Students from overseas will also have issues that are particular to their situation. Away from their home country, often for the first time, within a short space of time they are expected to have adjusted to an alien culture, strange food, the British climate, the British landlord and a new course of study, taught in a language in which they may be less than 100 per cent fluent! It is scarcely surprising that some overseas students feel bemused, perplexed and frightened for the whole first year of their stay. Perhaps it is more surprising that so many of them remain afloat and complete their courses successfully. In addition to these basic but profound upheavals, some will encounter racism here. For others, political instability in their home country can mean, at the least, potential financial hardship if their funding is interrupted, and at worst, anxiety about friends and family at home, or even doubts about the feasibility and safety of returning home.

Whilst some overseas students use their peers as a strong support network, others do not. Some are under great pressure to succeed; one may have a government loan to repay at the end of his course, another may have a huge sense of obligation towards his family who have made great financial sacrifices in order to send him to college in the United Kingdom. There can be a temptation to spend much of the time alone, studying. Students in this situation who find themselves increasingly homesick, or who are failing to do well at their studies, are unlikely to talk problems through with peers. Also, many overseas students come from cultures in which to acknowledge personal problems and to discuss them with others is perceived as weakness, and perhaps as disloyalty to one's family. Thus the students' distress is often not noticed until very late — when they have failed an examination, or actually break down under the weight of their stress.

The counselling room offers one clear point at which the overseas student who is in distress could receive help, and may experience some sense of affiliation with the college. However, unless some links have already been set up between the service and the overseas student community, unless the counselling service is 'visible' and obviously available, then overseas students are less likely than most to avail themselves of what it has to offer.

It is suggested that, for a variety of reasons, there exists the potential for many of the students who participate in further education to disaffiliate from the society in which they live, from their peer group and from the college as an institution; and that, further, their sense of alienation may lead them to seek counselling, or may lead others to recommend that they do so.

However, it has also been noted that, given certain circumstances, there is a real possibility that counsellors too may perceive themselves as marginal to and disaffiliated from the institution. In that case, we will have the disaffected counselling the disaffected! In order to consider how that undesirable outcome can be avoided, we need to look at a number of factors which affect the encounter between the counsellor and the student. Significant among these are the ways in which counselling as a service is presented to the institution, and the routes by which the student reaches the counsellor.

Students' Perceptions of Counselling

Counsellors in further education may have to work with quite inappropriate and inadequate facilities. Whilst this is damaging to the work itself, it is also harmful in terms of the statements it makes to potential users of the service about the value placed upon its activities by the college. Where a counselling service is unable to offer its clients the minimum requirements of a little comfort, privacy and freedom from interruption it is unlikely to be perceived as a potent source of help. Nor will its 'image' be improved if it is hidden away in remote parts of the building and poorly signposted, if it is only operational at limited times, and is inaccessible to students with disabilities.

It is of crucial importance that the counselling service is 'visible' in the college, and in ways that are friendly and welcoming. Some of the ways in which this can be encouraged include:

An accessible, well-appointed location for the service;
Counsellor involvement in induction programmes for new students;
Involvement/initiation by counselling staff of developmental groupwork to meet the needs of specific student groups;
A clear description of the service in college prospectus/student handbook;
A service that operates regularly and at times when students are able to use it (in some students' case, that might mean evenings).

Staff Perceptions of the Counsellor

Staff's perceptions of the counselling service are as important as those held by the students. Hamblin (1974) cites the 'hidden' counsellors who are secretive about their work and make few efforts to liaise effectively with other staff, whilst making self-important noises about confidentiality in a manner calculated to alienate and mystify other staff rather than to preserve the confidences of their clients. Such practitioners are likely to be viewed with hostility and suspicion by other staff, who may fear (sometimes with good reason) that they are being discussed behind their backs, and also that the counsellors are in collusion with students against them. It is really a part of the counsellors' role to help other staff to understand the work they do. Whilst they cannot of course discuss the cases of individual students with other staff, there are ways in which they can promote better understanding of their work. They can:

contribute to staff development and training programmes within the college: basic counselling and communication skills, study skills, stress reduction workshops, seminars related to specific problem areas such as anorexia or AIDS together with guidelines on the question of referral to the counselling service, are all potentially useful elements of a staff development programme;

use all available opportunities, formal and informal, to meet other staff and keep open lines of communication with them — they need to be 'visible' to staff as well as to students;

where appropriate, and where the student wishes it, enlist the support of other staff for a student who is in difficulties.

Counsellors will be unlikely to achieve any of these if they are either forced into, or have locked themselves into, a marginal position in relation to the life of the college.

Referrals

The route by which a student reaches the counsellor may have considerable impact upon their work together. Any counsellor knows that a self-referring client is, in general, more likely to work through his or her problems. However, anyone who has ever finally plucked up the courage to telephone a counsellor for a first appointment, or to knock at their door for the first time, will remember how great an effort this can require. Students will not feel able to take that risk unless they believe that the counselling service will take them seriously, and will be able to help them. When a service is operating professionally and students feel that they have been helped, they will generally recommend it to their fellows, and there will be little problem with self-referrals. Where the service is ineffective the student grapevine will operate and self-referrals may be low.

A referral made by someone else can be equally valuable, but it may also be problematic. Much depends on who has made the referral, and why. Whilst few counsellors will agree to see a student unless the appointment has actually been made by the student, or has been made with their consent, students may arrive in the counsellor's room under a sense of coercion. If the student has been referred with either an overt or covert message of 'get yourself sorted out — or else!', then the first issue the counsellor must address is whether the problem actually belongs to the student or to the tutor who has sent them. Unless counsellor and student are able to reach a point at which the student both feels that a problem exists and also that they wish to work through it, they can achieve little by working together. Even when a student has come along on the advice of a caring tutor who has noticed that something is wrong and is concerned for the student's welfare, unless the student feels safe enough to acknowledge that a problem exists, little can be accomplished. In such circumstances it may be that all the counsellor can do, for the time being, is to convey to the student that the counselling room is a safe and welcoming place to return to at a later date.

Confidentiality

A large element of 'feeling safe' for the student who is having counselling, lies in knowing that counselling sessions are confidential. Many will have initial difficulties in believing that confidentiality exists; as school pupils they will, unfortunately, too often have come to expect that they will be discussed behind their backs by adults. Therefore, in promising confidentiality, counsellors also need to describe its limits. They need to tell students that they have a professional supervisor with whom they discuss their work; they may need to discuss with the students those circumstances under which it might be valuable, or necessary, to discuss them with someone else, both with their consent and without it. What, for example, would be their stance if the student reveals in confidence, an intention to harm another person?

These issues are particularly difficult for the further education counsellor. The school counsellor, like other school staff defined as being 'in loco parentis' to the child in school, has a clear set of responsibilities towards clients; the counsellor in higher education is working with adults, who are legally responsible for themselves. The further education counsellor, working largely with a population aged between 16 to 19 years, has a client group on the borderline of legal adult status who may, under stress, veer wildly between child and adult in their emotions and behaviour.

Parents

The extent to which the counsellor has an involvement with the parents of clients may also be a vexed issue. Once again, the matter is far more clear-cut for those working in schools or in institutions of higher education. The counsellor in further education will almost certainly encounter parents who feel that they ought to be kept informed about their child's work, or who wish to discuss their child without the student's knowledge or consent. Whilst parents can be hard to gainsay, nevertheless the counsellor would not generally meet them without the student's consent. On the other hand, where that consent is willingly given, much can be achieved by working with the student and parents together, if all concerned are willing, and if the counsellor has the necessary skills.

The College

The student is not alone in having expectations of the counsellor, be they realistic or unrealistic; the college too will have expectations, both explicit and unspoken. Therefore it is essential that counsellors have sufficient status within the institution to negotiate about its expectations of them, and where necessary, modify them. There may be a need to educate other staff about the counselling process. For example, the author is aware of circumstances in which counsellors in further education colleges have encountered some of the following expectations about their work:

> that the counsellor will only need one, at the most two, sessions in which to work through problems brought by the majority of students;
> that they should deal instantly with every student who seeks help;
> that they will tell heads of department the names of students in their department whom they have seen;
> that they will only see the really 'ill' students — and that tutors must handle the rest.

It is important that counsellor and college are clear — and agree — about what is expected of them in terms of:

> the average length of their working contract with student clients;
> their availability to students;
> confidentiality;
> their teaching role and conditions of service;
> their need for professional supervision and on-going professional development;
> the degree of autonomy they exercise over referrals, both those which are made to them and those which they make to external agencies.

Where counsellors are working under conditions in which the expectations the college has of them are unclear, or are not in accordance with their own perceptions of the role, there will, at best, be constant misunderstandings, and at worst, a counsellor and an institution working against each other — disaffected and disaffiliated from each other. Ultimately, the student is bound to suffer. So how can the counsellor function most effectively within the institution?

The Effective Counsellor

It has been suggested that the more peripheral to mainstream college life they are, the less effective counsellors will be in meeting the needs of the institution as a whole. Unless the counsellor is able to make an impact on the institution in its totality then their work with students, though helpful, may be in the nature of crisis management. Although this will always be a part of a counsellor's work, the more effective counsellor is likely to be of help to students by working within the institution to influence its practices and procedures so that an environment is created which is congenial to the personal growth and development of its students and staff. Thus the counsellor may be seen to include the prevention, as well as the crisis management of problems, as a valid part of their role. It is likely that, in order to be truly effective, counsellors will need to be:

- an integral member of the staff team, with enough status within the institution to have 'clout'. This means that the counselling service is able to link into all the major college structures — academic board, administrative committees, student networks — at a senior level;
- provided with appropriate accommodation and facilities for their work;
- professionally trained and supervised;
- acknowledged as trained professionals in terms of status and remuneration;
- 'visible' within the institution, so that students are aware that the service exists, and are not made to feel that a visit to the counsellor is extraordinary or unusual;
- working within clearly defined role boundaries: they should not have to undertake welfare and advisory work as well;
- regular contributors to the in-house staff development programme;
- able to build and maintain effective links with other key members of staff, such as the principal, heads of departments, and special needs co-ordinator, and through them be able to feed back to the institution the impact made upon students by its practices and procedures;
- if required to have a teaching role, they may carry it out to good purpose through the provision of structured guidance programmes.

Hamblin (1983) has cited the following as potential areas for guidance for the 16–19 year old group:

— Careers Guidance: focusing on the development of a satisfying life style; the skills of job search and interview skills: the development and use of resources during a period of unemployment; and the skills of successful adjustment in a first job.
— Social and Life Skills: decision-making; social anxieties; stress management; relationships with authority figures.
— Group Interaction: mechanisms operating in groups; approval and

affiliation needs; conflict; roles and relationships; competition and co-operation.
— Learning about Learning: problem-solving; learning styles; questioning assumptions; information search skills; planning and organizational skills; self-monitoring; imagination and creativity.

The model suggested by Hamblin opens up the possibility of group work that could be offered to students covering a wide range of options wich might include:

— exam preparation groups
— assertiveness training groups
— personal growth groups
— stress management groups.

Because their position within the college is unique, counsellors have to perform the almost impossible feat of being able to stand back a little from the institution, whilst at the same time being involved with its functioning. It is not unlike the stance they need to maintain a rapport with their clients. In each instance, they must be able to understand the world of the other without becoming totally immersed in it, so that they are able to reflect back their perceptions to both the institution and the client. Counsellors who are able to achieve this paradox will be of immense value to both, and both will benefit from feedback that is objective and non-judgemental. Such counsellors can provide one of the conduits through which student and institution may affiliate to one another, and their price is greater than rubies.

References

ERIKSON, H. E. (1968) *Identity, Youth and Crisis*, London, Faber and Faber.
HAMBLIN, D. (1974) *The Teacher and Counselling*, Oxford, Basil Blackwell.
HAMBLIN, D. (1983) *Guidance: 16–19*, Oxford, Basil Blackwell.
ROGERS, C. (1942) *Client-Centred Therapy*, Boston, Houghton Mifflin.
TYLER, L. E. (1961) *The Work Of The Counselor*, New York, Appleton-Century-Crofts.
WALL, W. D. (1968) *Adolescents in School and Society,* Slough, NFER.
DEPARTMENT OF EDUCATION AND SCIENCE (1978) *Report of the Committee of Inquiry into the Education of Handicapped Children and Young People* (The Warnock Report) London, HMSO.

6
It's Almost Like Work:
A Study of a YTS Workshop[1]

Jenny Corbett

> On the dole, you've got a lot of problems. You have to keep
> bugging them for money and it doesn't always come through.
> While here it's almost like work really. It's different from school
> because you don't have to have people pushing you to do things.
> You can make up your mind if you want to do something.
>
> (Trainee at Hartworth Centre, December 1988).

Introduction

In this chapter I am concerned to investigate the social function of Youth
Training (YT) provision through examination of one urban workshop which
I shall call Hartworth Centre. My purpose is to share a closer understanding
of the culture of YTS (now termed YT). In evaluating the roles of
management, staff and trainees within the ethos of the workshop I shall
reveal the anomalous relationship between rhetoric and reality. The tensions
which ensue create complex and barely discernible layers of disaffection.
Within these layers a social function operates; one which I term *affectionate
patronising*. It is this covert practice, affecting all participants regardless of
seniority, which is the focus of my study.

I have selected this particular topic and am using this specific example
for several reasons. My earlier research in the borough in which Hartworth
Centre is located revealed that the drop-out rate for trainees with special
needs who were integrated into YTS programmes was over 50 per cent
(Corbett, 1987). I wanted to see how far borough YTS provision had been
adapted to accommodate a wide range of needs and whether these needs
were still causing the tensions among staff that they had done previously. I
selected this workshop because it responded to a diverse range of trainees and

would enable me to raise issues related to race, class, gender and disability.

I will not pretend that Hartworth Centre is representative of YT workshop provision generally. It is unusual in that it is placed in one of the most socially and economically deprived areas of Britain, according to DES statistics (DES, 1982). The young people who attend the scheme reflect the complex needs of a multi-cultural community experiencing urban stress. Of the trainees on the scheme 85 per cent are black, most of them Afro-Caribbean. However, it is also unusual in that it operates a policy of positive discrimination, reflecting borough priorities. This not only involves promoting equality of opportunity but the introduction of trade union practices and entitlements. About half of the staff in the scheme are from the same ethnic minorities as the trainees. In looking at the social function of YT, I have chosen a scheme which has many factors in its favour. Whereas some might say that all adult/adolescent relationships are, by their nature, patronising, an element of genuine affection and empathy between staff and trainees is a distinguishing feature of this scheme.

Whilst engaged in this research, between November 1988 and February 1989, I met with the familiar problems experienced by those who use ethnographic methods. I can only deal superficially with the heterogeneity of 'reality constructions' (Adelman, 1985, p. 39) within this complex setting. I have to acknowledge the effect of my role as a white, female researcher interviewing male instructors and black, male trainees. Davies suggests that 'women, because of their traditional invisibility, blend in with the wallpaper more, and are able to eavesdrop on conversations with greater insidiousness' (Davies, 1985, p. 86). Certainly, I found staff and trainees prepared to share experiences in which their perceptions might be subjected to critical analysis. This presented me with the dilemma of the rights of 'subjects' to comment on the final presentation. If my subjects are helpful and friendly throughout, how can I criticize their practice? As Woods (1985) reminds us, the problems of coping, in precarious situations, with logistical demands and ethical questions are uncomfortable realities for any ethnographer. He also emphasizes that ethnography is a highly personal affair.

This, then, is my inevitably subjective analysis of a YTS workshop in which I felt participants were valued and supported, where I felt at ease and where staff and trainees cared for one another. My expectations and perceptions have shaped my attempt to present an overall description of the workshop. I was expecting signs of disaffection under the surface and (only because of that, perhaps) found them. I was expecting YTS workshop-based provision to offer a poor quality of skills training and to focus on 'right attitudes' and (again, perhaps consequently) found this generally to be the case. Much of the interpretation of social function had to be 'read between the lines' and again this was my own (possibly faulty) reading.

YTS and Equal Opportunities

In examining the literature in this field I will look firstly at YTS generally before discussing the issue of equal opportunities.

From its inception, YTS has been subject to critical assessment. It has been seen as primarily concerned with preparing youth for the labour market rather than offering skill acquisition (Mac An Ghaill, 1988). Critics have regarded the reality of YTS as being diametrically opposed to its rhetoric:

> When the broad specification of goals is translated into detailed (and assessable) learning objectives, we have moved away from liberal demands for generic training to the illiberal social reproduction of a pliant underclass.
>
> (Jonathan, 1987, p. 105)

The social function of YTS is observed to stem from the emphasis on achieving the 'right attitude to the job' which 'is the most important criterion adopted by employers for recruiting young people' (Brown, 1987, p. 141). Young people whom Brown interviewed (like the trainee quoted at the beginning) appeared to find YTS acceptable only as an alternative to the dole.

Yet, some would see YTS as a last, precious opportunity for learning, in which the recruits are given:

> a *proper education* for the first time in their lives. The truth is that despite overall rising educational standards a minority of young people do leave school without proficiency in basic numeracy and literacy, however that is defined. Of course they always did.
>
> (Cohen, 1984, p. 161)

Whereas these young people were once able to obtain unskilled jobs despite their learning difficulties, the lack of such jobs is masked by the focus in the new vocationalism upon their need for skills.

The rhetoric of the Training Agency (TA) emphasizes choice in occupational competency, matching individual needs to required skills. This jars with the expectations of employers in which:

> the secondary labour market is organised on the basis of low commitment, high turnover and dependency, whilst education and training assumes high commitment, career orientation, self-fulfilment and individual choice.
>
> (Buswell, 1988, p. 178)

What emerged from much of the research in this area was the harsh fact that reconciling trainees to the reality of the limited choices which actually face them is one of the unwritten tasks of YTS. Having to make the coffee and do mundane office chores, whilst often resisted, was a reflection of their true status in the workplace (Buswell, 1988). A deficit model of disabilities was fostered by assessing all trainees against a general checklist of skills which might bear little relation to the actual tasks required (Rosie, 1988).

A Code of Practice on Special Needs in YTS (TA, 1988) might be seen as a direct response to the critical report on inadequacies found within the programme, which was produced by the Institute of Careers officers and the Royal Association for Disability and Rehabilitation in 1986. In the Code of Practice, the Training Agency acknowledges the need for specialist support for staff, for specific resources for individual needs, for extra time allowance for some trainees to complete their YTS programmes and for the opportunity within those programmes to accommodate social and educational difficulties.

In relation to promoting equality of opportunity, the Training Agency has expressed concern with the lack of access into YTS programmes for young people for whom English was a second language (TA, 1988). The need for positive discrimination to counteract disadvantage in YTS has led to the establishment of Development Officers to promote equal opportunities (Ghua, 1988). Posts within schemes have been created in which teachers of the same nationality as the trainees with English as a second language can offer support in chosen options.

Positive discrimination involves recognizing differences:

> Youngsters from ethnic minorities are different from their white peers: not better, nor worse, but different. We believe that enough is now known to suggest that these differences can and do act as a barrier between them and those from the white community who exert an influence over them and their futures.
>
> (Verma and Darby, 1987, p. 95)

Monitoring the progress of trainees could be open to discriminatory practices, so Verma and Darby suggest this should ideally be undertaken by staff of the same ethnic minority as youngsters on the scheme.

In addition to overt racial discrimination, black young people face difficulties in finding employment because of 'their perceived lower than average educational performance in a situation where credentialism is endemic' (Fenton and Burton, 1987, p. 37). The 'barriers' to which Verma and Darby refer can not only block entry to the labour market but can also equate 'ethnic minority' with 'special need' (Cross, 1986; Cross and Smith, 1987). This equation does not begin with the barrier to employment: this is just a later hurdle among many along the way.

Hall (1978) indicates that, from the remedial classes in schools to the lower end of the labour market, black youths experience a perpetuation of their marginal status. Stone (1981) suggests that the Afro-Caribbean community feel that the British education system regards them as 'basically inferior to people of European descent' (p. 174). There might be little evidence of racism from teaching staff whilst performing in the public arena, but Hammersley (1981) recorded a high degree of staffroom racism in an inner city school.

For some years, it has been evident that a tension exists between the value which Afro-Caribbean parents place on discipline and hard work and the liberalism prevalent in British state schools (Rex and Tomlinson, 1979). This dilemma was again evident in the findings of two recent reports — one on a primary school in ILEA (DES, 1989); one on a London borough (NFER, 1989) — highlighting parental wishes for increased discipline and higher academic expectations, both in multi-racial communities. As was found in the 1981 Scarman Report, Afro-Caribbean parents felt betrayed by the lack of structure in education, the failure of teachers to motivate their children and the lack of empathy for their cultural traditions.

Tomlinson (1984) demonstrates that a disproportionate number of children from ethnic minorities, particularly Afro-Caribbeans, are placed in some form of special educational provision, immediately furthering their disadvantaged status. Mackney (1985) records the progression of this cycle as young people move from school into YTS. He notes that, in Birmingham, there were a disproportionate number of trainees from ethnic minorities in the Mode B YTS rather than the more favoured Mode A. Whilst Mode A involved training with employers, Mode B was a simulation of work, at one remove from the labour market. The implications were that those trainees designated by careers officers and schools for Mode B were not yet suitable for employment.

Where does Hartworth Centre fit into this context? It offers an example of both positive and negative aspects of provision: positive, in that it has the potential to break the barriers Fenton and Burton (1987) outline by undermining traditional notions of educational success and by reducing discrimination among employers; negative, in that it is representative of workshop-based rather than employer-based YTS and, as such, offers a less favoured entry into employment.

The Function of Hartworth Centre

Hartworth Centre has a female manager which could be seen as a triumph for equal opportunities in a training workshop which has a traditionally male ethos. Fieldhouse (1987) emphasizes that there has to be commitment from the top for any policy in YTS to succeed and this commitment is clearly evident at Hartworth Centre. The manager makes her views on discrimination and access quite explicit:

> One of the things which is emphasised, both in staff and trainee induction, is our policy of equal opportunities and a strong policy against any kind of discrimination, including intimidation. We tell them that, 'You might have got away with picking on someone at school or you might have noticed it at school. We don't have anything like that here.' In the same way, we don't discrimate on the grounds of sex or race. So if you're the sort of person who's going to have problems in relating to people of other cultures, you need to think seriously about settling here.

> From our point of view, we have totally open access, whether the kids are directed here by the careers service or schools. If your first language is not English, you might not feel confident about going into a situation where you're with employers. If you've got learning difficulties, you might need extra time. We find the Training Agency is very amenable about extending programmes for up to 6 months.
>
> (manager, 1988)

One of the major social functions of the Centre, as the manager perceives it, is to 'unpick what schools have done to them' in terms of destroying their self-esteem and imposing no work discipline. She does not underestimate the daunting task of counteracting eleven years of negative school experiences but views it as requiring a fresh approach:

> We will recognise them and credit them for skills they have, in a positive way, rather than depending on reading and writing, although we do offer support for reading and writing. It's amazing how often you find a kid whose reading and writing was bad at school who, because they're motivated by something else, will work really hard to try and improve their reading and writing.

> We try to listen to them and to understand their behaviour; at the same time to make them accept responsibility for their actions. That's the biggest difficulty they have to take on board — the fact that if they behave badly it will affect their progress and other people's. It's always somebody else's fault.
>
> (manager, 1988)

Clearly, the manager is committed to offering trainees every opportunity to progress within YTS and to achieve to the maximum of their potential.

Yet she and her staff are patronised by a system which sets low ceilings on the potential of workshop trainees. The rhetoric of YTS offers skills; the reality offers survival tactics. Staff learn to modify the rhetoric. Although the manager values trainees and actively seeks to combat discrimination against them, she recognizes that they need grooming for employers and supporting every step along the way. They are not able to cope without considerable assistance:

> our place operates like a transitional process. You come into the workshop to gain basic skills in a vocational area which equips you to cope well in a work placement.

> We act as an impartial advocate to look after their interest so that, if there is any sexual harassment or exploitation, there is someone who can step in and say, 'What's going on here?'
>
> (manager, 1988)

Yet, despite emphasis on gaining the basics, preparation for employment appears to owe more to adhering to the programme, maintaining attendance and to the fluctuation of demographic trends than to the acquisition of marketable skills:

> I can make quite a strong commitment on induction that, if you follow a programme, you'll get a job. Particularly now, when the labour shortage is getting more noticeable and we get employers ringing us up saying, 'Have you got any kids who can do such and such?'
>
> (manager, 1988)

The primary social function of the programme is to develop acceptable social skills which will be the key to employment success:

> We've got a young black woman who had not very good social skills actually — rather strange in some of the ways she reacted. Now, after a lot of discussion and a lot of practice in how you operate in a work environment, she's gone out to be a typist in an Estate Agents and is now selling houses. So she's actually using very effective social skills and getting commission of hundreds of pounds a week.

The manager goes on to say:

> So we are actually in a position where we can intervene *in the traditional bias* against employing trainees.
>
> (manager, 1988, my italics)

When the manager refers to 'the traditional bias' is she really implying that there is a general bias against all YTS trainees? I think she is referring, rather, to the discrimination which her scheme is working to counteract. The *affectionate patronising* which results is not a systematic devaluing of the trainees concerned. It is more an acceptance of the inequities which exist and the level of cushioning and packaging required to work 'unacceptable' trainees into the establishment.

Perceiving a Social Function

There are layers of perceptions of the role of a YTS workshop. The Training Agency perceives it as a preparation for employment. The workshop manager sees it as part of the personal development of the young person, 'to help them recognise that there are key changes that need to happen if they're going to take responsibility for their own futures'. One instructor regarded his role in the proceedings as being to break down attitudes among some trainees of 'a total disregard of any authority whatsoever'. The perceptions of trainees themselves varied in relation to their length of stay in the scheme.

For some trainees, the stay was very short. The induction period, during which young people are introduced to the various options of wood-related skills, catering, office skills, computing, electronics, and graphic design, and are initiated into the work ethos, can prove to be a testing time for staff:

> With some, you just can't get near them. You can't find any way
> in. The trouble is, in a workshop like this, if you get one person
> like this, negative — then everybody polarizes towards them. They
> polarize towards the negative, not the positive. Whilst the YTS is
> an open-door system, we have to think seriously about the effects
> one person can have on the others. In the interests of the number,
> you sometimes have to look at one in the group and say, 'Well, we
> have a rotten apple in the barrel and we have to get rid of that
> one'.
>
> (instructor, 1988)

On my first visit to the workshop, I witnessed the suspension of two Afro-Caribbean male trainees who had failed their induction period on the grounds of displaying disruptive behaviour. It was clearly a stressful process for the manager who was having to cope with their vocal resistance to leaving the premises, in the exposure of the public arena of the lobby. Both young men challenged her decision and she was engaged in a protracted discussion with them in which she was justifying her position in relation to their 'attitude' to work and the general lack of commitment they evidenced. One young man left and his Careers Officer rang an hour later to say that she had him in her office and wanted to know the grounds for his dismissal. The other young man loitered around the lobby, gathering others around him. Sitting, waiting, on a chair in the lobby (perhaps, as Davies (1985) suggested, virtually 'invisible') I found the atmosphere becoming progressively more Afro-Caribbean, until I was able to distinguish little of what was being said. The young man at the centre was clearly elaborating on his feelings, supported and strengthened by fellow trainees, almost all of them Afro-Caribbean. They were using dialect which was effectively alienting me and, presumably, any other listener unused to the pace and use of such language. As staff passed through the lobby, I felt that this had been claimed as the trainees' territory and that we were perceived by them as the intruders. The 'disruptive' individual was being honoured with a cultural surge of solidarity. It was a small victory, no doubt, as the young man eventually left. He was told to return the following morning, by which time the manager would have been able to talk to more staff about his work.

Two issues emerge from the acknowledgment by staff that potential sources of disaffection have to be removed at the initial stages: firstly, that one of the distinguishing features of such 'trouble-makers' appeared to be their ability to articulate their feelings and to influence others (in another context, surely a sign of initiative and intelligence); secondly, that the borough Race Relations Unit makes the procedure for suspension a delicate and difficult affair and, therefore, it is easier to avoid enrolling possible problem trainees in the first place.

One instructor felt that positive discrimination in a policy of equal opportunites for trainees from ethnic minorities made him vulnerable:

> we have a distinct disadvantage as we really don't have any sanctions. The Appeal Committee is such that, if we suspend someone or we sack someone, we have to be absolutely one hundred per cent certain of our facts. We have to follow the procedure very, very carefully. Otherwise, given the situation of the Race Relations Unit, there can be terrible problems.
>
> (instructor, 1988)

The manager indicated that she wanted to share decision-making both with her instructors and with trainees' parents:

> All staff have the right to suspend trainees for up to two days, on the spot. You have to have that because, if they always refer decisions upwards, why should kids listen to them? A kid can appeal of course. But the first stage is an oral warning where the member of staff says, 'This isn't acceptable' or 'I don't want you to

do that'. The second stage is a written warning which is a recorded letter, either from me or one of the training officers. The third stage is suspension. Anything that involves a suspension means that a copy of the letter goes to the kid's parents. We used to have this thing about they're young adults but we often found that, when a kid got sacked, the parents would ring up and say 'Why has my son been sacked for being late once?' and it would be a kid who had been involved in intimidation, violence, vandalism and everything you can imagine but the parents had no idea and it was quite clear that, had the parents been involved, they would have tried to intervene in that downward spiral. We had a discussion with staff and trainee reps. and we thought the trainee reps. would be horrified by the idea of involving parents but they thought it was a very good idea. You just can't predict.

(manager, 1988)

The notion of involving parents in supporting their child's entry into the employment market reinforces the social function of YTS as a process of initiation into the rigours of working life. However, although I am sure it is not meant to be in the least condescending, I find the manager's constant use of the term 'kids' to jar with the concept of assisting young adults to accept responsibilities. Perhaps this is one of the reasons why I see examples of *affectionate patronising*. That the rapport between staff and trainees is warm and genuine I have no doubt — I saw instances of this all the time, in their chats together over lunch in the canteen, their smokes together over coffee, their sharing of jokes and patient repetition of routines together — but, in the process of moulding trainees to fit their roles, there was an unavoidable culture gap.

Trainees appeared to fall into three specific categories for the staff: those who spelt trouble immediately and were ousted; those who came reluctantly and were infrequent attenders; and those who became compliant workers. The infrequent attenders had generally been:

massaged in by social services because they'd like a bridging allowance, don't want a vocational area but have got to get some sort of YTS and have been through an initial training at college but it's not worked out. The family and general social problems that kids like that have quite often just militates against them succeeding.

(manager, 1989, my italics)

I emphasize the use of *massaged in* as an expression of entry to the scheme because it illuminates the coercive and contradictory function of YTS. The scheme is ostensibly all about *choice* of occupations. Yet, it denies choice to those who have not selected it in the first place.

The concept of 'open access', which was offered by the manager as one of the characteristic features in the policy of equal opportunities, can surely be challenged. There is open access for those who are prepared to comply with the system which exists and not attempt to sabotage it. There is also a form of *closed* access for those who want alternative provision but have been *massaged in*. For the trainees who are contented with the provision offered, there is the message of the opening quote: it is, at least, preferable to school or to the dole.

Trainees' Perceptions of the Role of YTS

I asked trainees what they felt they were getting out of YTS which they had not gained at school:

> To be disciplined. To get used to proper work. Like clocking-in on time. Behaviour.
>
> They want you to get on with your work. They don't want you to muck about. They just want you to get on with what you've come there to do.
>
> When you're doing work, you can go out when you want. You can go downstairs. When it's break-time, you make your own coffee. People are just more helpful.
>
> At school we used to be rioting. If you're asked to do something and you want to get some help, they just started shouting, 'Come on, come on' and they didn't come. Well, over here, they will come when you want them. They'll just take two to three minutes and they'll come.
>
> The teachers don't see us as children no more. They see us as adults now.
>
> (male and female trainees, 1988)

Some of the trainees were quite open about their school disaffection:

> I did do good but I kept fighting — fighting over stupid things like football. I can't tell you why I did. The teachers used to grab us by the scruff of the hair and pull us into the headmaster's office. I always used to get into trouble for that.
>
> (male trainee, 1988)

When this young man goes on to say that he no longer really feels the need to fight much beyond 'swearing at each other', it might be surmised that this is indicative of the maturing process. He saw it as part of the ethos he perceived in the YTS where:

> we should act like adults. They talk to us like they talk to other staff. In school, they used to talk like you was lower than them.
>
> (male trainee, 1988)

However, he observed inflexibility in the approach:

> I don't mind coming in on time but some of the discipline I don't like. If you're a little bit late, they send you home. I think they should let you stay and work late as you've come in to work.
>
> (male trainee, 1988)

I suggest that this last comment illustrates the cultural gap which exists between the world of work which the trainees are being prepared to enter and that which their instructors occupy. The former is inflexible because its primary demands are those of good time-keeping and attendance; the latter has room for flexibility because it values the skills on offer.

Some trainees are realistic about the limitations and possibilities in the YTS:

> I'm doing Graphics. I didn't really want to do it. I was going to go into the army. My teachers at school told me I was really good at Art and Design. At first I thought it was boring but then I liked it more and more. I've been on one work placement and I was good. I'd like to go on to a Graphic Design Office. I would have got a job from school as a painter and decorator as my dad has his own business. I do it sometimes at weekends with him.
>
> (male trainee, 1988)

For this young man, YTS might lead to work in Graphic Design or in his father's business — either way, he is sure of a job.

Getting a job of any kind is a powerful motivator into the YTS:

> I was on the dole before I came here, for about two years. Then I saw that advert for YTS on TV. Before I came here, I didn't know how to type at all. I didn't do typing at school or anything but I've learnt how to type letters and so on. For spelling you look it up in the dictionary and we have spelling tests on Fridays.
>
> (female trainee, 1988)

Whilst this trainee was eager to find work, she was disappointed with work placement, as it failed to match her expectations:

It was OK but I didn't really like it so I stopped. It was a different thing after I got there. I thought it was going to be nice but it was different.

(female trainee)

This perception of work not matching up to expectations is reiterated in my interviews with staff. Some see their roles as trying to 'bring home the reality of it'.

Staff Perceptions of the Function of YTS

In my examination of staff perceptions, I will draw upon interviews with a liaison officer, whose role is to act as intermediary between trainees and employers, and with YTS instructors and college lecturers. Both come to serve the trainees from different contexts and often with contrasting objectives. I will also make detailed reference to the diary whose pages were shared with me by an instructor who was leaving the workshop that week. I felt caught in a dilemma by the open access which this man gave me to his diary. He was quite contented to let me read the many anecdotes and observations he had made over the years, mostly related to the trainees and their sayings and habits. He knew I was researching for a chapter on disaffection and wanted to be quite frank in his opinions. I am most grateful for his open generosity for it enabled me, I feel, to gain a deeper insight into staff perceptions than by interview alone. However, in evaluating his diary, I could not avoid critical examination of his attitude towards the trainees, as it reflected his personal experience of *affectionate patronising* within the scheme.

The Liaison Officer noted three major functions of the YTS:

to require trainees to have a certain level of basic competence; especially, they need to have good time-keeping and attendance because that's the biggest thing employers are looking for; in the actual workplace they'll see the reality in relation to their ideals.

(Liaison Officer, 1988)

Supporting the employer in coping with the inadequacies of the trainee is seen as a vital stage, once these three functions are operating:

Frequently we're able to give advice to the employers on the best way of training young people. Quite often the employer will say, 'They won't do that' or 'They can't do that', when it usually just needs presenting in a different way. Employers will often say to us, 'They forget the most simple things' or 'Surely they know by now that this is their routine job'. We suggest writing down a list and sticking it on the wall so they'll remember. It's helping them get over problems. We have college tutors or workshop supervisors visit, if we're having a problem. They've got the expertise to say, 'If they're having trouble doing it in the workplace, this is the way we've taught them in the workshop'.

(Liaison Officer, 1988)

If the trainee was hoping to go into skilled work but is having to be weaned into the role of an unskilled labourer, this is done gently:

so that even if we get a young person coming out of the workshops that may not be the best electrician going, we can find them something in a related area — an electrical warehouse, where their knowledge of the bits that they know will be put to good use and they'll still be in that environment they want to work in.

(Liaison Officer, 1988)

Smoothing the path for employer and trainee, such that the former learns to accept a slow learner and the latter to settle to routine, is the compromise role of the Liaison Officer.

The Liaison Officer emphasizes the importance of gaining basic skills and of maintaining good time-keeping and attendance. Do instructors verify these priorities?

(Catering) We start off with basic skills: setting up counters; knowing what knives and forks are to go where; making teas, coffees and sandwiches; learning how a stock cupboard should be; how to hold a knife; how to walk around a kitchen without knives pointing out. From there, they get on. It depends what their level is when they start.

(Office Skills) They have to clock-in and do a 40 hour week. Their weekly rota of jobs includes: sorting the post; working the switchboard; recording the attendance list (transferring all the 'clocking-in cards' to a big sheet); photocopying; checking stationery, doing the laundry; making tea and coffee.

(Graphic Design) Basic skills — they get the jobs that had been delegated and delegated but that's only natural. The work placements would break down when the kids went out very starry-eyed and they were so quick to pack it in.

Yet there was clearly more to the scheme than preparation for work alone. The manager had enthusiastically developed an 'enrichment programme' which offered recreation, media studies, environment studies and 'Collective Employer Activities'.

Enriching the Programme

'Collective Employer Activities' was a short course run by the local college in which trainees were informed of their rights as members of a trade union and were initiated into the process of negotiation. I attended this one morning with a group composed of four Afro-Caribbeans, one African, and seven Bengali-speaking trainees (five of them only recently arrived in Britain and accompanied by their Bengali-speaking teacher). The tutor explained that if they learnt to write down details of what 'A' said to 'B' six months ago, this could help them in negotiating with management. Several of the Afro-Caribbean young men mumbled loudly that they had done this before and it was boring whilst the Bengali-speaking young women were coping with the translation.

Much emphasis was placed on the high cost of living and their prolonged dependence upon their families. I found this focus anomalous in relation to the accepted dependency of most 16 year olds. If this stage of life was still a period of relative irresponsibility for some, why was there this emphasis on assuming adult status for others? The irony of this disparity lies in the long-term prospects for both groups: those leaving school earliest would be most likely to remain in dependent and delegated roles whilst their more academic peers would ultimately become their managers.

The trainees were asked to reflect on their future aspirations:

Hope I just live in gold. If my dreams come true I will earn 25 thousand — dreaming, man! I want to work for a big company, have a big house in California, big car, a wife and child, and everything automatic.

(Afro-Caribbean male trainee, 1989)

a nice, cosy home and family car, two children, to live in a nice, safe, quiet area, get a job — knowing our husbands, I don't think they'd let us!

(Bangladeshi female trainee, 1989)

It is hardly surprising that trainees living in a violent, noisy inner-city area would aspire to quiet safety. The responses indicated that cultural values would inevitably influence future employment prospects, whatever trade union entitlements were available. The 'dreaming' of the young man seems particularly poignant to me in relation to a lecturer's perception of the function of YTS:

It's hard for us to bring home the reality of it. Regardless of what
we say to them, they cling to their beliefs and dreams.

(lecturer, 1988)

Professional Tension

Between the workshop instructors, who work full-time with the trainees, and
the college lecturers, who come to teach on one day a week, there appeared
to exist a degree of tension beneath the surface co-operation. For a start, the
trainees had made it quite clear that they rejected college in favour of the
workshop. Even this compromise was unsatisfactory for some college
lecturers who felt that attendance was still very poor on the day they came.
What caused them particular concern was that they perceived facilities as
superior at the college, academic demands higher and the ethos significantly
different.

The lecturers were sympathetic about and understanding of the
restrictions under which instructors were working. In carpentry, for example,
instructors were under pressure to produce goods for sale from the workshop.
This meant that they let trainees use electric saws to produce a smooth cut
and allowed them to use power tools in order to achieve successful results as
quickly as possible. When the college lecturers came into this situation, they
found themselves drawing lines on pieces of wood for the trainees to cut,
'using them as a labourer, not training them in carpentry skills'. Their
perceptions of the skills required to become a skilled carpenter differed
markedly from the concept offered by the workshop manager, that literacy
and numeracy were irrelevant to learning practical skills.

This notion clearly angered the college lecturers who saw themselves as
expert in a skilled craft, engaged in training others to develop expertise.
They suggested that a high level of literacy and numeracy was required to
cope with the range of demands involved in carpentry — it needed
intelligence and ingenuity and they deeply resented any implication that it
could be an easy option for slow learners.

They saw the focus upon training in carpentry and joinery as being
fraudulent: the workshop had neither the resources nor the trainees the skills
to justify such an emphasis. They felt, instead, that training was required in
warehouse and storeroom work and that the trainees ought to be prepared
properly as the labourers they were to become. Yet, the workshop was not
organized in such a way as to facilitate this:

The workshop is a mess: piles of junk, pieces of wood, very untidy
and disordered. There's no real organisation — tools are just lying

around in a haphazard mess. There's no coordination. The trainees are just left to their own devices.

What workshop would be so untidy and chaotic! The Wood Store is completely disorganised — almost unusable. The tools are in a very bad condition — very blunt and dangerous.

(carpentry lecturers, 1988)

They were concerned about a lack of structured learning:

There's no pattern to what they are doing here. So they are working on one job and move on to another job, having no idea of the skills they've gained and the skills they need to gain.

(carpentry lecturers, 1988)

Compared to the college carpentry training 'the learning process is more random, more *ad hoc*, less directed'. Their own college system was seen as clearly superior, in relation to the disorder they saw around them:

There is no filing cabinet resource or anything like that, with worksheets in it. We have worksheets, with a sequential series of tasks written on them, to lead trainees along a particular road. The instructors have one sheet only, with several diagrams of joints on it and the trainees are told to work through that. In our college workshop, for just two of those joints, we have a 20 page stage-by-stage learning pack, which gives full details of how the tools are used, what they're called, how to use them correctly, to maintain them and to give guidance as well. The majority of the joints on the sheet are very, very advanced joints — the sort you wouldn't even begin to attempt until you'd got quite an extensive training in woodwork, amounting to about 2 years.

(carpentry lecturer, 1988)

Underlying the practical details, which these lecturers are quick to elucidate, is the feeling of frustration at the political oppression inflicted by this type of YTS provision. They see the trainees as completely helpless pawns in the game being played with them, in which 'they don't know what is happening to them, they don't really know where they fit into this'. The lecturers see college as offering something better:

They go into YTS instead of college because of the allowance. They have no alternative. The YTS workshop prepares their attitudes to become a compliant, flexible workforce in unskilled labour, with the focus on good timekeeping and reliable attendance. At college we try to foster skills to improve the quality of life — to offer vocational education and open possibilities of more than dead-end jobs. College education is about the quality of learning; YTS training is about creating an attitude to work. It's keeping working class labourers compliant and submissive to authority.

(carpentry lecturer, 1988)

Whilst these are the views of individual lecturers and are not, therefore, necessarily representative of their colleagues' views, they do focus upon sources of disaffection within the layers of rhetoric and reality. These lecturers observed that young people with learning difficulties were requiring considerable support to grasp basic skills in vocational areas; the notion of 'occupational competence' bore slight relation to this experience. They also regarded the provision available within the workshop as quite inadequate to meet the criteria for Training Agency 'competencies'. The gap between the 'skills' rhetoric and the muddled reality of coping day-to-day in the workshop scheme created space for evident staff disillusionment and frustration.

The situation which has arisen is related to the confused function of Hartworth Centre, in a training structure which promotes a positive ethos to mask inequalities. A policy of equal opportunities gives trainees a taste of vocational areas which they may have no realistic chance of entering. In the case of carpentry, for example, one of the two female trainees among twenty males is in a wheelchair. She could only choose from carpentry or catering, for these are the only options available on the first floor and no other area is yet accessible. She says she enjoys being among the young men. As she is brought in on special transport every day, she is the most regular attender and clearly scores on that point. However, the instructor who works with her most closely admitted that the mallet she made was almost entirely done by him as she is unable to reach the bench properly and could not do the chiselling required from her wheelchair. He feels that she may be something of a 'token gesture' and thinks this is ultimately unfair to her.

I suggest that the *affectionate patronising* function of this scheme makes 'token gestures' out of most of the trainees. They are going through the motions of preparing for roles which staff (particularly college lecturers) will then cut down to size: not a carpenter, but a warehouse labourer; not a cook, but a cleaner; not a typist, but a coffee-maker; not a graphic designer, but a general helper. Of course the emphasis is upon good timekeeping and attendance: those are needed for the real parts they are to play. The 'skills' role is one that only a handful of them will be lucky enough to obtain. Yet, how can this reality be presented to the trainees as they go through the charade of their training? Realization of this 'con-trick' could lead to anarchy. Thus, those articulate and perceptive potential trouble-makers are quickly removed before they start to spread discontent.

The workshop staff are themselves caught up in this deceit. They have to fill many complicated forms produced by the Training Agency, forms which make the most simple act into a ten-stage procedure. Whilst this takes up a great deal of time, it offers the pretence of assessment and monitoring of 'skills'. What the instructors are good at doing is empathising with trainees for they share something of their lowly status and poor working environment. They have their roles to play in complying with the fragile work ethos: the factory hooter which goes off to divide breaks from working periods when they cajole trainees back from the canteen, the industrial and office simulation, the clocking-in and out. Trying to implant 'skill' can intensify their own frustrations:

> I walk out of this building at regular intervals during the day wondering what on earth I should do. One has periods of self-doubt, thinking it must be me. Then you meet the same problem again and again and again and you realise you're not approaching the problem entirely the wrong way.
>
> (instructor, 1988)

The instructor saw the 'problem' as being primarily cultural:

> to do with second generation Afro-Caribbean kids. They inherit a problem. It is in how they perceive themselves. Some are valid and rock solid. Quite a lot of them are confused over their identity. They don't see themselves as being West-Indian and they don't see themselves as being British.
>
> (instructor, 1988)

This issue of how people are perceived offers a useful insight into the value placed upon the trainees and the programmes themselves.

Find Out the Proper Name

In this final section I will examine extracts from the diary which one of the instructors shared with me. They were written over a period of three years at irregular intervals, in response to 'funny' sayings or incidents which he felt were worth recording for his later amusement. The following examples reflect the range of areas covered.

Some illustrate a misuse of the English language, as in, for example,

> (overheard) There was a very neopolitan crowd in Harrods.

and, *Trainee*: The sump is full of sentiment.

and, *Trainee*: Can I borrow that screwdriver what goes up and down?
Instructor: Find out the proper name and I'll lend it to you.
Trainee: (5 minutes later) Can I borrow your wankey ratchet.

Not all are concerned with trainees' sayings, as for example,

Inspector of FE: These measures will be very serious for parents, especially those with children.

and, (letter from trainee's father to Instructor)
Can my son have two days passionate leave?

Some illustrate certain characteristics in trainees, as, for example,

Instructor: The sum total of your work yesterday was to remove two sash cramps from that table.
Trainee: Yes, but I didn't come in till lunch time.

and, *Instructor*: Why are you late?
Trainee: I pulled a muscle in my leg. Then I had a Radox bath which relaxed me and I overslept.

and, Two trainees at college were allotted the task of decorating a practice booth
(one hour later)
Trainee: (to lecturer) We can't work in there. It's too dark.
Lecturer investigates. They had painted the flourescent fittings and the windows.

Others focus on cultural dissonance, as, for example,

Trainee: I'm going to stain this with that Jacob bean stain.
Instructor: Do you know how it gets its name?
Trainee: No.
Instructor: Well, Moses was leading the Israelites through the desert and they were starving. Suddenly, a man called Jacob saw a huge oak tree and it was covered in beans and those beans saved their lives.
Trainee: That's interesting.
Instructor: It takes 1 cwt of beans to make 1 gallon of stain.
(some time later)
Instructor: Seriously, it is Jacobean, not Jacob bean, and it comes from the Latin Jacobus meaning James. Jacobean means all the furniture made between the reigns of James I and James II.
Trainee: You're having me on.

and, *Indian trainee*: (on a residential) Can I change my boots? They are wet.
Instructor: Did you put them out to dry last night?
Trainee: No.

> *Instructor*: Piss off.
> *Trainee*: What it mean, 'Piss off'?
> *Instructor*: Fuck off.
> *Trainee*: Oh, all right.

(extracts from instructor's diary, 1988)

It is probable that these anecdotes served to diffuse the tension under which staff and trainees worked. It is interesting that they were recorded by a woodwork instructor, rather than an instructor in office skills or graphics. The evident tension between the methods used by college lecturers and instructors, the inherent hazards in working with dangerous tools and the largely male ethos served to foster nervous teasing. The anecdotes might also reflect the frustration and disaffection felt by some instructors, perceiving themselves as misunderstood by management and patronised by the better-paid lecturers.

However, they suggest a certain perception of the trainees: that they are feckless (many instances are offered of their laziness, deceitfulness and general irresponsibility); that they are under-educated, ignorant, inarticulate and generally stupid (their stupidity emerges as positively slapstick in some extracts); that they are both working-class and largely from ethnic minorities, therefore lacking any understanding of the dominant culture of Britain. Paradoxically, this 'culture' includes both historical events and use of swearing, confusion over either being used to tease and entertain.

Whilst this same instructor explained that he was very fond of his trainees, the Afro-Caribbean young men in particular, he saw them as sadly out of touch with the culture in which they were living. I see him as reflecting, most honestly, the *affectionate patronising* in the YTS.

Part of his paternal task was to rescue them from the crude state they were in. The role of the YTS was to gently and kindly smooth them out to become more presentable to employers. They were likely to remain stupid and lazy but they could, at least, become more compliant and learn to 'shape up'.

> It is a protected environment which is enough like real work for them to assess what they're doing, to see the relevance of it and for them to shape up.

(manager, 1988)

The reality of 'shaping up' to the moulding process of the YTS jars somewhat with the notion of opening up opportunities and choosing options. When it comes down to the real task of the scheme, 'shaping up' appears to combine the establishment of a work discipline with the destruction of dreams.

Conclusion

Does Hartworth Centre in any way reflect issues which emerge in the literature? It is concerned with preparing youth for the labour market, in terms of promoting the right attitude to the job (Brown, 1987; Jonathan, 1987; Mac An Ghaill, 1988). It is also concerned with reconciling trainees to the reality of limited choices and to mundane, repetitive chores (Buswell, 1988). One morning I watched as two male trainees and one female, all Afro-Caribbean, spent over half an hour preparing a tray of coffee, milk, sugar, cups, saucers and biscuits to take in and offer round to a board meeting of LEA officers. This constituted their morning's work and, despite being placated with broken biscuits, they moaned about how boring it was. Yet, some staff, perhaps quite realistically, suggested that the YTS had to reinforce the sheer tedium of work and to replace the work ethic that liberal secondary education had lost.

Both trainees and their parents appeared to support the disciplined framework imposed by the manager, a discipline which current literature indicates is sought by many Afro-Caribbean families (DES, 1989; NFER, 1989). She claimed that this is what they wanted and that staff were misguided if they attempted to become over-familiar and easy. Within this structure, there were clearly some trainees who had experienced difficulties at school in relation to learning, bullying or emotional problems who were now receiving the support and guidance they needed. The level of additional support was impressive, including a Bengali-speaking tutor, a counsellor, literacy and numeracy tutors and a system which provided flexible pastoral care. Yet there were signs of 'staffroom racism' (Hammersley, 1981) even if this was laced with affection.

Using the jargon of any one culture can effectively alienate outsiders to that culture (as I observed when ostracized by Afro-Caribbean dialect and as many trainees might have felt when made to look foolish because they were being challenged with completely alien historical and social concepts). Even using terms in which 'no offence is meant' can give offence and denigrate. There are moves within the Trade Union Congress Race Working Party (SERTUC, 1988) to prevent the language of trade unions becoming a barrier and to outlaw any terminology which could offend.

Clearly, it is a responsibility of Youth Training (YT) to work at positive discrimination. Hartworth Centre did this in many ways: employing staff from ethnic minorities; ensuring that male and female trainees had access to all options and were not stereotyped; and offering support to those who had missed out at school.

The manager was most eager to ensure that trainees experienced some form of success:

> . . .we had a trainee who couldn't read and write but could steer a
> narrow boat with no trouble at all. It was the first thing he could do
> that other people could not do as well as him.
>
> (manager, 1988)

This last comment seems to me to crystallize what is positive and negative about the scheme. It is a programme which cares, supports and fosters self-esteem. It is also one which fails to be honest with the young people, treating them like children who are not able to face the facts.

Seabrook (1988), interviewing young people in their first jobs, found them quite dismissive about their labour 'dispatching it in a single word. Factory. Warehouse. Messenger. Stores. Shop' (p. 13). Perhaps this YTS could learn to focus upon offering trainees more enrichment and opportunities for personal development with less emphasis upon a 'skill competence' which would bear little relation to the reality of their working lives.

In whatever ways the scheme itself could be altered, there remains the injustice of operating two systems of YTS, one attached to employers, the other removed into workshops, which preserves two distinct categories of trainee. In the case of Hartworth Centre, up to 85 per cent of the 'unemploy-able' trainees being black fails to match the ideology of promoting equal opportunities. As one newspaper observed, in relation to the Liverpool 8 inquiry report,

> 'Racism' is a term so often heard that it is possible to forget it is a
> form of injustice, not some strange offence existing in a category all
> of its own. A racist country is an unjust country.
>
> (*The Independent*, 19th August, 1989, p. 14)

At Hartworth Centre, the committed manager and her staff work on behalf of the trainees, to advocate to employers and to groom for the 'reality of work'. It is because that reality is a racist society which labels black youngsters as stupid, feckless and unreliable that provision such as Hartworth Centre is used as a buffer to protect the vulnerable and to ease an uneasy transition.

Acknowledgement

I am grateful to Martyn Hammersley for his observations on an earlier draft of this paper.

References

ADELMAN, C. (1985) 'Who are you? Some problems of ethnographic culture shock', in Burgess, R. G. *Field Methods in the Study of Education*, Lewes, Falmer Press.

BROWN, P. (1987) *Schooling Ordinary Kids: Inequality, unemployment and the new vocationalism*, London, Tavistock Publications.

BUSWELL, C. (1988) 'Flexible workers for fexible firms?', in Pollard, A., Purvis, J. and Walford, G. *Education, Training and the New Vocationalism*, Milton Keynes, Open University Press.

COHEN, P. (1984) 'Against the New Vocationalism', in Bates, I., Clarke, J., Cohen, P., Finn, D., Moore, R. and Willis, P. *Schooling for the dole? the new vocationalism*, London, Macmillan.

CORBETT, J. (1987) *Integration in Further Education*, unpublished PhD, Open University.

CROSS, M. (1986) *A Cause for Concern: Ethnic Minority Youth and Vocational Training Policy*, Coventry, University of Warwick Centre for Research in Ethnic Relations.

CROSS, M. and SMITH, D. (1987) *Black Youth Futures: ethnic minorities and the Youth Training Scheme*, London, National Youth Brueau.

DAVIES, L. (1985) 'Ethnography and Status: Focussing on Gender in Educational Research' in Burgess, R. G. *Field Methods in the Study of Education*, Lewes, Falmer Press.

DEPARTMENT OF EDUCATION AND SCIENCE (1982) *Statistical Bulletin 8/82, Additional Educational Needs*, London, HMSO.

DEPARTMENT OF EDUCATION AND SCIENCE (1989) *Highbury Quadrant Primary School, ILEA*, London, DES.

FENTON, S. AND BURTON, P. (1987) 'YTS and Equal Opportunity Policy', in Cross, M. and Smith, D. (eds.) *Black Youth Futures: ethnic minorities and the Youth Training Scheme*, London, National Youth Bureau.

FIELDHOUSE, P. (1987) 'Working on YTS: staff and training issues' in Cross, M. and Smith, D. (eds.) *Black Youth Futures: ethnic minorities and the Youth Training Scheme*, London, National Youth Bureau.

GRANT, V. (1988) 'Equal Opportunities in YTS' from *Youth Training News* 49, p.8, Sheffield, Training Agency.

GHUA, E. (1988) 'Exploring Equality in Black and White' from *Youth Training News, 49*, p.8, Sheffield, Training Agency.

HALL, S. *et al.* (1978) *Policing the Crisis: mugging, the state and law and order*, London, Macmillan.

HAMMERSLEY, M. (1981) *Staffroom Racism*, unpublished manuscript.

INSTITUTE OF CAREERS OFFICERS, ROYAL ASSOCIATION FOR DISABILITY AND REHABILITATION (1986) *The Youth Training Scheme and School Leavers with Special Needs*, London, RADAR.

JONATHAN, R. (1987) 'The Youth Training Scheme and core skills: an educational analysis' in Holt, M. (ed.) *Skills and Vocationalism: the easy answer*, Milton Keynes, Open University Press.

LIVERPOOL INQUIRY INTO RACE RELATIONS IN LIVERPOOL (1989) *Loosen the Shackles*, London, Karia Press.

MAC AN GHAILL, M. (1988) 'The new vocationalism: the response of a sixth-form college' in Pollard, A., Purvis, J. and Walford, G. (eds.) *Education, Training and the New Vocationalism*, Milton Keynes, Open University Press.

MACKNEY, P. (1985) 'YTS and Racism: the Birmingham Experience', London, *NATFHE Journal*, 10,6,pp.16-17.

ROSIE, A. (1988) 'An ethnographic study of a YTS course' in Pollard, A., Purvis, J. and Walford, G. *Education, Training and the New Vocationalism*, Milton Keynes, Open University Press.

SCARMAN, LORD (1986) *The Scarman Report: the Brixton Disorders* 10-12 April 1981, Harmondsworth, Penguin.

SEABROOK, J. (1988) 'Damaging expression of social anger', *The Independent,* 21 September, p.13.

SOUTH EAST REGION TRADES UNION CONGRESS (1988) *Black Workers and Trade Unions,* London, SERTUC.

STONE, M. (1981) *The Education of the Black Child in Britain*, London, Fontana.

SURKERS, S. (1989) '''Work us harder'' plea from pupils' (The Newham Inquiry), *Times Educational Supplement,* 7th April, p.A4.

THE INDEPENDENT (leader column) (1989) 'Racism in Liverpool', Saturday, August 19th, p. 14.

TOMLINSON, S. (1984) 'Minority Groups in English Conurbations' in Williams, P. (ed.) *Special Education in Minority Communities*, Milton Keynes, Open University Press.

TRAINING AGENCY (1988) *YTS Special Needs: a Code of Practice,* Sheffield, Training Agency.

VERMA, G. and DARBY, D. (1987) *Race, Training and Employment,* Lewes, Falmer Press.

WOODS, P. (1985) Ethnography and Theory Construction in Educational Research' in Burgess, R.G. *Field Methods in the Study of Education*, Lewes, Falmer Press.

Note

1. Although YTS became YT in May 1990, as my research took place in 1988/89 I have referred throughout to YTS as this was the current terminology.

PART TWO
THE CHALLENGE OF CHANGE

7
Obstacles to Overcome:
Higher Education and Disabled Students

Alan Hurst

Introduction: The Context of Entry to Higher Education

The decade of the 1980s has been marked by a number of special initiatives relating to people with disabilities. The period began with the International Year of Disabled Persons in 1981 whilst 1985 was proclaimed International Youth Year. Contemporaneously the European Commission, working through its Bureau for Action in Favour of Disabled People, has initiated two 'Action Programmes'.

Yet, amidst the wealth of publicity which surrounds such events, the situation of one group who are both young and disabled has been ignored: those intelligent and academically able men and women who wish to enter higher education. Such neglect is not new and it is possible to offer explanations for its continued existence. For one thing the numbers involved are not large and thus it is possible for them to be overlooked.

Recent developments in education for the post–16 age group have tended to be directed towards the large majority whose academic attainments are more moderate. Also it is perhaps assumed that because of their intellectual powers and qualities, disabled young people are able to present their own case and safeguard their position. What little evidence exists, suggests that this assumption should be rejected. The most recent full scale survey available in the United Kingdom, which looked specifically at disabled people in higher education, concluded on a pessimistic note:

> The proportion of disabled students to the total comparable student population was so small compared with that of disabled people to the population as a whole, that the conclusion is inescapable that there are obstacles which many disabled young people who would like to go to a university or polytechnic cannot overcome.
>
> (National Innovations Centre (NIC), 1974, p.125)

Such comment is now some fifteen years old. In the intervening period there have been other reports published which, whilst not specifically about higher education, do mention access. These fail to offer convincing evidence that the situation obtaining in 1974 has changed. A survey carried out for the Department of Education and Science by the National Bureau for Handicapped Students and Social and Community Planning Research in Autumn 1985 opens thus:

> A wealth of evidence from, among others, HMI, the Further Education Unit, and NATFHE, suggests that provision for students with special needs in further and higher education has expanded considerably over the last 10 to 15 years. This expansion has not been quantified however, and there have been no reliable estimates of the number of students involved, the type of college attended, or the course of study followed.
>
> (Stowell, 1987, p. 1)

On a more international level a report commissioned by the European Community's 'Bureau for Action in Favour of Disabled People' published in 1986 comments:

> The opportunity to go to higher education is open to all with the relevant entry qualifications. Handicapped students are not barred from ordinary higher education in any country solely on the grounds of their special needs ...
>
> No country was able to supply figures on the numbers of handicapped students in higher education although most professionals, voluntary organisations and handicapped young people themselves strongly believed that they were under-represented.
>
> (National Bureau for Handicapped Students, 1986, p.36)

Alongside this, there has been a more general concern with the potential effects of the falling birthrate on the output of graduates.

In 1988 the Training Agency funded a research project undertaken by the Institute for Research and Development in Post-Compulsory Education at Lancaster University. In describing its background the report states:

> Access is now one of the central concerns for higher education. There is widespread acceptance of the need for increased participation: labour market trends indicate that the demand for graduates, already buoyant, is likely to rise substantially in the medium term. The 1987 White Paper 'Meeting the Challenge' set ambitious targets for student numbers in the next decade, and the

Secretary of State for Education has recently signalled his hope of doubling the participation rate within twenty-five years.

(Fulton and Ellwood, 1989, p.7)

There are indications that the situation is changing and disabled people might benefit from the new 'expansionist' outlook. Following the NIC Survey of 1974, the educational context presented even greater difficulties for disabled students. The growing economic recession, coupled with contemporary government policy, meant that unemployment levels continued to remain at a high level. There is evidence to suggest that even in prosperous times, within a healthy economy, people with disabilities experience more difficulty than their non-disabled competitors in obtaining full-time paid employment. For many disabled people the key to a steady job and good career prospects is the possession of educational qualifications, particularly those at and beyond GCE 'A' level. Hence, the importance of further and higher education for disabled young people and their desire to obtain a place in a university, polytechnic or college of higher education. However, the process itself has become increasingly competitive, because of a lack of employment opportunities which in the past proved attractive to some young people who now choose to remain in the education system longer, and because many older people who, because of long-term unemployment, redundancy, or early retirement, are returning to study.

More certain was the increased competition resulting from the closer involvement of central government in higher education. This was part of a policy to control public spending and to ensure that the country obtained an appropriate return on its financial investment in education. The policy manifested itself in a number of ways. In both the more independent university sector and in the more closely controlled polytechnics, budgets were cut in terms of real value. The response of both sectors was to try to maintain the quality of student experience by trimming the number of places available. Government also tried to influence the distribution of a reduced number of places across the curriculum. There was some attempt to encourage the study of science, engineering and technology, whilst at the same time cutting down the availability of courses in arts, humanities and social sciences. The overall consequence was to increase the competition for places. Given the plentiful supply of qualified applicants, coupled with the possible need for an institution to incur additional expense in meeting the needs of some disabled students, it should be no surprise to find that disabled students have become increasingly disadvantaged. An additional argument could be proposed to suggest that this disadvantage is even greater than it might appear. If is accepted that, because of their disabling conditions, scientific, technical and a whole range of practical subjects are extremely difficult to pursue, the more severe cuts in available courses and places in the arts, humanities and social science areas will have had serious consequences for this group. Conjecture such as this indicates the need to consider concepts such as equality of opportunity and positive discrimination as they apply to physically handicapped students.

Concern about the flow of graduate labour, coupled with some more recent developments in the organization and provision of higher education, suggests potential for change in favour of disabled students. For example, in 1989, the government announced that institutions would derive much of their income from student fees and encouraged institutions to remove limits on numbers entering. However, very little is known about the way young people with disabilities relate to higher education and how higher education attempts to meet their needs.

Recent work in this country has examined further education giving detailed consideration to the curriculum, vocational preparation, social and life skills (Dixon and Hutchinson, 1979; Panckhurst, 1980; Rowan, 1980; Jowett, 1982). Higher education continues to be a neglected area. Even the report of the Warnock Committee (DES, 1978), established to investigate special educational needs, contains only four paragraphs on this area. Apart from brief autobiographical accounts from some students, often reported in the publications of various charities, there is no information derived from research studies about the progress of disabled people in education beyond school. This paper describes areas of common concern to disabled students, illustrating possibilities for improved provision through examples of current practice.

Application to Higher Education: Common Concerns

Official guidance to applicants has changed over time. In 1976 those with disabilities were given this information:

> Some universities can make special provision for disabled or handicapped students. If you have a major physical disability (for example if you use a wheelchair),
> (a) you are advised first to consult the universities to which you wish to apply to see whether they can offer you the special facilities you need; and
> (b) you are invited, if you so wish, to mention your disability or handicap in section 16 of the application form.

Eight years later the tone was more positive and helpful:

If you have a physical or other disability you should write well in advance of completing the UCCA form to your preferred universities indicating the courses in which you are interested, the nature and extent of your disability and any special needs you may have. This will enable you to find out before you submit an application whether the universities concerned can offer you the facilities you need. Your application will be considered on the same academic criteria as that of any other applicant, but universities will need to know in advance the degree of any disability so that they can discuss special provision with you. Universities will try to give as much help as possible, but there may be difficulties such as those presented by certain older buildings. Universities are bound by the Health and Safety at Work Act 1974, and must ensure that no individual (student or staff) is put at undue risk.

The guide then goes on to recommend contact with the National Bureau for Handicapped Students (NBHS — since renamed Skill: The National Bureau for Students with Disabilities) and with the Royal Association for Disability and Rehabilitation (RADAR).

When considering applications for places on courses in polytechnics the procedures have now become centralized in a similar fashion to the UCCA system. From Autumn 1985 onwards, most candidates have made use of the PCAS system. The Operations Manual devised in connection with this contains a lengthy appendix on 'Guidelines for dealing with applicants with disabilities', although it is interesting to note that this opens in the following way:

The following statement has been prepared by NBHS. It does not represent PCAS policy but polytechnics may wish to consider its impact when assessing its admissions procedures vis-à-vis disabled applicants.

Thus much depends on individual institutions and so the next step is to examine their public statements and admissions policies relating to disabled students.

More welcoming trends are evident in the prospectuses of institutions offering higher education courses. Many universities and polytechnics have produced special versions of the prospectuses for disabled applicants, often providing the name of an individual with particular responsibilities for disabled students, to whom any queries can be addressed.

Disabled students are invariably presented with more restricted choices than their peers. Where, for non-disabled applicants, choice of institution and choice of course can be wide, disabled students might have to restrict their choice to those institutions with the special facilities able to meet their particular needs. As an example, students with impaired mobility might choose the University of Sussex, not because of the merits of its geographical location or the course on offer, but because of the residential and care facilities available there.

Most application forms contain a section which allows applicants to indicate the nature of their disability and their special needs (see the comment earlier concerning the UCCA guidelines). Whilst this is intended to be helpful, some individuals might feel uneasy about a public declaration of their position at this stage, and anxious lest those reading the application envisage problems. Even at the interview stage demands placed upon disabled applicants are considerable, for example when asked to travel long distances, perhaps using public transport. Nor should the expense involved be overlooked particularly if overnight accommodation is required. If the NBHS guidelines are followed, disabled applicants will have to make two visits to the particular institution.

In recent times, there has been an increasing trend towards the provision of special courses to try to overcome any difficulties. The University of Nottingham has a long tradition of holding open days for any interested disabled people. More recently the University of Strathclyde has organized a short transition course (Graham, 1985) whilst at Easter 1987 NBHS sponsored a similar venture held at Reading University.

Access and Accommodation

Some universities, polytechnics and colleges have specially adapted accommodation for disabled students. For example, in the university sector, both Southampton and Sussex have established national reputations for their facilities to meet the needs of those with mobility impairments. Whilst this might solve some difficulties, it might create others. Some people question the social consequences of accommodating disabled students together in separate facilities, thus raising the issue of integration. In other institutions accommodation is associated with the Student Health Centre and again this is a controversial point since it associates 'disability' with 'sickness'. Whilst some disabling conditions do require regular medical attention others do not and yet there appears to be some feeling that, in the past, medical considerations might have assumed a somewhat dominant position: the appropriateness of this is open to question. In the case of motor impairments some students are able to manage most, if not all, of their care needs (e.g. feeding, bathing, going to the lavatory) without assistance.

Others, who are more severely affected, require help. If such help is needed, especially for a considerable portion of the day and night, it raises problems of provision, accommodation and cost.

Access to buildings is always problematic:

> Almost all polytechnics are multi site: fewer institutes of higher education are. Nonetheless both types of H.E. college suffered from inaccessible buildings: not one reported full access for students with disabilities to all buildings. As a consequence three quarters of the higher education colleges said they would in some circumstances have to deny a place to students with a mobility problem.
>
> (Stowell, 1987, p. 94)

Finance

All students have become increasingly outspoken in recent times about the adequacy of the grant they receive. For many it has become a necessity to obtain some kind of paid employment to subsidize their stay in higher education. This alternative is unavailable for almost all physically handicapped students and yet there is much evidence to indicate the additional costs which a disability brings (Younghusband, 1970). Both NBHS and the students' own union (NUS) have tried to inform disabled students about their financial entitlements especially with regard to the additional LEA Disabled Students Award and to DHSS provision.

Staff Development

Tutors need to acquire knowledge and information about disabilities in terms of their medical and social aspects.

For example, for some disabled students normal assessment methods might need to be amended because:

> A three hour written examination paper, for example, may be just as much a test of physical endurance and writing speed as a test of knowledge; a profile or practical demonstration may contain within it an element requiring physical dexterity or sight-edness . . . In all of these cases, if adjustments are made to account for an impairment, care has to be taken to ensure that the resulting changes retain an equivalent value . . .
>
> In other instances, where more integrated provision is made,

> there may be a need to negotiate individual arrangements... in
> the Netherlands, for example, handicapped university students
> are normally given freedom to sit an examination as they wish, on
> the grounds that if they have already proved themselves capable of
> getting to university, a further rigid test at the end of the course is
> unnecessary.
>
> (NBHS, 1986, p.55).

The recent survey of public sector institutions states that nine polytechnics
and eleven institutes of higher education had held in-house staff
development sessions for their lecturers teaching students with special needs.
These are usually general disability awareness sessions or else training in
specific skills, e.g. in relation to deaf students (Stowell, 1987).

Social Development

An important part of higher education is the opportunity to meet people
and to develop interests. Here, the social interaction between disabled and
non-disabled people might be facilitated or inhibited both by some of the
factors already described and by social-psychological variables. Some writers
have commented upon the potentially strained interaction when disabled
and non-disabled people meet (Davis, 1961; Goffman, 1969; Finkelstein,
1980).

Obstacles to Overcome: a Case Study

The following example shows the problems faced by a disabled applicant.

Alec

Alec has cerebral palsy and uses an electric wheelchair. His home is in
Northern England but all his educational experience had been obtained in
residential schools in different parts of the country. At the stage when he was
applying to enter higher education he had already obtained a grade B pass at
GCE Advanced level in Pure Maths with Statistics together with passes in
seven subjects at Ordinary level. He was taking further Advanced level
examinations in Pure Maths with Computations and Computer Science. He
wished to obtain a place on a Computer Studies course at university.

Alec's first choice was Bestley University which happened to be the one nearest to his home. He had some personal contact with a tutor friend there and he knew that the university had previously accepted disabled students on some of its courses. His application was rejected but, rather than the standard letter informing applicants of this disappointing news, the University provided a detailed letter outlining their reasons for taking this decision. The letter reads:

> Our reply to your UCCA application has been delayed as we have given it very careful consideration.
>
> We reluctantly have decided that we cannot make you an offer of a place. This decision has been reached after obtaining advice from the University's Director of Student Services, who consulted our Senior Medical officer. He in turn obtained information from your college doctor.
>
> The conclusion that we arrived at was that it would be very difficult indeed to provide the facilities which might be needed to support you during a three year degree course. We have considerable experience of catering for certain disabilities, notably blindness. We now realise that it is desirable that the University should provide more than the bare minimum of facilities in order to maximise a disabled student's chances of success. In your case we do not feel that we can provide such an environment. In particular we are concerned about the difficulty of access to our present computing facilities and these may become even worse if we move elsewhere.
>
> We have checked your application status with UCCA and can see that you have had three conditional offers from other universities. We are naturally very pleased that this gives you a good choice from universities who do feel that they can provide the support necessary for you.
>
> We are therefore forwarding to UCCA a reject reply to your application but we felt you would prefer to hear the news directly from us. We will inform UCCA that we are rejecting you because we are unable to provide appropriate facilities. They should then write directly to you offering one more choice of university.
>
> Naturally we wish you success in the A-level examinations in June and in your subsequent university career. (Admissions Tutor — Computing).

Whilst Alec was disappointed to receive a rejection from the university which had been his first choice, he was encouraged by the attempt to offer a full explanation. Having said that, the letter raises some interesting issues. For example there is a claim to have expertise in meeting the special needs of students with a particular condition (i.e. blindness). If this is an indication of the way in which provision for special needs might be offered in a cost effective and efficient fashion some applicants will find their range of choice restricted. Secondly, the letter points to the need to offer students 'more than the bare minimum of facilities'. It is not clear if this refers only to classroom experiences or whether it is indicative of a broader concern to ensure that the total student experience is of a high quality. Thirdly, it is not clear how much the decision has been influenced by medical and personal care considerations rather than academic ones.

At this point it is appropriate to consider Alec's relations with the university selected second in order of preference. Again the university, in this case Lowville, sent a personal letter informing Alec of their decision not to offer a place. This letter bears similarities to the previous one, even to the extent of the opening apology:

> Thank you for your application for admission to the University. I am sorry that it has not been possible to write to you about it until now. The University likes to try to help disabled students and you may know that a number of students from your College have come to the University in recent years. However, the University Medical Officer has to be satisfied that the necessary arrangements can be made. I have therefore consulted him in detail and he has, I understand, discussed your case with your present College Medical Officer.
>
> I am sorry to have to tell you that the University Medical Officer judges that we will not be able to provide proper care for you at Lowville. Accordingly, I am afraid it will be necessary for us to reject your UCCA application. Since however this decision is not being taken on academic grounds, it would seem to me right that you should have the opportunity to substitute an application to a different university for the one that you have submitted to us. I am therefore sending a copy of this letter to the UCCA to inform them of the situation and if you wish to name another university as an alternative to Lowville may I suggest that you write to UCCA as soon as possible naming the university and course in question.
>
> I am very sorry we cannot help you but I hope you will understand that the University Medical Officer has the final responsibility in these matters and I must respect his decision.
>
> (Deputy Registrar)

The most obvious similarity between the responses of the two universities is the apparent influence of the medical personnel. In the case of Lowville, it seems clear that the refusal of a place is on medical grounds rather than being based on academic judgements. In recent times many institutions, when advertising for people to join them, often as employees, issue a disclaimer that they are in favour of equal opportunities and that individuals will be offered opportunities irrespective of gender, ethnic origin, religious belief, political persuasion, or disability. It is interesting to speculate on the potential consequences had such a disclaimer appeared on UCCA application forms.

Alec's third preference was for Murly. His first contact with this institution was the arrival of a standard letter sent to all those who were to be made conditional offers of a place on a course via UCCA. The letter gives 'a little more information about the special features of our course and this Institute' and concludes by offering to arrange visits. This offer of a place came prior to any decisions from Alec's first and second preferences being known. Alec responded to the letter from Murly immediately stating:

> I note that it is not your intention to invite me to attend an interview, but as I am disabled I would very much welcome the opportunity of visiting the University and to discuss with the staff and the support services my own particular needs. If this could be arranged during my half-term holiday this would be most helpful.
>
> (Alec A., January, 31st, 1984)

Within a few days, a reply was received offering a choice of dates during the period Alec had requested. The visit took place and soon afterwards Alec began to plan his accommodation, having by this time received the rejections from the two preferred choices. Prior to writing, the College Vice-Principal had been in touch by telephone. Alec indicated in his letter that he hoped to have the support of two CSVs who would also need accommodation and that he had contacted his local Social Services Department seeking financial help for this provision. He asked that he be allowed to visit the accommodation, preferably during the Easter vacation. A prompt reply followed, giving a date in the vacation and providing directions. At this meeting, the Warden of the Halls of Residence expressed some anxieties in relation to the need to begin converting facilities early, the additional expense that this would incur, and the possibility that Alec's examination performance might not meet the conditions attached to the offer of a place. When this visit took place no reply had been received from the Social Services Department on the CSV provision. Following this, Alec, together with his mother and the Admissions Tutor, made an appointment to see the Vice-Chancellor.

The feeling that Alec had after this meeting was that there was a lack of enthusiasm at the prospect of his possible arrival as a student but that, if he met the conditions of the offer, he would have obtained suitable qualifications and therefore could not be denied a place. By this time the examinations period was imminent and Alec gave his attention to the 'A' levels. After returning to his home and over the Summer, both before and after the publication of the examination results, he and his family made several trips to the university to arrange accommodation. In his own words:

> The special rooms available for the disabled were far too small and totally unsuitable. Fortunately, the rooms at Gordon Plaza were larger and they made over a suite of rooms for myself and two helpers. These consist of three bedsits, bathroom, ante-room (suitable for recharging and keeping spare wheelchairs) and kitchen. It is only a ten minute walk to the university.

In connection with his application to the institution which had been his third preference Alec had been successful but his experiences highlight several points. Firstly, there was the welcome and support he received from the department in which he hoped to study. Secondly, the length of time needed and the various processes that have to be set in motion are evident. The system of making conditional offers which can only be confirmed some six weeks before the start of courses creates additional pressures. The conditional nature of the agreement between the institution and the individual is emphasized by the Warden's hesitancy in agreeing to pursue alterations to rooms. Finally, one can note that the lobbying had to take place and agreement obtained at the highest level.

Still to be considered are Alec's fourth and fifth choices. The University of Nestterly was the fourth choice but was first to make a conditional offer of a place. This arrived shortly before Christmas and came directly from the University rather than from UCCA. It took the form of a standard letter and concluded with the following paragraph:

> We normally ask applicants to attend for interview and a tour round the Laboratory before making an offer of a place on our course. I have decided to dispense with this visit in your case since you have us so low on your choice list and/or because of the very large number of applications we have received this year.

After he returned to college, Alec wrote to the university drawing attention to his disability and using the wording set out above in which he asked to visit Murly. The department responded by offering to arrange such a visit but then revealed:

> The Department is not ideally set up for this (i.e. students with disabilities) as we have floors 1, 2, 8 and 9 and the basement of

Clement Building. Perhaps you could give us some further information before you come.

Alec wrote back to arrange the visit and gave a brief outline of his needs and his intention to seek the help of a CSV. The visit took place in the half-term holiday and after visiting the campus Alec declined the offer of a place. He himself felt that the environment would be unsuitable. In this instance, it seemed a little negligent on the part of the university in making a conditional offer without acknowledging that Alec was disabled. It was also at Alec's prompting that the visit was arranged.

The fifth university selected was Loxleyford. Early in January, Alec was sent a standard letter making a conditional offer. The letter contained an invitation to see the campus and to discuss the course. For this purpose the university was setting aside two days and those who participated would be accommodated overnight in a hall of residence. The letter gave no indication that Alec's special needs had been recognized. However, attached to this formal letter was a note from the assistant registrar offering Alec a private visit 'in view of your disability' if this was preferable. In fact, this was Alec's preference and he and his parents visited the campus in March. After this visit he accepted the conditional offer but he was not enthusiastic about the prospect of taking up the place. In his discussions with the staff he gained the impression that he was being admitted to the course 'rather as a guinea pig' and that the tutors were not whole-heartedly in favour of the 'experiment'.

This is interesting in that it raises a point in relation to an institution which is attempting to bring disabled students on to its courses for the first time. Obviously, the institution and its tutors needed to build up experience and test the feasibility of offering places to students with impairments similar to Alec's and yet Alec was unwilling to pioneer the way.

In relation to polytechnics and colleges of higher education, Alec felt confident that he would be successful in his 'A' level examinations and would meet the conditions of the offers made by the universities to which he had applied. For this reason he did not make applications outside the university sector. Given that he had already obtained an 'A' level pass with a high grade and was made aware by his teachers that his work was of some quality his decision not to apply is understandable. It should also be remembered that further applications would take time as would any interviews and visits.

When the results became known it was clear that Alec had met the conditions set by Murly and he took up the offer of a place.

Lancashire Polytechnic: Meeting the Challenge of Change

Introduction

So far the focus has been on the process of application and admission from the perspective of the students. There is now a need to try to balance this by outlining how institutions approach the matter, what facilities are provided and how they are organized and financed. This might provide greater insight into the background in which some of the experiences and exchanges described above took place.

Meeting Needs

Lancashire Polytechnic was mentioned in the House of Lords debate on the 1988 Education Reform Bill as having made some progress in trying to meet the needs of disabled students (Hansard, June 28th 1988, p. 1348).

It was established as part of the binary system of higher education in the expansionist period of the late 1960s and early 1970s. As well as the Preston site, it incorporated two colleges of education located some distance away but which were later closed as teacher training contracted. Hence, split site working no longer occurs. The main buildings are astride a busy main road on the edge of the town centre. Most are modern although the building originally occupied in late Victorian times is still in use. The academic structure consists of five faculties, together with a combined studies degree programme and these are supported by a range of other sections: the library, student services and the registry. In 1988–89, there were approximately 5000 full-time and 3000 part time students enrolled. Of these, over 100 declared a special need, relating to vision (twenty students) hearing (ten students) mobility (twenty students) or other difficulties (e.g. dyslexia, epilepsy, etc.).

From its earliest days the polytechnic has been concerned to be seen as a resource available to everyone in the community and also to improve access to higher education for disadvantaged groups. Provision for disabled students has been an important part of this. In order to ensure this occurred, a working party was established under the aegis of the Head of Student Services. The members represented students, accommodation, health, library and the five faculties. Many matters of interest were debated and recommendations passed to the policy makers. In particular in those early days considerable attention was given to the information provided to prospective students and comparisons were made with the prospectuses produced by other institutions. Over time the working party became a polytechnic sub-committee with a chairperson and with a formal line of communication to the Academic Board.

An important achievement at this time was the production of a comprehensive guide to the campus for disabled people. When it was produced it was innovative and contained ideas later taken up by other institutions in their own guides. Throughout, there had been student involvement in the sub-committee although often the changes in student union representation caused by elections made for a lack of continuity. The minimal participation by disabled students was also a cause for concern.

This situation was to change considerably in 1986. At that time three events coincided; the appointment of a new Head of the Students Services section, the election of a group of student union officers who had an interest in disabled students and the appearance of an active group of disabled students. Both the student groupings viewed the progress of policy development and provision as too slow and the mechanisms for instituting change as too ponderous. Consequently, they took action. A pressure group was formed, the Special Needs Action Group (giving the acronym SNAG), and a meeting was arranged with the Polytechnic Directorate. In response, it was agreed that a member of the academic staff who had some knowledge of disability should be seconded from teaching duties on a half-time basis for six months in order to initiate, co-ordinate and develop policy more quickly.

The initial step was to provide a central focus for all aspects of policy and provision relating to disabled students and to draw more attention to issues relating to disability. Within the polytechnic, some faculties and schools had acquired expertise in successfully meeting the needs of disabled students. It was essential to draw upon this experience and to spread the good practice to others. This could be facilitated by asking one individual to act in a co-ordinating capacity.

Having such an individual would also help with another issue. Some of the correspondence cited above illustrates the point that when disabled students first contacted an institution they did not know to whom their enquiry should be addressed. If they wrote to a particular department the person receiving the letter might have had no experience of disabled students and might be unaware of their particular needs and how these might be met. A solution is to have a 'named person' to be responsible for handling all contacts with disabled enquirers. All polytechnic publicity would contain the name of this contact.

Two further aspects needed to be addressed: staffing and finances. In relation to staffing, whilst the secondment of a member of the academic staff (and prior to this the valuable efforts of a member of the library staff) was an improvement on previous provision, it became clear that further development needed full-time staff. Accordingly, it was proposed that a new post should be created with the title of Welfare Officer for Students with Special Needs, with the Head of Student Services as line manager. This proposal was accepted and the individual appointed began work early in the 1987–88 academic year.

Despite having a full-time appointment, it was decided that it would be valuable to retain a link with the academic staff and so the secondment of the tutor continued but on a reduced basis. To clarify roles, this individual took the title 'Adviser for Students with Special Needs'. It was intended that the Adviser should focus on academic concerns (e.g. admissions, classroom difficulties and assessment) whilst the Welfare Officer would look after accommodation, personal care and grants. In practice, it became clear that such a division of labour was inappropriate and that the title 'Welfare Officer' was misleading. The new title of Co-ordinator was introduced with an amended division of work in which the Adviser was to become more closely involved in the regional and national aspects of provision for disabled students, while the Co-ordinator's involvement was in all aspects of provision within the polytechnic.

Staffing resources allocated to working with disabled students were growing but one important area remained to be tackled. This is particularly significant in relation to students with impaired mobility. By allocating rooms on the ground floor, some students who used wheelchairs had managed to live in the halls of residence adjacent to the main campus. However, the halls do not have lifts and so access to some facilities, notably laundry rooms, was impossible. The kitchens in each block do not have cookers, plugs or sinks at a level appropriate for wheelchair users. Thus disabled students were disadvantaged. In order to alleviate this and to remove any need to ask favours of friends, the polytechnic appointed a number of part-time care assistants. On a rota basis, they were available to offer help with washing clothes, running errands, cooking and serving meals for a short period at the beginning and end of every day, including weekends. While this falls short of providing full-time twenty-four hour care, it does mean that some of the delays incurred by disabled students in their everyday living are diminished and more time is available for study purposes. It means, too, that the polytechnic is in a better position to offer places on its courses to disabled students. From very little, the staffing resources allocated to meeting the needs of disabled students had grown considerably.

Staffing costs money and this leads to an examination of how finance is provided. It is a sign of Lancashire Polytechnic's committment to disabled students that it is prepared to pay the wages and salaries of the Adviser, the Co-ordinator, two full-time and one part-time staff in the support unit and the part-time care assistants. However, finance is needed for other purposes, too. Prior to 1986, any finance for meeting the needs of disabled students was made available on an *ad hoc* basis from both central and departmental budgets. Partly as a result of SNAG and the campaigning of the sub-committee, the polytechnic allocated a budget to special needs in September 1986. This has been renewed annually since then. Apart from small items and consumables, the budget is used to purchase a range of aids and equipment. Its use is not confined to academic support and can be directed towards items which improve the general quality of life. For example, in relation to students with impaired dexterity or mobility, a number of microwave ovens were bought for use in the kitchens in the halls of residence. Not only do these reduce the time needed to prepare and cook meals, they also remove some of the difficulties and dangers encountered in independent living. The special needs budget is limited and, prior to incurring expense, requests from disabled students are considered carefully.

Some equipment purchased is of benefit to many students and can be used year after year; this is probably the most efficient way to use the money. Other equipment relates to the needs of a particular individual and might not be used by others (e.g. special puncture resistant wheels were obtained for an engineering student who uses a wheelchair in a workshop). Money also has to be set aside as a contingency since, because the GCE 'A' levels are used to determine entry for many students, it is difficult to predict which disabled applicants will actually arrive at the polytechnic. There have been other changes which have incurred expense and which have benefited disabled students. Many of these have been incorporated in the minor works of the buildings section, the provision of ramps and handrails being a good example. However, considerable expenditure was incurred in the installation of a lift to allow access to the three floors of the polytechnic's oldest building. It is unlikely that this project would have been given its high priority had it not been for a commitment to make all areas and all courses accessible to disabled people.

Having obtained suitable staffing resources and been allocated a budget, the time was right to try to make further progress. Like most other polytechnics, Lancashire Polytechnic published its mission statement setting out its aims and objectives. It was necessary for all publicity material to mention the polytechnic's commitment to disabled students and the name of the person to contact. In addition a small folder was devised as a guide for disabled applicants. There is also the handbook for students with special needs which contains information about access to buildings, routes between buildings, lifts and toilets for disabled people. This information can be made available on cassette tape or in braille to meet the needs of visually impaired people.

In recent years the polytechnic has developed a policy on admissions.

This was produced by a working party on which those working with disabled students were represented and who ensured that this group of applicants were not overlooked. A particular section of the policy document outlines the procedures to be followed. On receiving any indication of a special need, either from information on the PCAS application or from an informal enquiry, the individual concerned is invited to visit the polytechnic to discuss with the Adviser and the Co-ordinator potential difficulties and how these might be overcome. This allows individuals to experience the campus for themselves and to be involved in making realistic decisions about the future. If it is felt by the Course Leader that a formal interview is necessary, this is arranged to coincide with the visit and either the Adviser or Co-ordinator takes part in this so that tutors can be made aware of any special equipment which is available. In cases where no formal interview is needed, an attempt is made to arrange an informal meeting with course tutors. This strategy allows some forward planning in relation to adaptations, obtaining equipment and altering room timetables to cut down on cross-campus travel between teaching sessions. Usually this cannot be definitive since entry to the course depends on 'A' level grades which become known in mid-August. An individual might obtain grades higher than expected and go elsewhere or fail to obtain the grades required for entry to the course. Problems also arise in late August/early September if disabled students are referred via the PCAS clearing house system. This does not really allow adequate time for making appropriate provision.

Having encouraged disabled students to join the polytechnic, there is an obligation to try to ensure that they have an educational experience of the best possible quality. With this end in view, a range of strategies has been introduced. This includes regular meetings with disabled students. Whilst acknowledging that there is an issue in bringing together people only on the grounds that they share a disability, it has been found useful to hold these meetings. Some students have found them useful because they can be put in touch with others who share similar problems. Those working with disabled students obtain valuable feedback. Occasionally, students themselves have organized their own meetings to allow any students who might feel inhibited by the presence of staff to raise matters of concern.

More staff have come into contact with disabled students as the numbers have grown. This has produced the need to consider how their daily customs and practices might need modification to meet the needs of some students. One example of this relates to the strategies and techniques used to assess student attainment. Generally, there has been a recognition of the needs of disabled students and a willingness to meet these by flexibility in patterns of assessment. Occasionally, this has led to problems. To try to avoid these, students and tutors compiled a procedure to be followed when making assessment arrangements for students with special needs. This was brought into operation for the first time in 1989. Its efficiency and effectiveness will be monitored annually.

As part of its efforts to improve provision, strong links have been established with other higher education institutions in the region. Lancashire Polytechnic hosted the first meeting of a group of staff working with disabled students in higher education institutions in the north-west. This meeting, which took place in March 1987, was found to constitute a valuable forum for the exchange of ideas and practices. It has continued to meet once each term, each institution taking it in turn to act as host. At the meetings, the group has often focused on particular themes (e.g publicity, admissions, finance). A written record is kept and copies are circulated to everyone. Those unable to be present have found this especially useful for keeping in touch. Since the establishment of this group which, until May 1989, was unique to north-west England, there has been a growth in informal contacts between members seeking advice and information from each other. Firm links are being developed with a similar group which has been established in Yorkshire, Humberside and the north-east.

In addition to these activities at regional level the polytechnic has been very supportive of the work of Skill: the National Bureau for Students with Disabilities. Staff have attended a number of conferences which have been helpful in indicating ways in which provision might be improved.

Of crucial importance is continuing financial support. In 1989, as a consequence of government policy, Lancashire Polytechnic was given corporate status with new Articles of Government and new financial responsibilities. While there is no reason to suspect that the current commitment to disabled students will be discontinued, the polytechnic will be concerned to avoid a deficit budget. Often admitting disabled students to courses incurs additional costs and, in order to keep these in check, new sources of funding are being investigated. To begin with, disabled students are being encouraged to make as much use as possible of the LEA additional discretionary award. Also, rather than purchasing equipment for students using the polytechnic's own budget, it is possible that money for purchase might be loaned to the students who can then repay the loan interest-free whilst they are members of the polytechnic. Both strategies have the advantage that any equipment belongs to the students and they are able to retain it after leaving the polytechnic.

In relation to students with impaired mobility, currently there is no specially adapted accommodation. Students who use wheelchairs have been allocated ground floor rooms in the halls of residence or have occupied suitable rooms in a housing association development, bordering on the polytechnic. The possibility of converting some of the more spacious rooms in the halls of residence is being examined. Normally such rooms can be occupied by two students, so to accommodate one disabled student brings a loss of revenue. One should remember too, that the projected upsurge in student numbers in higher education, following the government's recent encouragement to institutions to recruit as many as possible, will also make demands on the already scarce accommodation.

A final issue of concern is careers advice. Whilst it is not intended to treat disabled students in ways different from other students, it must be recognized that they do have particular needs. There is already much evidence about how difficult it is for disabled people to obtain suitable employment, even in times of economic growth. Bringing together these two points suggests that disabled students might benefit from good careers guidance, perhaps from someone with specialist knowledge. The polytechnic's own careers service is already subject to a huge demand; it lacks the experience of placing well qualified disabled people and cannot devote sufficient time to developing this. A partial solution is to make links with the Disabled Graduates Careers Information Service. Looking at this problem from another angle, some of the difficulties are created by the resistance of employers to having disabled employees, a position based more on ignorance than hostility. Consequently, attempts are being made to forge stronger links with employers, who make regular visits to the polytechnic.

The Changing National Context

In the United Kingdom a system of student loans is in the process of being introduced. In 1988 the government put forward its proposals in a White Paper entitled 'Top Up Loans for Students' (HMSO, 1988). Towards the end of this document mention is made of the creation of access funds to be available to students:

> where access to higher education might be inhibited by financial considerations or where students, for whatever reasons, face real financial difficulties.

> (para 3.21)

Whilst this offers some hope, one must question the extent to which the government is aware of the additional expense incurred in coping with a disability. Certainly some of the other proposals in the White Paper seem impractical for disabled students. Thus it is suggested that, to minimize borrowing, students can obtain part-time or casual work (Annex G10). For many disabled students this is hardly a possibility. The White Paper states that the proposed changes will have no effects on subject choice; students will pursue the courses they desire. This ignores the potential consequences where courses take a longer period or where special aids are needed (Annex G9). The proposals relating to the repayment of loans also ignore the wealth of evidence which demonstrates the greater difficulties experienced by disabled people in obtaining employment; even when they secure jobs disabled graduates often earn below the income their qualifications and potential suggest. From the point of view of disabled applicants seeking entry to higher education the situation is worrying.

A second aspect of recent government policy which is also a cause for concern is the changed structure and organization of higher education. The Education Reform Act 1988 established two new bodies to oversee higher education provision: the Universities Funding Council and the Polytechnics and Colleges Funding Council. At the time of writing, it is not clear what their influence on individual institutions might be. Both Councils have the potential to exercise considerable influence since they have responsibility for distributing a major part of the finances on which institutions depend. In this respect there is also the potential for them to act in a pro-active capacity. Whilst there is a desire to allow institutions considerable autonomy in financial matters, a case can be made for some kind of central support being made available.

This could operate in a number of different ways. Given the reliance on GCE 'A' level grades which characterizes the operation of admissions procedures at the present time, institutions cannot engage in too much forward planning for potential disabled students. Thus the institutions might be faced with additional costs as a result of accepting disabled students on to their courses. This can be a disincentive since institutions are, in effect, bringing financial penalties upon themselves. On the other hand, if places are not available the penalty is against the interests of disabled students. To overcome this, the Councils could establish a contingency fund to which institutions could apply for the reimbursement of costs. This should allow institutions to feel more secure in terms of their ability to meet the needs of disabled students. Rather than focus on the institution, the Councils might consider individual students by creating bursaries or scholarships for people with disabilites which could be used to cover expenses in excess of the current discretionary disabled students' award administered by LEAs.

One suggestion which has been made is that higher education institutions should decide amongst themselves, perhaps on a regional basis, to specialize in providing high class facilities to meet the special needs of particular groups of disabled students. Thus, whilst university 'A' might develop provision for students with visual impairments, within the same region polytechnic 'B' would meet the needs of those with mobility impairments. This strategy might appeal on grounds of cost-effectiveness but it would go against the principle that students can apply to any institution. It might also introduce a greater potential for segregation. Much of the cost of providing appropriate facilities is directed towards accommodation. Resulting from this, a second cost-effective strategy is for disabled students to live at home and to attend the higher education institution nearest to them. If the predicted increase in student intake occurs, the already hard-pressed accommodation resources will be under further pressure so all institutions will be exploring ways of housing their students. If more disabled students participate in higher education from their homes, they might be the precursors of a trend likely to involve a large number of their non-disabled colleagues.

These policy changes have been accompanied by a series of reports concerned with access and admissions to higher education. In 1987 another White Paper, 'Higher Education: Meeting the Challenge', urged institutions to consider widening access. Making suitable provision for disabled people, so that they might take advantage of the opportunities offered by higher education, appears to be an important way of doing this. Yet, in many subsequent documents this group continues to be ignored. In August 1987, Maurice Plaskow compiled a report on admissions policies in higher education for the Education-Industry Forum (Plaskow, 1987). This contains only a passing mention of 'the physically handicapped' as part of a paragraph on widening access, which also mentions mature, unqualified people, women and ethnic minorities. The groups appear together again in Section 7: 'An Agenda for Action' which states:

> More effort is required to reach and provide for disadvantaged groups especially the handicapped, members of ethnic minorities, married women with children.
>
> (page 22)

The strategy of bringing together women, ethnic minorities and disabled people is also to be found in the recent HMI report 'The Widening of Access to Higher Education' (DES, 1989). However, the attention given to the first two groups is far greater than that directed towards disabled people. In fact issues relating to disability appear at only two points — a mention of dyslexia in paragraph 50 and of buildings 'unsuitable for use by disabled students' at one particular institution (para.52).

A final illustration of this serious neglect is the Training Agency Report, 'Admissions to Higher Education: Policy and Practice' (Fulton and Ellwood, 1989). Specific references to disabled students are notable for their almost total absence. Whether this reflects an omission on the part of the researchers or whether it results from a lack of concern on the part of the institutions and their admissions officers cannot be determined. However, there are many general points which are highly relevant to disabled people. Examples of this are the discussion on 'A' levels as admissions criteria and the potential of non-standard entry requirements, the effects of developing modular courses, and the formulation and application of policy statements.

These reports, together with the recent policy changes, give no grounds for optimism about disabled people wishing to enter higher education. There has been a heightened awareness of equal opportunities but mature students, women and ethnic minorities have secured the limelight. One reason for this might relate to cost; any imbalances in student numbers from these groups can be redressed without serious implications for cost-effective provision.

However, perhaps there is an avenue through which change and development might be introduced. As the social, economic, administrative and political barriers between European countries diminish, the possibility of learning from others increases. There are growing numbers of student exchanges. Encouraging disabled students to participate in these could bring greater awareness. Comparing provision will be facilitated. With this knowledge, pressure for change can be put upon the less enlightened, either directly to the particular national government or through European Community channels.

Voluntarism and market forces have proved inadequate in meeting the higher education needs of an important minority of people. Policies to date have been re-active rather than pro-active. What is needed is a more forceful central initiative. The changes currently taking place in the administration of higher education offer an opportunity for this to occur. This group of disabled young people, who have the potential to make an important contribution to society, might then be given the consideration they deserve.

References

DAVIS,F. (1961) 'Deviance disavowal: the management of strained interaction by the visibly handicapped', *Social Problems*, 9, pp. 120–132.

DEPARTMENT OF EDUCATION AND SCIENCE (1978) *Report of the Committee of Enquiry into the Education of Handicapped Children and Young People* (The Warnock Report) London, HMSO.

DEPARTMENT OF EDUCATION AND SCIENCE (1988) *Top Up Loans for Students*, London, HMSO.

DEPARTMENT OF EDUCATION AND SCIENCE (1989) *Report by HM Inspectors on the Widening of Access to Higher Education*, London, DES.

DIXON, K. and HUTCHINSON, D. (eds) (1979) *Further Education for Handicapped Students*, Bolton College of Education.

FINKELSTEIN, V. (1980) *Attitudes and Disabled People*, World Rehabilitation Fund.

FULTON, O. and ELLWOOD, S. (1989) *Admissions to Higher Education: Policy and Practice*, Sheffield, The Training Agency.

GOFFMAN, E. (1969) *Stigma*, Harmondsworth, Penguin.

GRAHAM, B. (1985) 'Transition to higher education for disabled students' *Educare*, 23, pp. 30-33

JOWETT, S. (1982) *Young Disabled People*, Slough, NFER.

NATIONAL BUREAU FOR HANDICAPPED STUDENTS (1986) *European Students with Disabilites*, NBHS/EEC.

NATIONAL INNOVATIONS CENTRE (1974) *Disabled Students in Higher Education*, NIC.

PANCKHURST, J. (1980) *Focus on Physical Handicap*, Slough, NFER.

PLASKOW, M. (1987) *Admissions Policies in Higher Education*, unpublished report for the Education–Industry Forum.

ROWAN, P. (1980) *What Sort of Life?* Slough, NFER.

STOWELL, R. (1987) *Catching Up? Provision for Students with Special Needs in Further and Higher Education*, London, National Bureau for Handicapped Students.

YOUNGHUSBAND, E. *et al.* (1970) *Living with Handicap*, London, National Bureau for Co-operation in Child Care.

8
Changes in Social Education Centres: Aspects of Disaffection

Colin Carnie

Introduction

I have been the Manager of a social education centre for many years and have been instrumental in making changes which I hope will have been of benefit to our members.

Social education centres are the responsibility of the Local Authority Social Services Directorate. They provide day care and training and attempt to meet the social needs of people with learning difficulties over the age of 16 years. Around the middle of the sixteenth century, the Spanish Conquistadors debated as to whether the slaves they had captured in Africa were fit to be anything other than slaves in the 'new world of the Americas'. Perhaps a similar debate is going on today but the subject has been changed to that of people with learning difficulties. Are they, will they ever be, other than clients requiring some form of care?

The clients are admitted to the day centres via social workers and through panels, school leavers conferences and interviews. When admitted, it is expected their names will remain on the register until such time as they leave the district, become too old, refuse to attend or become one of the 3 per cent who get a job. These centres could be called social education centres or adult training centres. Multi-purpose day centres provide training, occupation and management of people with challenging behaviour and give respite care to families who otherwise would have to provide day and night care.

Colleges arrange fixed period courses for students who are offered a place on a formal or informal contract and this applies equally to students with special educational needs as to all other students. Colleges can be more selective in their choice of clients than social education centres but they still have an expected percentage of disaffected students.

Day centres for children excluded from the education system were beginning to be set up in the late 1930s but the start of the second World War resulted in these closing. So it was not until the 1950s that pressure from parents resulted in occupational centres being set up in church halls and similar places. There was no question of handicapped children refusing to attend as their parents 'had fought for this service'. Section 12 of the 1959 Mental Health Act made it compulsory for children under 16 years to attend junior training centres but I do not think it was ever used. Most children stayed on at these centres well after they were of school leaving age, with their families and themselves believing there was some compulsion regarding their attendance, particularly as, up to 1960, there was statutory or voluntary supervision by the local authority of all mental defectives. Questions were asked about the defective's care, accommodation and occupation. There was a gradual introduction of the term 'Adult Training Centre' in the early 1960s. This title was used solely up to 1977 when the National Development Group suggested the alternative name 'social education centre' for those places which provided specific training, assessment and services. Staff training became the responsibility of the Central Council for Education and Training in Social Work. They took over the existing Diploma for Teachers of Mentally Handicapped Adults and later incorporated it in the more generic Certificate in Social Service. During all this time people with learning difficulties were being brought to the day centres by coaches and there was little chance of them not attending. Though children, from 1971, were not excluded from the education system, there was a widely accepted assumption that they would, on leaving school, transfer to the local social services day centre. It was difficult for an individual who was part of this process to see any alternative to attending the day centre five days per week. He or she was a slave in the system with the carers all acting on his or her best interests.

A Period of Change

The changes that are currently taking place in social education centres can, in my opinion, be backdated to the 20th December, 1971. It is the date when the United Nations Declaration on the Rights of Mentally Retarded Persons was adopted by the council. The principles of equality, integration, individualized habitation and natural justice were all incorporated in this declaration. There were specific articles to define rights to personal advocacy, protection from degrading treatment and any unwarranted restriction of rights. It amazes me that this did not have more impact at the time.

It took the initiative of other people and organizations to help people with learning difficulties to claim some, if not all, of these rights. Advocacy

Alliance was launched in 1982 by five voluntary organizations (Mind, Mencap, One to One, The Spastics Society and The Leonard Cheshire Foundation). The Campaign for Mental Handicap produced helpful papers on aspects of mentally handicapped people's lives and fought against injustices. Some day centres have 'student unions' or 'trainees' councils' which have some influence on their daily routine. They are also given an opportunity, through Mencap, to hold day conferences where they can meet others who are trying to make changes in their own lives.

These organizations have got to become more effective. The members need practice at being better committee members, representatives and advocates. This takes time, just as a new member of parliament or new local councillor needs time to get to 'know the ropes'. However, other people with learning difficulties hear of these things and are realizing they have rights, can say 'no' and can question authority.

Staff of social education centres are being made to face up to such issues as their authority over others, their responsibility to their clients and the need to offer the service which the client wants.

Disaffection and Change

Disaffection in social education centres is generally seen as a situation where individuals or groups are not attending or are only attending occasionally. This situation can be changed by the person returning to the centre, albeit with some concessions being made by both parties.

The Pocket Oxford Dictionary defines 'disaffected' as 'Inclined to sedition, ill disposed to rulers'. At first I ignored this definition, as the word 'ruler' seemed not to describe the day centre staff or manager, and then I tried thinking from the point of view of the client who has become disaffected with the centre. In Webster's Dictionary of 1852 'Disaffection' is defined as 'Alienation of affection, attachment or good will, want of affection, or, more generally, positive enmity, dislike or unfriendliness; disloyalty'. It generally signifies more than indifference: as in the disaffection of people from their prince or government; the disaffection of allies; disaffection from religion! This definition implies that the 'disaffected person' can be friendly, loyal and have good will but not to a particular person or organization for whatever reason. If there are causes for disaffection they could be with either party, so teachers and managers should be prepared to examine their own long-held views.

It is very difficult to change your attitude, especially when you know how *right* you are. We use various strategies and ploys to defend our attitudes: by joining with like-minded colleagues; drawing on our vast experience; letting the 'disaffected' get on with it, without the usual help, and see what happens. This strategy of self fulfilling prophecy is one which the conquistadors used to prove that slaves could only be slaves. I am not sure whether attitudes are best altered by gradual modification, total reversal of ideas or by conversion. Sometimes real life happenings best illustrate the consequences, the pressures, the emotions, the actions, the support or lack of support that are brought to bear on people who do not accept the plan of action mapped out for them.

John: a Study of Disaffection

John first became known to the day centre when he was introduced by the social worker. He had been living at home since leaving school, and was unable to find a job due mainly to his learning difficulties. His main occupation at home was the garden. He had over £20 per week spending money. It took two false starts at the centre (half day on the first occasion and two weeks on the second occasion) before his attendance became regular. A pattern of life developed which included him walking to his girlfriend's house in the morning and walking with her to the centre. The staff felt very pleased that they had succeeded in getting him to attend regularly. With hindsight, it is easy to see how the centre staff accepted that the problem of his not wanting to attend the centre had been solved and did no more to investigate the original problem.

Plans for the opening of three group homes were nearing completion and John applied for a place. There was tremendous parental opposition. He stood up to his parents and was admired and supported by the centre staff. In spite of threats that he would never be allowed home again if he left, and letters from his GP, John accepted a place in a group home. Parental opposition continued but the most difficult factor for John to accept was his reduced amount of spending money. He continued attending the centre. At this time, the centre staff were seeing this as a victory for a disabled person standing up to unwarranted restriction of rights and securing individualized habitation. They felt they were part of this victory but what had they actually done to meet John's needs?

John's medication for his epilepsy was reviewed, which resulted in him having time off from the centre for hospital appointments, and he was temporarily having more fits. He changed girlfriends and had to accept the bitter feelings of his ex-girlfriend. It became evident that his poor attendance was not solely due to hospital appointments and change in medication. According to his residential social worker, John did not want to attend the centre as he did not like boring industrial work. He could attend literacy and numeracy classes in college and he did not need the other subjects. John was persuaded to visit the centre and discuss the situation. He seemed happy about most of the industrial jobs. He would accept some of the other centre activities. He wanted more money and a real job. There was no long term improvement and the disaffection continued. The centre staff put all the blame for this disaffection on the residential social worker, who had failed to see the significance of the change of medication, and on the girlfriend who was also the person influencing John, using his own bias against the day centre's industrial work.

Two other members of the group home became disaffected with the centre. They were arriving at the centre progressively later in the mornings and sometimes not at all. It was as the result of a complaint from another house member, who said she was kept awake all night by others listening to videos late into the night, that we learnt of the two people's pattern of life. They were going to bed late, around three or four o'clock, and not getting up until the afternoon. Eventually they ceased attending the centre. Late to bed, late rising and late to the centre became a feature for some other people, though they continued to attend. Discussions with the same residential social worker focused on boring industrial work, people having a right to choose what time to go to bed and whether they would attend adult education classes. The result of the discussions was that a less disruptive way of watching late television was devised, adult education classes were found and one person agreed to attend two days a week. The staff members blamed the residential worker for not being firm with John, thereby allowing him to be a bad example. They also knew that those people concerned enjoyed industrial work, and they could prove it. The education department could not offer better than that which was offered at the centre.

John and two clients of the centre began working on a gardening scheme which was supported by the local branch of Mencap and introduced by the residential social worker, with my assistance as the day centre manager. This scheme later received funding from what is now the Training Agency. So John is occupied doing what he wants, which may lead to a 'proper job'. He has more money and there is no reason to keep his name on the centre register.

Changes have taken place in all house members' lives, though not all were planned. Professional people should try to avoid being defensive. If teachers or instructors are agents for change they should accept the changes initiated by others.

Trapped by Restrictions

There is virtually no choice of establishment available to people with learning difficulties. Generally they attend the day centre provided by the local authority's area in which they are resident. Even if there is more than one day centre within the authority, each could have its own catchment area. It would be unlikely, therefore, if everyone attending the centre was an enthusiastic member. There must be people, who, though they still attend, dislike being there, feel positive emnity or have no good will towards the place. People with learning difficulties can see no way out of this situation. Most people in their lives are authority figures: parents who will probably have control over their money; brothers or sisters who may see them as the youngest sibling in spite of their actual position in the family; social services staff who tell them what to do and the GP who listens to parents. It is a classic case of powerlessness which can lead to aggressive, even violent behaviour. Feeling trapped in a marriage can be a cause of physical abuse, trapped in a poor employment situation can lead to industrial sabotage and trapped in a poor social environment can be a cause of delinquency.

It is easy enough to identify those whose attendance is irregular, though this does not necessarily mean they are disaffected with the centre, but it is more difficult to identify those who resent attending, particularly if they have limited means of communication. Perhaps the centre staff should look for signs of disaffection within the social education centre and not assume that all is well. There will be areas where changes could be made. The use of Individual Programme Planning or similar schemes can make people feel less helpless and encourage staff members to understand them better. Assuming normal family, social and employment considerations, a person's daily, weekly or yearly activities should be as much in their control as possible. This includes planned activities within the social education centre.

Under the Disabled Persons Services Consultation and Representation Act, 1986, clients are entitled to a full assessment being made of their needs which they can use with the help, if required, of a representative of their own choice, to obtain appropriate services. It is a major task in a social education centre to determine the needs and wants of everybody, allocate the appropriate amount of time, train the staff members and find the physical and monetary resources to implement initiatives. No wonder when someone says 'Horse riding!' the answer is all too often, 'We don't do it'. When clients want to change their programme it should be easy.

In this country we have learnt not to give people whose first, and perhaps only language, is not English an explanatory leaflet in the English language. Or if we do, we should provide a person who can translate for them. So, in a social education centre, we should offer every assistance necessary to help the clients get what they want. Or is it that, by creating this choice of activity, we are concerned that nobody will elect to be occupied in the workshop areas which require less staff and make the least call on resources? How do we reconcile planned goals and aims for an individual with the client being offered a choice?

Negotiating Change

It is useful if there is, at least, an informal contract drawn up between the client and the day centre. The centre should have clearly stated in writing the training, occupation, education and recreation which is available so that the contract is not a one-sided affair. Each client should have a named advisor to help them reach an agreement about their planned activities. Where appropriate, their families should be part of this agreement.

Would the implementation of the above begin to reduce the amount of disaffection experienced within the social education centres? It would certainly help, but there are other factors. For the person with learning difficulties, there are three main influences on their lives: those which they exert themselves; those applied by their family; those imposed by the providing agency. Most people have similar forces on their lives and accept the balance which is reached, but in social education centres the staff often feel that the parents have a far greater influence than they should. Parents, in turn, feel that the staff ignore their needs, expertise and knowledge of their child. It could well be that the person with the learning difficulty, in being forced to make a choice, becomes disloyal to the centre, or even to the family.

I was concerned that members were not being as independent as they could be and I thought it was largely due to the influence of parents. I know that some parents believed that I was pushing people too far and was unrealistic about their ability to lead a more independent life. This caused stresses within the family. A working party was set up to consider this problem. The working party consisted of parents, centre staff, clients, representatives from the local Mencap and a social worker. As part of the group's work, a questionnaire was devised and completed by most of the centre clients and their parents. Many useful actions resulted from the group's work. One of the most interesting findings was that members felt both parents and centre staff had poorer expectations of their ability to become more independent than should have been the case. This was a source of disaffection which I had not considered. I was able to encourage changes to promote dignity and to offer new experiences.

Traditionally people who attended the adult training centres were paid a wage of between 30p and £4.00 per week for the assembling and packing jobs they did in the centre. One of the factors taken into consideration in determining the amount was attendance. This small sum of money has had an influence on regular attendance out of all proportion to its value. Four years ago, I changed this weekly payment into an annually credited sum of money, called training allowance, which could be withdrawn any time of the year, in any amounts, for a wide range of purposes. The amount was not related to attendance but to a contracted amount of attendance. One of the weekly incentives for attending had been lost but others have been developed. The centre is one of the members' main opportunities for social contacts. To make full use of these contacts they require mobility skills, knowledge about relationships, ability to use places of entertainment and have the use of their own homes for socializing. It cost only £100 to run a project which taught seven people to use the cinema. As horizons widen and social and personal relationships give increased pleasure, affection towards the centre has strengthened.

There comes a time in everybody's life when it is right to leave the parental home and this also happens to the members of the centre. As with most of us, there are worries about managing money, lack of knowledge and, perhaps, loneliness. The centre should make it known to the clients that it is there to provide a service to overcome these worries. It is not just a matter of the client attending the classes which have been planned, but of positively seeking out or even demanding an individual programme to meet their assessed needs. This developing of affection with the centre rather than waiting to deal with disaffection should be a part of the strategy for change.

Up to now, social education centres have neither had to advertise for customers, as colleges do, nor had to compete with other centres. Therefore, a greater self discipline on behalf of the staff is required to innovate and to maintain standards. What can people do when they become dissatisfied with their centre, want changes made or want injustices put right? Many of the staff are members of a trade union and/or professional association. Minimum standards and conditions are agreed and maintained. Each member pays a subscription to remain a member and enjoy the benefits. Earlier in this chapter I spoke of student unions or trainees' councils and of how they needed more practise at running committees. However, they need more than that. I have known trainees' councils disbanded because a new manager was appointed to the centre and that person did not approve of them. Consider what is normal practice with regard to trade unions and professional associations. The union provides its own legal advisors, administrators and consultants. It has control of its funds and would decide whether to merge with another union or whether to cease functioning. Most student unions are dependent on the centre for advisors, funds and secretarial help.

This need not always be the case. Money could be raised independently of the centre. They could affiliate with other organizations which exist for disabled people. They could pay for legal advice. The result of this would be a more normal balance of power within the social education centre.

Looking for Alternatives

During the 1980s services have become available which offer alternative options. These have developed through the influence of: community mental handicap teams; sheltered placement schemes for employment; raising earning limits; part-time employment; sheltered housing; Mencap Homes Foundation; welfare rights benefit groups; the opening of special needs units; various college courses; and the British Sports Council. Community mental handicap teams are a specialist service usually combining the expertise of the Health Service and Social Service. Clients who have become disaffected from the social education centre are usually known to the team. Their records have become the basis for the compiling of registers of mentally handicapped people in authorities where records are kept. Sheltered placement schemes give an opportunity for people whose rate of work is below that of the average worker to be gainfully employed in full time work. They would have all the other criteria for employment such as good work habits, knowledge and skills. There are people who have become disaffected with the social education centre, resulting in poor attendance, who have been successful in keeping a job through this scheme. It would have been all too easy for centre staff to have said 'If you can't attend here, how do you expect to keep a job?'

Some people with learning difficulties become tenants of council houses when their parents die, as a tenancy can be transferred to them. They may then be offered sheltered housing accommodation which could also offer some day time activities. By providing these smaller housing units, larger council houses become available to families requiring council accommodation. Some people living in group homes are asking whether or not they require full time attendance at the day centre. Welfare rights benefit groups have demonstrated the poor take-up of available benefits by disabled, low income and elderly people. They are also advisors to people seeking alternative accommodation where Income Support, Family Credit or Housing Benefit are factors.

Special needs units are the service most appreciated by families or carers who need this respite care. Even though the clients are not usually in a position to refuse to attend, the level of acceptance shoud be monitored, as there has to be a close watch kept for disaffection in this group of clients.

Differences in behaviour from home to centre, screaming, self-mutilation, head banging, not eating, incontinence, biting, scratching and sleeping disorders, could be signs of dislike, enmity and unfriendliness. A good special needs unit will treat people as individuals and will find alternatives before deciding the behaviour is unmanageable. The Health Service provides a range of services for the most severely disabled people.

Colleges now offer a wide range of full-time and part-time courses. There have been bridging courses and literacy and numeracy courses. More recently, positive action has been taken to introduce students with special needs into integrated classes. Buildings have been modified, 'helper student' schemes have been started and tutorial staff have received training. Colleges are now becoming a realistic alternative to social education centres.

Sports associations are becoming aware of the need to provide sports facilities for disabled people. There has been the Year of the Disabled and the Seoul Olympics for disabled athletes. Many sports facilities are underused during the weekdays and can provide a better service than that which is available in day centres.

The Centres and their Clients

Though many adults with learning difficulties attend adult education centres or social education centres, these centres vary considerably, depending on the policy of the local authority and the current manager's philosophy. Some centres have nearly everyone brought in by coach; others have most using public transport, walking or cycling. Some have a 'school meals service' and others have a 'staff canteen service'. Some carefully control who leaves the building at lunch-time and others encourage everybody to use local facilities unescorted. Therefore it is not surprising that people, using what appears to be a similar service, can vary so much. Whelan and Speake, in their 1977 survey (published in 1979), found that the absentee rate in adult training centres was 15 per cent, which is over double that found in industry. How much of the 15 per cent was due to disaffection by the client or their parents is not known. Today, we do not know how many potential clients there are, their distribution around the country or even their distribution within a town. This is in spite of very good surveys having been done in Cardiff, Sheffield and other places. There are people with learning difficulties who attend day centres and hospitals, there are those who once attended, those known to social services departments who do not want to attend, or who do not require a service, but statistically there should be many more.

The Social Services Directorate are compiling registers of people with learning difficulties and their needs, which will be used as a planning tool to provide the service required for the number of people wishing to use it. To establish and maintain these registers or information systems requires a computer and two staff for a population of 250,000. When this work is completed we may begin to see to what extent disaffection is a factor in those rejecting the service. Some of the reasons for non-attendance or for leaving centres are known and recorded. They include: progressive infirmity; the age of parents, no longer able to get their son or daughter ready in time or needing them at home to fetch and carry; insufficient places for multiply handicapped people; insufficient places for people with 'challenging behaviour'; gaining employment; finding alternatives; refusing to attend; pregnancy; leaving the district and not seeking another place. This does not tell us how much is due to disaffection nor does it tell us if, by improving the service, there will be less disaffection. Confidentiality and disabled people's rights should be taken into consideration when compiling a register, especially when it contains personal details of themselves and their families. Amongst professional workers there are debates as to whether or not they should advise their clients to co-operate fully with giving information about themselves. However, unless the register is at least 90 per cent accurate, it will be an ineffective tool. The percentage of accuracy aimed for is 94 per cent.

When a person leaves a day centre, whether through indifference, positive dislike or emnity, they should not automatically have cut themselves off from all other services. It may still be that the centre staff, with their expertise and experience, are the best professional people to continue to meet the needs of that person. Some centres are providing peripatetic instructors to work with people in their homes, colleges or work places. Often social workers are now based in the day centres and there is a close liaison with community mental handicap teams.

Conclusion: Meeting Needs?

Large hospitals were built to provide care and to protect the public from the effects that people of low intelligence might have by breeding and thus lowering the intellectual stock of the county. Today, medical services train nurses to work with people who have learning difficulties. Medication is used to help with the management of people with behavioural problems. Genetic counselling is expanding. There are operations and dietary strategies to overcome specific conditions. Clinical psychologists use behaviour modification techniques, provide detailed assessments and develop treatment plans. Educationalists have shown that every child can learn and, since 1971, no children have been excluded from attending some form of schooling. Universities and colleges have provided training for professional staff and are expanding their service to meet the needs of all students. The Education Departments provide lecturers and teachers in day centres. Individual research and voluntary organizations have been influential in causing particular patterns of service to evolve. Clarke and Clarke (1974) showed how people with learning difficulties could be productive and well able to sustain this effort. Adult training centres of the 1960s and 1970s tended to have large workshops producing goods for local industry.

Recent developments have led to the redesigning of these centres into several smaller workshops or to the closure of workshop provision and the opening of more diverse recreational activities. Some centre members have expressed their discontent with the changes and demanded a return to the old style of sheltered workshop as a relief from boredom. Would getting back the industrial work bring back affection for the centre? It is the nature of disaffection that more than merely the presenting problem has to be dealt with. For a couple of centuries, local authorities have had the responsibility of catering for people with learning difficulties in the community. Through the Guardians Committee they provided relief from poverty, workhouse accommodation and statutory supervision. This has developed over the years to the present community care service with mental handicap being seen as part of the service to all disabled and disadvantaged people. The introduction of the Certificate in Social Service for day care, residential and field work with the Social Service Directorate reflects this. More recently, the Department of Employment has provided training schemes to get people back to work or to introduce people into employment by giving experience, supervison and training. Many of these schemes are suitable for people with learning difficulties.

Medical, educational, social service or employment departments are all training staff to meet their department's needs, but how many training schemes are there to meet the overall needs of the client? When someone becomes disaffected with one service and changes to another (as John did from Social Services to Employment) then no harm is done. Indeed, it is good that choices exist. Unfortunately, the various services can be so isolated, like stepping stones across a stream, that the client can fall between two stones.

References

CLARKE, A. and CLARKE, A. D. (1974) *Mental Deficiency: The changing outlook*, London, Methuen.
WHELAN, E. and SPEAKE, B. (1979) *Learning to Cope*, London, Souvenir Press.

9
Transitions in a Transient Organization

Paul Jeffcutt

Introduction

This chapter is concerned with a study which considers the process of 'second chance' education, i.e. post-experience, non-formal educational provision for adults (Hutchinson, 1978; McDonald, 1984). The fieldwork setting was a transient educational organization brought into being by sponsorship from an agency of central government. The educational activities of this transient organization were focussed on the re-training of the female adult un-employed. This chapter will focus upon trainee experience of transition in this setting, one of a number of significant themes which were identified through an ethnographic case study (Jeffcutt, 1989). Over the past ten years, in concert with a substantial rise in adult unemployment, there has been a proliferation of 'second chance' education for the unwaged (Charnley *et al.*, 1985; Fraser and Ward, 1988; McGivney and Sims, 1986; Senior and Naylor, 1987). A significant proportion of this provision has been targeted exclusive-ly or predominantly at unwaged women (Thompson, 1983; Hughes and Kennedy, 1985; Wickham, 1986; Groombridge, 1987; Coats, 1987; Kearney, 1988; Waddington, 1988). Such programmes can be divided into two types (McGivney and Sims, 1986), 'return to learn' and 'return to work'.

'Return to learn' programmes for unwaged women are primarily organized as 'outreach' or 'extension' activities of formal education, e.g. higher education institutions (Mezirow, 1978; Hutchinson, 1978; Wolpe, 1980; Lovell, 1980; Thompson, 1983; Gardiner, 1986), adult or further education institutions (Wickham, 1986; Hughes and Littlewood, 1986) and the voluntary sector (Kearney, 1988). In character, such provision is predominantly part-time (e.g. one or two days a week for a period of an insti-tutional term or year), and normally targeted at access to and educational progression within the formal educational system.

'Return to work' programmes for unwaged women are primarily

organized as 'preparations' for entry into the labour market. Such work preparation is both generally rehabilitative and specifically preparatory in terms of training in respect of particular jobs or skills. This type of provision is organized in both the public sector, predominantly through further education colleges (Burrow, 1985; Wickham, 1986) and the private sector (McGivney and Sims, 1986; Wickham, 1986; Senior and Naylor, 1987). This latter category would include both training organizers ('managing agents') and training providers ('training agents') with private industry often fulfilling both roles (Benn and Fairley, 1986). Such programmes (or 'schemes') usually provide both 'on' and 'off the job' training, and frequently involve a mix of private and public sector agencies (as in the fieldwork setting). These programmes are predominantly full-time in character and of short-term duration (i.e. 4–6 weeks), following sponsorship from national or local government. 'Return to work' provision is frequently targeted at specific groups of the female unwaged, e.g. housing professionals, (Dean, 1987) or specific skills, e.g. science and technology (Stoney and Reid, 1981).

A Remedial and Rehabilitative Focus

Both types of provision have a remedial and rehabilitative focus towards access to and progression within, either the labour market or the educational system. The ethos of 'second chance' education (Kearney, 1988), is one of 'entitlement' (providing access to work or education for those individuals who had previously been isolated by barriers to their participation), through a process of 'empowerment' (a process of transition that enables individuals to achieve more control over their own lives).

The separation of return to work or learn as a focus for the second chance education of the unwaged, would appear to reflect a current position in a long standing educational debate between liberal and vocational education, that has been evident throughout the development of the compulsory and post-compulsory education system (Sanderson, 1987). The educational objectives of developing general all-round capabilities versus the development of specific skill based competencies (Mezirow, 1981) has been strongly argued recently in terms of a 'great debate' between education and training (Watts, 1983; Dale, 1985; Bates *et al.*, 1984; Benn and Fairley, 1986; Finn, 1987; Jeffcut, 1988). The terms of this debate concerning national education and training policy, and economic and social transition, can be seen in microcosm in respect of debates concerning the curriculum for the education and training of the long-term unemployed.

On the one hand this curriculum is structured towards 'employability' and 'opportunity creation', and on the other hand towards 'coping' and the use of 'leisure' time (Watts and Knasel, 1985). This separation between the formal economy and employment, and personal and community development (Johnston, 1987) embodies a further division between waged and unwaged work.

The numerous critics of these educational, occupational and economic separations argue that rather than empowering and entitling the long-term unemployed, such approaches maintain and reinforce their disability. Thus, 'second chance' education would be understood as a process of social and economic stratification (akin to initial education), in terms of class (Willis, 1977; Bates *et al*, 1985; Finn, 1987) and gender (Cockburn, 1985; Wickham, 1986). Correspondingly, 'second chance' education which was seriously concerned with empowerment and entitlement would thus be focused at challenging such restricted social definitions (Thompson, 1983; Freire, 1985). In curricular terms, the needs of the long-term unemployed could not be simply dichotomized (Johnston *et al*., 1988) and subsequently prescribed (McGivney and Sims, 1986; Senior and Naylor, 1987).

Traditionally, unemployment has been conceptualized in respect of loss of status and (male) identity (Hayes and Nutman, 1981), with women assumed to be occupying either an 'invisible' domestic role (Finnegan, 1985) or a parallel domestic and marginally employed role, earning a subsidiary income. In such a situation female occupational identity is structured around the 'invisible' role of domestic labourer. With female employment thus being seen as marginal, any unemployment would be consequently perceived as unproblematic, being overcome by greater reliance on a male breadwinner and an increase in compensatory domestic activities. However, such assumptions need to be considered against increasing female participation in paid work (Dex, 1985), the routine and permanent nature of that participation (Martin and Wallace, 1984), and the predominantly financial needs that motivated that participation (Coyle, 1984). A recent study (Coyle, 1984) of female redundancy and unemployment found that the female experience of unemployment, far from being marginal and subsidiary to the male experience, was indeed closely comparable.

> Women work primarily for money and economic independence, and when they lose their jobs they suffer a serious financial loss. At the same time their self image suffers too; for many consider work (though not necessarily the 'male' model of work) to be central to their lives (Coyle, 1983, p. 83).

In such a situation unemployment means financial hardship, isolation and depression for both men and women. Whilst for men, unemployment may be conceived of as a crisis of gender identity (hence the search for extrafamilial compensatory activities); for women, unemployment is often experienced as a crisis of autonomy (Coyle, 1984). In such a situation of a loss of independence, a domestic role is not a compensation, particularly for older women (Martin and Wallace, 1984), but rather a return to drudgery and dependence following the loss of an escape route. For unemployed women, the family thus acts as a comfortable and familiar trap, in a discriminatory rather than compensatory relationship with paid work (Finnegan, 1985).

Restricted Social Stereotypes

In the light of recent reconceptualizations of the formal and non-formal economies (Sparrow, 1986) and of waged and unwaged work (Deem, 1985), the term 'unemployed' becomes less accurate (hence the use of the term 'unwaged', which best encapsulates the experience for women as well as men). From such a basis, not only do the demarcations between 'work' and 'leisure' for the unwaged become artificial and irrelevant (Johnston, 1987), but also essentially patronizing. Such separations in the curriculum for retraining the unwaged can thus be examined as based in a stereotypically male experience of employed work and non-employed leisure time (McGivney and Sims, 1986; Senior and Naylor, 1987; Johnston, 1988). The empowerment and entitlement of the female unwaged is thus not only focused on an experience of powerlessness (Bryant, 1983) and alienation (Mezirow, 1981), but also of oppression (Coyle, 1984). Yet as we have observed, 'second chance' education is typically remedial and rehabilitative, having evolved from an educational tradition in which the concept of 'disadvantage' has been central.

> The language of 'personal deficit', 'affliction' and the need for 'treatment' to 'rehabilitate' the 'malfunctioning' adult into 'normal' society runs like a medical checklist through the literature. The tone is one of mission and concern for the less fortunate in areas in which the distinctions between therapeutic, educational, and welfare needs become very difficult to establish.
>
> (Thompson, 1980, p. 87)

Thompson (1983) describes such provision as 'role education', a subordinating outcome of patriarchy that defines women's needs and education in terms of restricted social stereotypes. Patriarchal 'second chance' education for unwaged women would thus confirm rather than challenge women's allegiance to their domestic and traditional roles. For some educators, 'second chance' education is not concerned with such prescriptions for the participants' 'return' to a particular position or stratum of society, but with a 'revolutionary transformation' (Freire, 1985) of the learner's social world. The achievement of this latter objective for the female unwaged requires the critical exploration of the issues of empowerment and entitlement (Mezirow, 1981; Thompson, 1983, 1988; Freire, 1985; Senior and Naylor, 1987) with the objective of stimulating a 'critical consciousness'. Education is thus perceived as a process of 'liberation' (Thompson, 1983) and 'emancipation' (Mezirow, 1981), a critical process through which the social world can be clarified and social order revealed as an experience in the making (i.e. 'conscientisation' Freire, 1985).

This theoretical and philosophical underpinning is clearly most relevant to the 'second chance' education of the unwaged, and has been put into operation in a number of ways. Johnston (1987) discusses the development of a resource base and a learning exchange which 'belonged' to the unwaged participants, as a contrast to the powerlessness and alienation of their experience of being unwaged (see also Groombridge, 1987). Senior and Naylor (1987) in a critique of 'employability' and the 'work ethic', discuss community-based programmes for the unwaged which focus on 'redefining' skill, creativity and competence as part of a process of transformation to a 'post-industrial' society.

By far the largest area of development has been in programmes of 'second chance' education for women which have been concerned with 'consciousness raising' in respect of gender inequalities. Thompson (1983) discusses the establishment and operation of a women's education centre which was organized by and for women.

> We began with the assumption that the traditional roles of women are discriminatory and restricting ones, so that rather than offering a curriculum content designed to reaffirm or reinforce them, we adopted a different definition of social relevance as our starting point. The topics chosen for study were to provide a vehicle for the examination of the shared condition of being female in our society, to examine how sexism and patriarchy operates, what the consequences of this might be for ordinary women and what, if anything, can be done to escape from the limited and limiting expectations which a society like ours still reserves for women.
>
> (Thompson, 1983, p. 152)

Further operational examples of this form of 'second chance' programme can be found in Hughes and Kennedy (1985), Groombridge (1987), Coats (1987) and Waddington (1988). The autonomy of these programmes appears to have evolved largely through a process of struggle, in which their 'critical consciousness' has developed. Indeed, the women's centre that Thompson

(1983) describes, evolved from an 'outreach' return-to-learn programme of a university. Thus all women's 'second chance' education has the potential to facilitate 'consciousness raising', and indeed many 'outreach' programmes have an apparently 'feminist' philosophy. Yet many such programmes (e.g. Wolpe, 1980; Gardiner, 1986; Hughes and Littlewood, 1987) do not appear to achieve their objectives of autonomy and liberation.

The NEW Programme

The setting in which the above significant issues have been considered in detail (Jeffcutt, 1989) was a transient educational organization located in an industrial city in northern England. This 'pilot' programme (NEW), received short-term sponsorship from the MSC (as it was then titled), an agency of central government, and was organized by a privately-owned training consultancy company. The NEW programme was concerned with the re-training of the female adult unemployed and operated during the period September–December 1983.

Trainees who undertook the NEW programme ranged from 28 to 57 years old (mean 43) with the majority having been unemployed for between one and three years. A wide background of occupational experience was evident in which office, shop and assembly work predominated. A further significant trainee characteristic was the proportion (75 per cent) who lacked any recognized educational attainment. Whilst trainees were all female, trainers were predominantly male, younger (mean 35) and with professional or managerial work experience. Trainers had all, at some time, participated in higher education, and had relatively little personal experience of unemployment. No ethnic minorities were represented in either group.

Trainees participated in the programme on an open access basis, remaining registered as unemployed, receiving benefit and an additional subsistence allowance. The duration of the programme for a trainee was four weeks, whilst for trainers this transient educational organization operated for three successive trainee cohorts. The programme was organized into three distinct phases which were replicated over time. An initial period of group work and individual guidance took place at the programme base (a set of rooms hired from a Public Library), leading to a period of occupational experience (predominantly 'work sampling' at a local Skillcentre), followed by a further period of group work and individual guidance at the programme base.

A three stage process is commonly identified in studies of planned educational programmes:– in schooling (Willis, 1977; McLaren, 1986), in youth training (Bates *et al.*, 1985; Finn, 1987; Pollard *et al.*, 1988), in adult training (Van-Maanen, 1973; Light, 1979), in female 'second chance' education (Mezirow, 1978, 1981; Lovell, 1980; Pitman, 1988). In such programmes a participant experiences a process of transformation between an entry and exit state, or set of conditions, through the catalyst or threshold of the programme itself. Such a process of change is described as a 'rite of passage' (Van-Gennep, 1960; Turner, 1974) and is elaborated in three processual stages which shape the participant's transformation; 'a passage from one position, constellation or domain of structure to another' (Turner, 1974, p. 238).

Processes of Passage: Patriarchal and Patronizing

The NEW programme was the setting of a transitional process for both trainers and trainees, symbolized as a 'bridge' between entry and exit states. Trainees were projected to be transformed from unemployed to employed through the agency of the 'vocational preparation' of the programme. At the same time, trainers were projected to be transformed from temporarily funded (a 'pilot' programme) to more permanently funded (a 'renewed' programme) through the agency of trainee success in gaining employment. Trainer and trainee transitions through the NEW programme were thus projected as both integrated and harmonic.

In practice, the nature and focus of trainee passage through the programme towards the objective of employment was contested by trainers. Through the content and organization of the 'vocational preparation' provided, two contradictory models of training the long-term unemployed can be observed. On the one hand, a prescriptive process was described which led fairly directly to a job: trainee deficiencies were identified by trainers (i.e. inadequacy in terms of ability and motivation), a remedial process was prescribed and enacted (predominantly group confidence-building and attitudinal reconstruction), trainees then exited this intense transformative process both empowered and re-directed into employment. On the other hand, an exploratory process was described which was the first step on the road to employment: trainees were identified as unknowing (both of their own selves/skills and how these could be employed) rather than deficient, a process of guided discovery was initiated (individual assessment, guidance, skills tasting), trainees then continued this process of discovery and change under their own power in the direction of their own needs (e.g. further training towards a particular goal). Thus oppositional processes of passage were constructed for trainees, both of which embodied significant restrictions and limitations in terms of the women's origins, process of change and destinations.

Trainees were either conceived of as 'deficient' and thus requiring 'prescription', or 'unknowing' and thus requiring 'guidance'. In each case, trainers assumed trainees to be 'traditionally conditioned' and 'working class'. Both transitional models had pictures of successful outcomes for trainees; which were on the one hand bright, confident and motivated individuals who could 'sell fridges to eskimos', or on the other hand knowing, realistic and integrated individuals who could 'take steps along their own road'. In either case, successful functioning for trainees was conceived of as their learning of 'trainer-like' roles which were depicted in both 'male' (the successful sales*man*) and 'middle class' (the self-actualized person) terms. The roles which trainers constructed for trainees in the NEW programme were thus both patriarchal and patronizing.

The NEW programme as a process of passage is thus concerned with trainees on the one hand losing their 'female' employment identities and acquiring 'male' employment identities, whilst on the other hand losing their 'working class' social identities and acquiring 'middle class' social identities. The rite of passage of the NEW programme can thus be seen as initiated by the 'death' of the trainees as 'trainee-like', and by their 'rebirth' as 'trainer-like'. However, as we shall see, these passages were unsatisfactory for trainers and trainees alike.

As Turner (1974) observes, the ritual subject's experience of a rite of passage is one of ambiguity and paradox in which social structures are perceived as being in a state of flux. For NEW trainees this was intensified since the model of observances of the process of passage (i.e. the tribal lore, myths, taboos, invocations etc.) were contested by the programme elders (the trainers). On the one hand there was a stable and replicable (temporal and structural) pattern to the programme process, yet on the other hand this process was contested and oppositional in a number of key issues. This situation resulted in a number of particularly puzzling conflicts and inconsistencies.

Conflicts and Inconsistencies

The 'return to work' transition was largely translated into the group activities curriculum. However, rather than challenging the perceived traditional conditioning of these 'working class' women, this process celebrated and sustained their perceived deficiencies. Confidence-building training activities were patronizing (conducted through a 'Coronation Street script') rather than developmental. The programme base was projected as 'a home from home', in which trainees were encouraged to take on domestic ('tea making') and passive ('the audience') roles. Any trainees who challenged this regime were perceived as deviant, whilst those whose abilities were beyond the standard provided were threatening (described as 'red lights'). These trainers assumed trainees to be a relatively homogeneous group of deskilled deficients, and scapegoated those who contradicted these projections. The passage of these 'housewives' to their rebirth as putative male trainer-like 'employables' was thus enacted through a disabling process which was patriarchal and patronizing. Hardly surprisingly, these trainees did not become empowered to 'sell fridges to eskimos', with only the most independent and resilient trainees achieving any developmental progress.

The 'return to learn' transition was largely translated into the individual activities curriculum. This process was essentially one of guidance through which individuals would uncover their own needs. A trainee's desire for employment could thus be seen as a presenting need which initiated a process of discovery which could lead in a different direction. Trainees were thus perceived as 'unknowing', and the programme's role was one of providing insight through a series of individual experiences (assessment, guidance interviews, skills tasting). These experiences were presented as intensely focused and worldly, a means of getting in touch with the 'real world'. Through this process, trainees would receive insight into their own situation and thus be empowered to make decisions about their own future (i.e. to take steps along their own road).

Trainees were thus assumed to be 'out of touch' or 'lost' rather than deficient; they did not suffer so much from inability as from a lack of realization of their abilities. Yet, whilst trainees were perceived to be individuals rather than a homogeneous group, the range of guidance experiences available was limited and occupied a standardized pattern that was largely invoked for all trainees. In curricular terms, individual trainee needs were assumed not to extend beyond a fairly limited menu of educational experiences; whilst in temporal terms, individuals were assumed to be able to start taking steps along their own road by the end of four weeks, (as trainee testimony showed, there was great difference in the level of need over time). Little attention was paid by these trainers to trainee post-programme support, with the formation of a trainee support group only being effectively undertaken with the last cohort. The programme was also not part of a network of agencies to which trainees could be referred for further guidance. Trainee guidance, it seems, was an intensive formalized process from which only the most capable or confident could gain. Those trainees who required more detailed or extensive attention could not be catered for within the programme.

Though trainees were not the discrete homogeneous group, in respect of their 'disadvantage' (in terms of age, work experience, educational attainment, socio-economic group, etc.) that had been projected, there is considerable commonality in their experience of passage. Following Lakoff and Johnson (1980) and Moch and Fields (1985), common metaphoric structures were identified in trainee discourse across cohorts; which following Turner (1974) and Srivastva and Barrett (1988) have been taken to indicate phases of development during a transitional period.

'Waking Up' and 'Simmering Down'

The first phase of a 'rite of passage' is one of 'loss' (a separation from pre-existing structures and conditions) which trainees commonly perceive as both 'dormant' and 'unseeing' (e.g. they feel 'stale', 'blindfolded', 'asleep', 'lost'). The second phase is one of 'liminality' (a marginal state of transition, 'betwixt and between', Turner 1974), which trainees again initially experience in common terms of 'revelation' (e.g. images of 'light' and 'clarity'). By the end of the first week of the programme trainee images are becoming more confused and ambiguous, expressed in terms of 'good health' ('a tonic', 'refreshing') and 'bad health' ('exhausting', 'draining'). As the programme continues, such paradoxical imagery increases with trainee experience characterized by 'disorientation' (e.g. trainees are both 'going on' as well as 'slipping back'). Throughout the varied activities of the 'work sampling' phase of the programme, trainee imagery contrasts the 'togetherness' and 'sharing' of the trainee group with the 'isolation' and 'depression' ('flatness'/'falling') of being apart from the group. The third phase of a rite of passage is one of 'reaggregation' or 'rebirth', and trainee imagery of their entry into this phase is oppositional in character — whilst some trainees are 'waking up' and 'simmering down', others are still 'high on a drug' (i.e. 'addicted' to their liminal experience). This opposition continues through the point of leaving, when some trainees feel they have 'got something', whilst others feel as if they have been 'dumped', needing to 'go on' in order to 'get something' from the programme. Beyond the end of the programme trainee imagery becomes even more stark and oppositional, with their experience of the programme being summarized as a 'holiday entertainment' then 'going back to before', or about 'finding yourself' and 'breaking free'.

The increasingly oppositional character of trainee transition is clearly closely related to the contradictions of trainer transition; there are however, important tensions which need to be aired in advance of this discussion. As we have considered, the female experience of unemployment is essentially one of loss of autonomy (Coyle, 1984), with a consequent entrapment in the private and isolated world of unpaid domestic labour (Finnegan, 1985). However trainee participation in the programme represented only a transient and partial 'escape' from this domestic world. On the one hand, the programme offered alluring prescriptions of a return to work or learning (McGivney and Sims, 1986) but without an effective change of status for trainees, who were occupied for a temporary four-week period without any change in their contractual or financial circumstances (i.e. conditions which effectively denied them any gaining of autonomy). On the other hand, trainee participation in the programme offered some release from a private domestic world through the communal experience of 'togetherness' and 'sharing'. Yet this participation was continually mediated by the encroachment of domestic labour, in terms of the double burden of work experienced by employed women (Pollert, 1981), and the 'emotional blackmail' of the family in respect of a contest of allegiances between the private and public worlds of trainee experience. Hence the paradox of trainee 'addiction' to the sharing and togetherness of the group (an experience of 'communitas', Turner, 1974) as well as the perception of this experience as transient (a 'holiday'). Indeed at the height of this tension, trainees appear unable to differentiate between which experience (the home/the programme) can be constructed as 'real' and which can be considered a 'fantasy'.

The experience of trainees sharing and uncovering common problems is identified as a significant 'consciousness raising' process in second chance education (Wolpe, 1980; Lovell, 1980; Burrow, 1985; Gardiner, 1986; Hughes and Littlewood, 1987). This collective experience is opposed to the individualism of traditional 'role education' and provides the lateral development space of 'respectable feminism' (Thompson, 1988). In such space trainees can develop from passive to active learners (Burrow, 1985) and develop strategies of resistance to domestic limitations (Wolpe, 1980; Lovell, 1980). However, supportive and developmental as such sharing processes can be (Gardiner, 1986), these consciousness raising strategies have limitations which mean that they fall short of the goal of 'liberation'. As has been already discussed, these limitations are twofold: firstly, in terms of the educational exchanges themselves; secondly, in terms of the organizational practices which sustain such exchanges. The central issue is one of control and empowerment, and can be identified as a process which sustains a particular set of educational power relations and a particular sexual division of labour, or a process which challenges and transforms them. Thus empowerment not only means solidarity and resistance, but also transformation and reconstruction. As Freire (1985) and Thompson (1988) argue, the former opposition is a respectable form of dissent which maintains rather than transforms inequalities. The logic of transformation as posed by these dialectical theorists is a creative process of empowerment through which both individuals resist oppression and transform the social order that structures such oppression. Thompson (1983, 1988), Freire (1985) and Mezirow (1981) suggest such transformation is effected by the development and sustenance of a reflective critical consciousness which has its origin in a strategy of resistance. In respect of the women's movement, and particularly the empowerment of mature unwaged women, such processes are inevitably concerned with women's educational and economic subordination to men: as Freire (1985) puts it, a process of liberation or domestication that is in relation to patriarchy (Thompson, 1988).

The Limitations of NEW

As we have seen, despite a series of disputes between trainers concerning opposing models of training the long-term unemployed, NEW was a limiting rather than transforming experience for trainees. Whether concerned with a return to working or learning, NEW was focused on restructuring individual trainees rather than any collective empowerment focused on transforming any social order. In fact both these contradictory processes of trainee transition can be understood as inadequate, embodying different forms of 'role education' (Thompson, 1983). As a course projected to transform incapable females into employable 'males', NEW provided a limiting 'Coronation Street script' which celebrated female 'deficiencies' and enforced passive, dependent and domestic roles for trainees. As a programme projected to provide lateral space for trainee self development, a restricted menu of educational activities occurred in a stable pattern for all trainees over a limited time period. Thus trainees were not empowered either to take on male occupational identities or to question and develop their current selves and needs. Clearly these objectives were mutually antithetic, and given the degree of conflict evident in NEW, undermined one another, contributing to their mutual inadequacy.

Unsurprisingly, trainees displayed different levels of attachment to the ambiguous transitional process of the NEW programme. For some the programme was an entertainment, a holiday, before an inevitable return to pre-existing limitations. Thus these trainees achieved a transient escape from their isolation (and oppression) through a collective experience of sharing and potentiality. However, their low investment in the programme's potential outcomes meant little risk of disappointment, or gain. Hence the programme represented a 'holiday', even if this were only 'a change being as good as a rest' (i.e. the reformulation of an oppressive social order in a fresh setting). For those trainees with a big investment and a strong attachment to transition, the programme was really about change and 'breaking free'. These trainees had 'burnt their bridges' and could not go 'back to before';

thus they had a sense of desperation about needing to go on to get something. Their experience of the programme was not enough to sustain them (as a holiday effect), as they physically returned (unsupported and isolated) to the oppression of their former lives. The programme was thus a glimpse of a different world that they would have to strive alone to re-discover. One trainee in particular (Cathy), alone, was determined enough to pursue this long hard road; others had to return embittered to accept the restrictions of their former lives. Thus NEW was on the one hand a delicious fairy tale, a fantasized and transient holiday, whilst on the other it was a catalyst, a cathartic and traumatic process that exposed needs that were either unrealizable or if potentially available had to be realized alone and unsupported.

It would seem that in respect of both employment and personal development, NEW was inadequate. In terms of employment, trainees were actively disabled rather than enabled to achieve projected job outcomes. In terms of personal development, trainees were encouraged to embark upon processes of change which they were unable to effectively sustain and support. In both cases trainees were not being empowered; firstly, through limiting and restrictive expectations; secondly, through over-optimistic and unrealistic expectations. Thus NEW as a transient educational experience was more disabling than enabling, and more destructive than constructive.

The liminal stage of a rite of passage is replete with ambiguity and paradox (Turner, 1974) and the trainees' experience of NEW certainly provided contradictory and competing understandings of their transition. Not only were tribal lore, myths and taboos invoked and interpreted differently by different elders (trainers), but each interpretation was internally inconsistent. In such a confusing situation the one consistent and fresh experience that the programme provided was the formation and interaction of the trainees as a group. A culture of female solidarity is strongly and consistently evident, becoming both the motivation and the support to overcome difficulties and problems in participation, and the lateral space in which useful learning is both created and discovered. Indeed as Thompson (1983) and others argue, the formation of such a women's learning group is the basis for challenging patriarchy. It would seem that whilst one can indeed take steps to facilitate such an outcome, it is at the same time difficult to prevent such developments spontaneously occurring even in the most inhospitable settings. As we have discussed, all second chance education, and particularly those programmes exclusively for women can have a consciousness raising effect; however, according to Thompson, (1988) particular philosophical, educational and organizational practices are required in order for such developments to achieve liberation.

It would seem that NEW trainees did achieve a collective experience which was both supportive and developmental (an experience of 'communitas' — Turner, 1974). Though such trainee progress was apparently what trainers espoused, it would appear that this was achieved more despite than because of their ministrations. The significance of this communal experience is indicated by the common experience of loss and fear of the future that trainees have at the end of the programme. Whether trainees were committed to the various transitions proposed through the programme or not, they all exhibited a strong dependence on their collectivity. This reinforces the conception of the programme as a rite of passage, since trainees did not want to exit from their liminal (and communal) state to be reaggregated into a different social world. Whether the passage was an experience of a 'holiday' or a 'catalyst' in a process of 'breaking free', trainees would inevitably be entering a world in which they would be more isolated and unsupported. From a liminal state of possibility and potentiality (however gendered and domesticated) they would be re-entering a limited and stratified world of disadvantage. The collective experience of 'communitas' was clearly transient, since it did not survive the trainees' 'rebirth' (as they left the programme) — all attempts to preserve their collectivity (post-programme support groups) were either unable to become established, or soon foundered. This is understandable since the preservation of a liminal state requires particular social and physical conditions which are lost at the point of leaving. Trainees through leaving and reaggregation were embarking on coping with a range of different needs that had all been agglomerated and subsumed in the liminal stage of transition.

Cathy's Experience

> The programme was a springboard. I'm diving in deep, going where it's dark. I'm going further and needing a bit of support. Some of the others are paddling, some are drying their feet already.
>
> (Cathy, NEW3, day 65).

As we have observed the most significant aspect of trainee 'liminal' experience was that of 'sharing' and 'togetherness'. Here this experience of 'communitas' (Turner, 1974) appears to have offered developmental potential (Gardiner, 1986) which was largely unrealized in terms of trainee empowerment and 'liberation' (Thompson, 1983). The experience of Cathy appears to offer the only example of the development of 'critical consciousness' (Freire, 1985). Her long lonely struggle exposes the catharsis of 'breaking free' through the contradictions of 'role education' (Thompson, 1983), exemplified by the double burden of sexually stratified work roles (Pollert, 1981). Cathy's progressive rejection of her domestic role in the family is sustained by the female solidarity of the group. However, the 'high' from this 'drug' is a transient experience, and Cathy suffers the trauma of leaving and losing support. Her isolated struggle to preserve this transformation (symbolized as the relaunching of a sunken ship) is focused on the achieving of autonomy through employment (Coyle, 1984). However, through this struggle to succeed in the labour market, Cathy appears to have adopted the persona of a 'token male' (Cockburn, 1985), and subsequently characterizes other trainees' lack of progress in terms of feminine 'deficiencies'.

Other trainees' transitions were interrupted and diverted (Pitman, 1988) by the interference of domestic 'responsibilities', manifest in various forms of 'emotional blackmail' (Wolpe, 1980; Lovell, 1980). However, the limitations of these undoubted domestic burdens may have also represented a framework of safety and security amidst the ambiguity and tension of liminality. As we have observed, a majority of trainees conceived of their transient experience as a 'holiday', a therapeutic but temporary communal experience in which the 'holiday effect' was a relaxing change of setting and companions, rather than a challenging transformation of consciousness. Thus these trainees actively denied the potentiality of their liminal experience (perhaps through justifiable fear of experiencing the trauma of unsupported change, e.g. Cathy), by choosing 'safe' options and passively accepting the limiting and stratified roles which were constructed for them (Griffin, 1985). As Hughes and Littlewood (1986) found, trainees resisted adopting more active and challenging roles in their 'second chance' education, and sought the 'parental' support of trainers through their process of passage. From this perspective the apparent lack of trainee resistance (which would have been anticipated particularly by theorists concerned with structural inequalities — Alvesson, 1985; Ray, 1986) to the stratified and limiting roles which were constructed for their transition, appears more explicable.

Trainer Perceptions

Such ambiguity and paradox in trainee experience is clearly related to the conflict and tension of trainer experience of the programme. As we observed, trainers constructed structurally compatible but mutually antithetic processes of transition for trainees. From a common starting point in trainee disadvantage and trainee needs, the process of change and their primary objectives showed contradictions in construction. Hence trainers articulated competing transitional processes for trainees which projected opposing concepts of success. On the one hand, 'employable' images of performing, polish and persuasion; on the other hand, 'learning' images of self-knowledge, insight and personal development. However, these contradictory trainee outcomes were also projected as the agency by which the programme's transience would be resolved (i.e. the 'success' of trainees being understood as the major criterion for the 'renewal' of the 'pilot' organization).

The conjunction of trainer and trainee processes of passage in the NEW setting thus produces an experience that is more disabling than enabling for all participants. The most significant feature of this experience is its paradoxical nature; on the one hand, those transitions which are projected are also proscribed; whilst on the other hand, those participants who are most committed to the process of passage, experience the least satisfactory outcomes.

Both the conflicting transitions of 'role education' articulated in the NEW setting shared common assumptions of 'disadvantage' (Thompson, 1983), whilst embodying roles for trainee passage which were male rather than female, and trainer-like rather than trainee-like. Thus trainees were anticipated to lose the disadvantages and deficiencies of being female and trainee-like, and become re-born with the advantages and characteristics of being male and trainer-like.

However, as we have observed, the roles which were enacted through the liminal phases of passage were disabling, and domesticating rather than emancipatory (Mezirow, 1981; Freire, 1985). On the one hand, gender stereotyping was enforced through domestic labour (tea ceremonies), patronizing talk ('the Coronation Street script') and passive and dependent trainee roles (the audience). On the other hand, a routinized and institutionalized programme structure was constructed for trainees as a homogeneous group which both suppressed trainer deviance, and characterized trainees with non-programmed needs as deviants (e.g. 'red lights', drop-outs).

Trainee passage was concurrent rather than interdependent with trainer passage (as trainers assumed). Given the role limitations and stratifications that were constructed by trainers, the trainee experience of transition seems peculiarly separate. Indeed the 'holiday' experience that the majority of trainees' liminal phases are characterized by, is predicated upon their failure to become committed to the role objectives which trainers had constructed for them. This passive or 'silent' resistance (Griffin, 1985) rather than active resistance to trainers' ministrations was built around the 'togetherness' and 'solidarity' of 'communitas' (Turner, 1974).

However, as we considered earlier, these trainees both denied the potential, and were denied the educational and structural conditions, by which this experience of female 'solidarity' could become liberating (Freire, 1985). Thus, paradoxically, this sharing of the experience of being female (Thompson, 1983) also became expressed through the observance of domestic duties in the programme. In this way, these trainees accepted the double burden of 'role education', as the programme became literally a 'home from home'. Trainee 'rebirth' thus resulted in the continued practice of the dual role of domestic work, in terms of domestic tasks in the public sphere of paid work (as 'green labour' — Wickham, 1986), and as private unpaid domestic labour. Yet even this stratified and limiting outcome was only achieved by a minority of trainees (20 per cent), with most returning reluctantly (from their 'holiday') to an isolated world of invisible and unpaid work (Cockburn, 1985). Those minority of trainees who were committed to the role objectives constructed (particularly Cathy), became 'addicted' to the female solidarity of liminality. However, as we have observed, this is a transient condition which is structurally disabled from becoming emancipatory. Thus these trainees experienced the competing responsibilities (Thompson, 1983) of role education whilst searching for 'liberation'. 'Rebirth' thus came as an abrupt awakening to the loss of solidarity, support, and the realization of a long and rough road to travel.

Thus, what was projected for trainer and trainee transitions was also proscribed through the process by which these passages were enacted. Hence those trainers who believed the effectiveness of the programme would be judged by the transformation of female inadequates into 'token male' employables, enacted domesticating and limiting roles for these trainees. Whilst those trainees who sought to break free from the female private world of unpaid work and enter the male public world of paid work, encountered a learning experience which, whilst providing the potential for consciousness raising (female solidarity), was enacted through conditions which disabled these emancipatory or liberating influences. So, (in a painful paradox) the developmental processes of these trainees who sought to move on were handicapped and impeded by the limiting and stratifying training conditions enacted by trainers (thus disabling rather than enabling the very outcomes they sought to achieve).

Paradoxical Transitions

Parallel paradoxes are also evident: trainers who believed that the success of the programme lay in the personal development of individual trainees (being transformed from the female 'disadvantaged' to the 'self-actualized person'), enacted a relatively routinized and restricted guidance curriculum for all trainees as a homogeneous group. While those trainees who sought to experience the programme as a 'holiday' or a break from their private world of domestic labour, found their 'sharing' and 'togetherness' interrupted by an institutionalized programme of activities which both differentiated and stratified them. Thus the limited and simplified escape of these trainees (symbolized by their acceptance of domestic duties in the programme), represented simplistic and limiting obstacles for trainers who believed that trainee success would be demonstrated by their 'taking steps along their own road'.

Such paradoxical transitions, characterized by denial and symbolic inversion are clearly different from the transitional breakdowns identified by Pitman (1988). Although the ritual passengers of the NEW setting clearly experienced the tension and ambiguity that Pitman (1988) identifies as 'social dissonance', these contradictions led to paradoxical outcomes rather than to breakdown. Similar paradoxical transitions have been identified in studies of the transition from school to work, in which expressions of autonomy and resistance by young men (Willis, 1977) and young women (Anyon, 1983), become transformed into conformist and stereotypical outcomes. Such paradoxical transitions appear to be characterized by the processes of contradiction, symbolic inversion and denial.

Theorizing that has explored this ambivalence in organization studies, has identified such a conceptual division in terms of the formal and informal organization. Yet, the formal has typically assumed primacy over the informal (Gregory, 1983) as has the functional over the expressive (Jones *et al.*, 1988). Hence, the rational and ordered structures the irrational and disordered. However, if we were to perceive these oppositions as both mutually constructive and mutually destructive, the focus of our investigations would become the structuring of the boundary or the division between them (Cooper, 1986). One is therefore examining the process of 'cultural production' (Willis, 1977, 1983), whereby through their creation of meaning in an institutional setting, participants are actively reconstituting their structures of oppression. Thus, the paradoxical interconnections of trainers and trainees in the NEW setting meant that the particular outcomes that were projected, were proscribed through the process of participation itself.

At the outset of the 'pilot' programme, trainers had projected that 80 per cent of trainees would find work within three months of leaving the programme. Follow-up research with all participants indicated that the 20 per cent of trainees that had gained employment had done so in work which was poorly paid, transient, deskilled and vulnerable. It is here highly debatable whether trainees' employment prospects were significantly altered by their experience of the programme. On the one hand the turnover in such employment of 'green labour' (i.e. 'inexpensive, inexperienced and unorganized' — Wickham, 1986) is sufficient for such work to be relatively easily available. On the other hand a 20 per cent employment rate is common for 'return to work' courses (Gardiner, 1986) with 50 per cent being exceptional (Burrow, 1985), whilst the projected 80 per cent had not been recorded in any study.

Correspondingly, the trainers who needed to receive the reward of a further period of sponsorship to indicate the innovation of their training activities, scapegoated trainee deficiency as the 'cause' of NEW's 'failure'. The trainers' report (in a celebration of 'male' motivations and values, with a corresponding derogation of the female) recommended the redesign of the programme to select more effectively and stratify trainees. They proposed the separation of trainees into 'succeeders' and 'failures' (determined by their abilities to adopt male occupational roles); these two groups would then be located in two separate training programmes (following the employment/leisure divide of Watts and Knasel, 1985). Thus, in an intensified extrapolation of the limiting and stratifying transitions of the NEW programme, women would either be returning to work as token men (Cockburn, 1985) or returning to learn as a social therapy for their disadvantage (Thompson, 1980). However, since an extension or renewal of NEW's funding was not granted by the MSC, this transient organization ceased operations.

Conclusion

In the context of the national training policy of the MSC, the NEW programme represented a distinct change of funding for MSC sponsored adult vocational preparation courses. In 1983, such training places were normally funded under a national training grants scheme (TOPS) rather than 'benefit-plus'. Subsequently this form of funding has become increasingly commonplace through a series of national 'benefit-plus' programmes of adult training (e.g. the 'Adult Training Strategy' of 1985, MSC, 1983). The NEW programme can thus be seen as an early 'pilot' of 'benefit-plus' training for unemployed adults, that has subsequently come to be known as 'workfare' (Finn, 1987). This form of provision links welfare benefits for the long-term unemployed to prescribed work or training activities (e.g. such provision is commonplace in the USA, Zacharakis–Jutz, 1988). As Gardiner (1986) and Senior and Naylor (1987) have argued, such provision is ineffective in terms of both skills training and post-programme employment. Additionally, as Wickham (1986), McGivney and Sims (1986) and Cockburn (1987) have argued, such programmes extend and enforce, rather than challenge, the limiting occupational opportunities available to women. As we have observed the 'vocational preparation' of the NEW programme was predicated upon particular behavioural changes taking place in trainees who remained contractually and financially 'unemployed'. Thus a further paradox is added to the incapacity of this projected 'bridge' from a 'home' to a 'work' environment.

Organizationally the NEW programme represented the continued privatization of national training initiatives (Benn and Fairley, 1986), through an increasing redistribution of MSC training funding from educational institutions to private training agencies and employers (MSC, 1985, Finn, 1987). The private company which operated the NEW programme thus represented one of these newly empowered training organizations which was consequently more concerned with profitability than educational outcomes (Small, 1985; Jeffcutt, 1988). From this basis we are thus empowered to decode the focus of the 'pilot' status of the NEW programme (an issue that was never clarified during operations). On the one hand, to the MSC (the programme sponsor), NEW represented the piloting of a cheaper form of training the long-term unemployed. On the other hand, to the programme organizer (a private training consultancy company), NEW represented the piloting of a more profitable form of training the long-term unemployed. This mutual advantage would seem to be the only harmonious relationship established through the NEW programme, since the assumed harmony and interdependence between trainer and trainee needs was nowhere achieved. Indeed, the marginal and peripheral status that training the female long-term unemployed had with both the programme sponsor and organizer was not unconnected. Maintaining a simplified and stereotypical sexual division of labour meant, on the one hand, cheaper, and more profitable training; and, on the other hand, the protection of the programme sponsors' and organizers' patriarchy from any form of challenge. In this way the provision of women-only training can be an enterprise that is safely liberal and limiting (Waddington, 1988). This is quite different from the dangers to men's roles and work inherent in 'consciouness-raising' and 'liberating' education for women (Thompson, 1988). Hence, the recent widespread development of second chance provision for women (e.g. Groombridge, 1987; Kearney, 1988; Coats, 1987) has not led to corresponding changes in the educational institutions which 'host' or sponsor this provision (Waddington, 1988). Indeed, such provision may well be manifest as a peripheral substitute for mainstream change (Thompson, 1988), and a further example of the marginalization of women in the face of male power (Cockburn, 1985). Thus the transitional processes of the NEW programme can be interpreted as both patriarchal and patronizing, perpetuating both a discriminatory sexual division of labour (Dex, 1986) and the marginalization of educational provision for women.

References

ALVESSON, M. (1985), 'Organizations, Image and Substance', *Dragon*, Vol. 1, No. 2, pp. 45–55.

ANYON, J. (1983), 'Intersections of Gender and Class', in Barton, L. and Walker, S. (Eds) (1983), *Gender, Class and Education*, Lewes, Falmer Press.

BATES, I., CLARKE, J., COHEN, P., FINN, D., MOORE., R. and WILLIS, P. (1984), *Schooling for the Dole*, Basingstoke, Macmillan.

BENN, C. and FAIRLEY, J. (Eds) (1986), *Challenging the M.S.C.*, London, Pluto Press.

BRYANT, I. (1983) 'Some Aspects of the Educational Needs of Long Term Unemployed Adults', *PLET* Vol. 20, No. 4, pp. 218–223.

BURGESS, R. (Ed.) (1985), *Field Methods in the Study of Education*, Lewes, Falmer Press.

BURROW, M. (1985) 'Wider Opportunities for Women and Work', *Adult Education*, Vol. 58, No. 2, pp. 158–162.

CHARNLEY, A., McGIVNEY, V. and SIMS, D. (1985), *Education for the Adult Unemployed*, Leicester, National Institute of Adult Continuing Education.

COATS, M. (1987), *Consulting Women*, Leicester, National Institute of Adult Continuing Education.

COCKBURN, C. (1985), *Machinery of Dominance*, London, Pluto Press.

COCKBURN, C. (1987), *Two Track Training*, Basingstoke, Macmillan.

COOPER, R. (1986), 'Organisation/Disorganisation', *Social Science Information*, Vol. 25, No. 2, pp. 299–335.

COYLE, A. (1983), 'An Investigation into the Long Term Impact of Redundancy and Unemployment Amongst Women', *Equal Opportunities Commission Research Bulletin*, No. 8, pp. 68–84.

COYLE, A. (1984), *Redundant Women*, London, The Women's Press.

DALE, R. (Ed.) (1985), *Education, Training and Employment*, Oxford, Pergamon Press.

DEAN, R. (1987), *Return to Work*, Sheffield, Manpower Services Commission.

DEEM, R. (1985), 'Leisure, Work and Unemployment', in Deem, R. and Salaman, G. (Eds) (1985), *Work, Culture and Society*, Milton Keynes, Open University Press.

DEEM, R. and SALAMAN, G. (Eds) (1985), *Work, Culture and Society*, Milton Keynes, Open University Press.

DEX, S. (1985), *The Sexual Division of Work*, Brighton, Harvester Press.

FINN, D. (1987), *Training Without Jobs*, Basingstoke, Macmillan.

FINNEGAN, R. (1985), 'Working Outside Formal Employment', in Deem, R. and Salaman, G. (Eds) (1985), *Work, Culture and Society*, Milton Keynes, Open University Press.

FRASER, L. and WARD, K. (1988), *Education from Everyday Living*, Leicester, National Institute of Adult Continuing Education.

FREIRE, P. (1985), *The Politics of Education*, Basingstoke, Macmillan.

GARDINER, J. (1986), 'Working with Women', in Ward, K. and Taylor, R., *Adult Education and the Working Class*, Beckenham, Croom Helm.

GREGORY, K. (1983), 'Native View Paradigms: Multiple Cultures and Culture Conflicts in Organisations', *Administrative Science Quarterly*, Vol. 28, No. 3, pp. 359–376.

GRIFFIN, C. (1985), 'Qualitative Methods and Cultural Analysis', in Burgess, R. (Ed.) (1985), *Field Methods in the Study of Education*, Lewes, Falmer Press.

GROOMBRIDGE, J. (1987), 'Learning for a Change', Leicester, National Institute of Adult Continuing Education.

HAYES, J. and NUTMAN, P. (1981), *Understanding the Unemployed*, London, Tavistock.

HUGHES, M. and KENNEDY, M. (1985), 'New Futures: Changing Women's Education', London, Routledge and Kegan Paul.

HUGHES, M. and LITTLEWOOD, M. (1986), 'Women as Unwaged Learners', *Occasional Paper No. 17*, Centre for Adult and Higher Education, University of Manchester.

HUTCHINSON, E. (1978), *Learning Later*, London, Routledge and Kegan Paul.

JEFFCUTT, P. (1988), 'Education and Training: Beyond the Great Debate', *British Journal of Education and Work*, Vol. 2, No. 2, pp. 51–59.

JEFFCUTT, P. (1989), *Persistence and Change in an Organisation Culture: a Longitudinal Study of a Retraining Scheme for the Female Adult Unemployed*, Doctoral Thesis, University of Manchester (unpublished).

JOHNSTON, R. (1987), *Exploring the Educational Needs of Unemployed Adults*, Leicester, National Institute of Adult Continuing Education.

JOHNSTON, R., MACWILLIAM, I. and JACOBS, M. (1988), *Negotiating the Curriculum with Unemployed Adults*, London, Further Education Unit.

JONES, M., MOORE, M. and SNYDER, R. (Eds) (1988), *Inside Organisations*, Beverley Hills, Sage.

KEARNEY, P. (1988), *Second Chance to Learn?*, London, Further Education Unit.

LAKOFF, G. and JOHNSON, M. (1980), *Metaphors We Live By*, Chicago, University of Chicago Press.

LIGHT, D. (1979), 'Surface Data and Deep Structure', *Administrative Science Quarterly*, Vol. 24, pp. 551–559.

LOVELL, A. (1980), 'Fresh Horizons for Some', *Adult Education*, Vol. 53, No. 4, pp. 219–224.

LOVETT, T. (Ed.) (1988), *Radical Approaches to Adult Education*, London, Routledge and Kegan Paul.

MCDONALD, J. (1984), *Education for Unemployed Adults*, London, Department of Education and Science.

MCGIVNEY, V. and SIMS, D. (1986), *Adult Education and the Challenge of Unemployment*, Milton Keynes, Open University Press.

MCLAREN, P. (1986), *Schooling as a Ritual Performance*, London, Routledge and Kegan Paul.

MANPOWER SERVICES COMMISSION (1983), *Towards an Adult Training Strategy*, London, HMSO.

MARTIN, R. and WALLACE, J. (1984), *Working Women in Recession*, Oxford, Oxford University Press.

MEZIROW, J. (1978), 'Perspective Transformation', *Adult Education*, Vol. 28, No. 2, pp. 100–110.

MEZIROW, J. (1981), 'A Critical Theory of Adult Learning and Education', *Adult Education*, Vol. 32, No. 1, pp. 3–24.

MOCH, M. and FIELDS, W. (1985), 'Developing a Content Analysis for Interpreting Language use in Organisations', *Research in the Sociology of Organisations*, Vol. 4, pp. 81–126.

PITMAN, M. (1988), 'Developmental Stages and Institutional Structure', *Anthropology and Education Quarterly*, Vol. 19, No. 2, pp. 139–154.

POLLARD, A., PURVIS, J. and WALFORD, G. (Eds) (1988), *Education, Training and the New Vocationalism*, Milton Keynes, Open University Press.

POLLERT, A. (1981), *Girls, Wives, Factory Lives*, London, Macmillan.

RAY, C. (1986), 'Corporate Culture: The Last Frontier of Control', *Journal of Management Studies*, 23:3, pp. 287–297.

SANDERSON, M. (1987), *Educational Opportunity*, London, Faber and Faber.

SENIOR, B. and NAYLOR, J. (1987), *Educational Responses to Adult Unemployment*, Beckenham, Croom Helm.

SMALL, N. (1985), 'A Continuing Dilemma; Responses to the Adult Training Strategy', *Discussion Paper No. 13*, Association for Recurrent Education.

SPARROW, P. (1986), *The Erosion of Employment in the U.K.*, Working Paper, Centre for Corporate Strategy and Change, University of Warwick.

SRIVASTVA, S. and BARRETT, F. (1988), 'The Transforming Nature of Metaphors in Group Development', *Human Relations*, Vol. 41, No. 1, pp. 31–64.

STONEY, S. and REID, M. (1981), *Further Opportunities in Focus*, London, Further Education Unit.

THOMPSON, J. (Ed.) (1980), *Adult Education for a Change*, London, Hutchinson.

THOMPSON, J. (1983), *Learning Liberation*, Beckenham, Croom Helm.

THOMPSON, J. (1988), 'Adult Education and the Women's Movement', in Lovett, T., *Radical Approaches to Adult Education*, London, Routledge and Kegan Paul.

TURNER, V. (1974), *Dramas, Fields and Metaphors*, Ithaca, Cornell University Press.

VAN–GENNEP, A. (1960), *The Rites of Passage*, London, Routledge and Kegan Paul.

VAN–MAANEN, J. (1973), 'Observations on the Making of Policemen', *Human Organisation*, Vol. 32, No. 4, pp. 407–418.

WADDINGTON, S. (Ed.) (1988), *Working With Women*, No. 2, Leicester, National Institute of Adult Continuing Education.

WARD, K. and TAYLOR, R. (Eds) (1986), *Adult Education and the Working Class*, Beckenham, Croom Helm.

WATTS, A. (1983), *Education, Unemployment and the Future of Work*, Milton Keynes, Open University Press.

WATTS, A. and KNASEL, E. (1985), *Adult Unemployment and the Curriculum*, London, Further Education Unit.

WICKHAM, A. (1986), *Women and Training*, Milton Keynes, Open University Press.

WILLIS, P. (1977), *Learning to Labour*, Farnborough, Saxon House.

WILLIS, P. (1983), 'Cultural Production and Reproduction', in Barton, L. and Walker, S. (Eds), *Race, Class and Education*, London, Croom Helm.

WOLPE, A. (1980), 'Fresh Horizons', *Feminist Review*, No. 6, pp. 89–104.

ZACHARAKIS–JUTZ, J. (1988), 'Welfare to Work and Adult Education', in Zukas, M., (Ed.) *Transatlantic Dialogue*, Leeds, University of Leeds.

ZUKAS, M. (Ed.) (1988), *Transatlantic Dialogue*, Leeds, University of Leeds.

10
Business and Education:
Motivating the Workforce

Derek Wheeler

Introduction

The ubiquitous commercial manager, if given the opportunity to reflect upon both his own and his company's performance over the last decade, would no doubt wryly smile and award himself some accolades for his successes. Unprecedented de-regulation, increased competition, and company rationalization, all set against the background of the explosion of information technology have been an exciting and stimulating environment. Resources, whether human, capital or plant, have been shrewdly deployed, resulting in an increase in both performance and profit.

Unfortunately, that smile would soon freeze on his lips as he considers the future. Armed with Tom Peters' latest book *Thriving on Chaos, Handbook for a Management Revolution* (1987) he would realize that his company could no longer be merely excellent. It would have to constantly adapt, and respond to the shifting circumstances, and take advantage of them, creating new products and markets. Further, product life cycle is inexorably shortening, and global competition, whether new or from a post-1992 EEC, is intensifying.

Yet, within this maelstrom of activity, what would cause him the greatest anxiety would be the future composition, size and skills of his workforce. He would have to consider what innovative and radical solutions would be needed to recruit, train and retain the personnel required to take his organization into the next decade and the next century.

The problem is considerable. In the United Kingdom, the number of 16–19 year olds in the population will drop by nearly 25 per cent between 1987 and 1995. Further, because of an increasing tendency to enter higher education, the number of 16–19 year olds active in the labour market will decrease correspondingly by 29 per cent. Allied to this is the ageing of the remaining labour force; by 1995, 78 per cent of the labour force will be aged between 25 and 29, compared with 72 per cent in 1987.

The Acceleration of Change

As companies continue to reappraise products and services, they will require a more highly skilled and adaptable workforce. My own company, Marks and Spencer, traditionally recruited large numbers of school leavers as full-time sales assistants. Ten years ago that sales assistant was probably responsible for one counter of stock. The display would have comprised possibly five styles in four colours and sizes, a catalogue of eighty ways. That stock would have been drawn from an internal stockroom, and the merchandise counted once a fortnight to ascertain sales.

Now, that same sales assistant will look after an autonomous section of several counters and racks. The catalogue has exploded to fulfil customer expectations. Internal stockrooms have been ceded to extended sales floors, so that the assistant now orders her stock using a hand-held computer terminal from a distribution centre up to thirty miles away.

Products are entered by unique product code at the point of sale, which results in instant sales information being available. Each week computer print-outs detail sales, stock and 'on-order' composition to enable the assistant to display her wares in the most advantageous and effective manner.

New products, enhanced selling techniques and methods of customer payment have not even been touched upon, and all these changes have taken place in less than five years.

The scenario is being replicated elsewhere in banking, finance, local and central government, health authorities and education. Thus, just as the number of school leavers falls, the requirement for more skilled and motivated staff intensifies.

Recruitment Inducements

There are some solutions. Companies can simply 'bid up' their starting salaries, for example, 'A levels? Become a computer operator, £9,750, local' (an advertisement outside a Hammersmith job agency). Organizations can investigate new pools of employees: the mother returning to work, or the older job changer / early retireee.

This, in turn, is leading to some highly innovative practices. Johnson & Johnson in America have a policy that looks at employees as parents. Crèches, and a flexible view on holidays coinciding with those of schools, ensures that employees (particularly mothers) are free of the worry of what is happening to their children, and more able to concentrate at work.

McDonalds are now advertising for staff aged over 50 at twelve stores in difficult recruitment areas in the South-east. In the United States, such older workers are known as 'McMasters'. Training will be given to managers in how to treat these older workers. McDonalds believe that not only will they have a more reliable workforce, but that it will encourage older customers.

These initiatives are pragmatic and commercially astute, although it could be argued that in certain instances employers are simply looking for a replication of the existing workforce, but in a differing age bracket.

Current School Population — a Perspective

Where employers will have to look more assiduously is to those young people whose academic ability, racial origin, or home environment has precluded them from entering mainstream employment, particularly within prestigious 'blue chip' companies. Often these pupils are the ones who are most disaffected within both our society and education system.

I have recently undertaken a two year secondment from my company, and am currently the director of the West London Compact (an area covered by the City of Westminster, the Royal Borough of Kensington and Chelsea, and the Borough of Hammersmith and Fulham). Compacts are a partnership between education and business. They are an educational initiative aimed at motivating young people to achieve their full potential by enriching their educational experience.

From this new position, I can now view the perspective of the tenuous links that exist between education and business differently than when in my old role as an employer in central London. Most importantly, even after a few months in the educational arena, I have a clearer understanding of the aspirations of current school pupils, and how they match with the employment market in London.

It would be fair to accept that the top 25 per cent of our educational achievers bear comparison with any in the rest of the world. Where Japan scores over us is that it has the 'best bottom quarter', when 98 per cent of all their pupils are still in full-time education at 18. Thus, with our declining young population, we can no longer afford to throw away the bottom 30 per cent if we wish to compete as an effective economy.

Why do Pupils Leave School?

The Inner London Education Authority Research and Statistics Branch, undertook a study in Tower Hamlets in 1988, examining the attitudes of pupils in the fifth form (RS 1177/88 and RS 1205/88). The report found that the major reason pupils leave school is a desire to earn money, and a dislike of school or studying. Conversely, those pupils who decide to stay in full-time education do so in the belief that they will benefit in terms of employment later, when they have additional qualifications. My discussion with heads, teachers and pupils has led me to similar conclusions.

Another finding from the report was that the first major ethnic groups in Tower Hamlets that left school were the English, Scottish and Welsh. Some 52 per cent of these pupils chose to leave school at the end of the fifth form as compared with 32.7 per cent of all scholars.

Further, many of these early leavers already had a job which had been found for them by relatives or friends (40 per cent of all leavers found jobs this way compared with 24 per cent through application and 21 per cent using the Careers Service). This network of employment certainly bears out my own experience in Marks and Spencer, where a number of staff joined the company directly because close relatives already worked for us.

Caribbean and Bangladeshi pupils, on the other hand, tend to stay in education beyond 16, with 21.8 per cent of Caribbean and only 9.5 per cent of Bangladeshi pupils choosing to leave school at 16. This, though, may not be because these pupils have a propensity for academic learning. It is more likely that they do not have a network of ready employment, and thus additional qualifications are required to allow them to compete with the early school-leaving adolescent.

Class, as well as race, can be a deciding factor upon those who leave school at 16 or 'drop out' of education before then. The ILEA report showed that, where pupils' fathers had manual occupations, they were more likely to seek work straight from school than those students whose fathers had non-manual employment. (50 per cent of the children of fathers who had unskilled manual jobs left school at 16 compared with 31 per cent of all pupils.)

The survey concluded that there was little evidence that these pupils left because of financial pressures. Only eleven pupils out of a survey of 756 said they were leaving because they could not afford to stay on.

The Part-time Employment Network

Another way that pupils can enter the work place using personal networking is via part-time work, as I have recorded from my experience in Compact. Whilst running a Compact Induction Day for third year students at a girls school, part of an 'ice breaker' exercise was to ask the pupils to explain to the group of forty what was the best thing that had happened to them recently. The second pupil who was asked explained that she was starting a new job that week. Knowing that the girl was only 14 I expressed surprise, but, when I asked the group, over 50 per cent of those present gleefully admitted to doing paid work of some kind, such as jobs in shops, markets and restaurants, and not traditional paper or milk rounds. Further discussion showed that several students had more than one job. Clearly, there are a significant number of pupils in London with this 'portfolio' of employment. With 'cash-in-hand' available, it is unlikely that they will be anxious to stay in education.

Legal part-time work has long been a traditional transition into full employment. One of my previous assignments was for the training and development of Marks and Spencer staff in the South-east of England. A major part of that job was the organization and administration of both my company's graduate and 'A' level Management Training Schemes. A large percentage of our intake had worked with the company previously in a part-time capacity, generally on Saturdays or at vacation time. Because they know the company philosophy and jargon they integrate quickly, and are operationally effective much earlier. As a result of this early acceleration many are swiftly promoted.

Nevertheless, in recent years there has been a perceptible change in people applying for part-time work. Apart from students and middle-aged women, a much younger person is considering part-time work as a job in itself. Extended trading hours, geared towards changing customer shopping habits, is resulting in a requirement for a more flexible working day in retailing. When I left my store in March of last year, fourteen members of our staff were single parents. This was not a policy we had actively pursued (application forms do not ask this question). Simply, the hours were convenient for mothers with young children. Again, no doubt, some subtle networking system had been in operation where vacancies had been passed by 'word-of-mouth' from current employees to friends, and in certain cases had allowed individuals to re-enter the work place.

Work Experience

It is, therefore, reasonable to assume that school pupils do understand about work via part-time employment. Where they are critical is that they feel their school's preparation for employment is lacking and, in some cases, inadequate (ILEA reported 20 per cent as feeling the latter). However, this attitude might be seen as part of a general disaffection as those pupils intending to leave were more likely to truant (11 per cent of leavers admitted frequent truancy as against 4 per cent of stayers) and may have been absent during career's advice.

When asked what could have been done to prepare them better, 73 per cent cited more work experience. This has been taking place within schools for some time, using 'Project Trident' or local business links and is now proposed for the National Curriculum. Within the Compact partnership, two weeks' work experience is one of the four goals students need to attain to become 'Compact Graduates', the three others being 85 per cent attendance, 90 per cent punctuality and the completion of the pupil's course together with accreditation or certification in English, mathematics / numeracy. In West London, 800 pupils were placed in various work experience schemes for two weeks during the summer term. Schools found that the pupils who particularly benefited were those who showed signs of disaffection and had poor attendance records. At the end of the exercise 85 per cent of pupils had been successful in completing the project.

What work experience can best do is break down the barriers of prejudice which exist on both sides of education and business. Pupils (and teachers visiting them) have a clearer understanding of the qualifications and requirements needed within companies. They also understand that an organization such as BBC Television is not just the glamour of production, but that a multifarious assortment of jobs are required to service the corporation. Similarly, hotel work is not purely being a chambermaid or waiter, but that there is also reception, maintenance and computer work.

Some employers produced highly innovative programmes for pupils. The Department of the Environment constructed a course geared toward those pupils for whom English is their second language. At the end of their two weeks, the students were able to use a telephone, arrange a simple meeting or complete filing. The Body Shop spent their time not just showing pupils retailing, but also explaining 'make-up' techniques and how that company uses natural ingredients in their products.

Work experience can be effective on all levels. One of the most satisfying results was at a special school for pupils with moderate learning difficulties, which was in the Compact. There, the eleven pupils who made up the fifth form took part in a twenty-six week work experience programme, where pupils spent one day a week with an employer. The raising of those pupils' confidence, coupled with the enthusiasm of their teachers, resulted in the entire school (aged 6–16) completing a project on 'the world of work'. Five of the pupils actually entered employment as a direct result of their work experience. All those employers who came into contact with the school were impressed with the commitment, reliability and enthusiasm of the pupils, so much so that the 'Royal Mail' donated a video camera and equipment for curriculum development.

It would be naive to assume that all the work experiences were totally without fault. Some failed because employers were ill prepared and line managers were not aware of attachments until the preceding Friday. Consequently, some pupils were disruptive, bored or simply failed to attend.

Nevertheless, structured work experience is a 'win-win' situation for both schools and employers: it can be the fillup which enables the pupils to complete their schooling; it can show them how to enter a company or industry and it charts the ways in which the student can successfully progress. For the employer it is not purely altruistic. They can see the skills and maturity of the current school population and be more certain of how to induce them into their company. They can maintain contact and offer (legal) part-time work, eventually leading to full-time employment. Finally, even if that pupil chooses not to pursue employment in that company or occupation, often there can be a commercial bonus for the employer, in that the student becomes a customer, simply because they have a good feeling towards them! (The Disney corporation always take the view that ex-employees are potential customers!)

Teacher Secondment

Another strategy available to enhance the transition from school to work is teacher secondment. Within my eight Compact Schools, funding available from both the Training Agency (The Department of Employment) and Inner London Education Authority (ILEA) has allowed over fifty teachers to spend one week within commerce and industry. Their secondments have been either simple work shadows, researching a specific management issue such as appraisals and performance ratings, or accruing additional information which can be used to enhance their school's curriculum. Funding for this year will enable another sixty teachers to undertake this experience.

Contacts are made, so that reciprocal visits to schools are made by employers.

Reflections from 'The Outside'

Having been positive about so much I have seen in schools, it would also be true to say that there are elements in modern education which can explain why pupils become disenchanted and drop out.

Admittedly, until last April I had not been into a secondary school since

I left school in the mid-1960s. Nevertheless, noise, activity and an almost Pavlovian response to 'the bell' was intimidating to an outsider. Further, conditions within classrooms, staff rooms and toilets were such that they would be deemed unacceptable within many commercial operations. Much decision-making within commerce and industry is based on effective meeting practice. Quiet meeting rooms (with a secretary acting as 'gatekeeper' to allow the meeting to continue without disturbance, and a knowledge that tea and coffee will arrive at the appointed time) will often mean that management is able to focus quickly on issues and resolve them. Having been asked by one head to take INSET training for the heads of department, I realized that this same service is not generally available in education, particularly when I had to make the coffee for the rest of them! With Local Management of Schools (LMS), heads now have to be effective managers who are able to produce school business plans, marketing programmes and financial profiling of their budgets. In addition, they and their senior management will increasingly have to consider appraisal technique and performance payments. Many heads that I have met possess these management skills, as well as vision and leadership, but others, who entered the teaching profession to 'educate', clearly do not have the ability to motivate and lead an increasingly disaffected teaching workforce. In short, the demands are for a very different type of skill from that traditionally expected in heads of schools. As a result, it can become increasingly difficult for some heads to raise the morale of their staff.

It is a truism that the most successful companies (Tom Peters' 'excellent organisations' (1987)) are so because of the high motivation and commitment of their workforce, who are prepared to innovate and contribute far in excess of their position or salary. Conversely, poor performance within companies can be attributed to the active disenchantment of their workforce.

In my final year at Grammar School, back in the 1960s, whilst I saw my career as becoming an advertising executive I was told that I would be a 'natural teacher'. Having undertaken many presentations in schools, I now realise what poor careers advice I was given. I find large groups of sullen adolescents intimidating and apparently non-receptive. Individually, the same students can be lively, enthusiastic and offering refreshingly open views. The effect of peer pressure seems to nullify students' obvious attributes, making the education of them even more difficult for their teachers. In addition to coping with disaffected students, teachers are burdened with a damaging public image. Both the serious and tabloid press have produced many articles, informative or misleading, about teachers and their conditions of pay. This is rarely conducive to raising the status of educators or education, especially in the eyes of their disaffected students.

Recruitment Into Employment

I should like to consider the actual entry into the workplace of school students. Employers generally look towards some kind of past criteria on which to base the future performance of prospective employees. Often that was, and still is, examination attainment. This can, unfortunately, produce a record of failure, rather than achievement. The London Record of Achievement can give employers a far better framework within which to interview school pupils. Certainly this portfolio of achievements will enable nervous students to 'sell' themselves more assiduously at interviews. It will also mean that employers may have to re-assess interview testing and reference procedures.

Employers are investigating their initial training programmes in the light of both company and industry changes. The clearing banks, large employers of 'O' Level (now GCSE Grade 3) maths/English pupils are either re-appraising or even abandoning this benchmark. They realize that instead of staff with a clerical bias they require employees with interpersonal skills, more able to sell financial services to their customers.

The other way in which employers are looking towards integrating their new workforce is through additional education. This particularly applies to those pupils who have English as a second language, where a mentor guides that new employee into the company.

Nevertheless, few employers will invest in this educational training. They will simply reduce their workforce if they believe the educational system is not delivering pupils with sufficient basic skills.

Drop Outs

Finally, there is the issue of pupils who become so alienated by education that they 'drop out' of school prior to the end of the fifth year. As described earlier, employers will look to past performance and will require to see some type of work pattern.

If there is an irregular or, in certain circumstances, no model of employment, then that applicant will not obtain a job. Several charitable organizations such as Workwise, Task Undertakings and Full Employ, together with the Department of Trade and Industry, are involved in integrating these individuals into the workplace.

Conclusion

Employers will have difficulty in recruiting and retaining staff during the 1990s. They will need to re-appraise the requirements of that workforce against the ability of current school leavers. There will be a need to invest more time in fostering industry–school links, particularly through work experience and teacher secondment. Finally, employers should consider what new testing and recruitment techniques are required.

Education will have to develop a greater range of technical and vocational courses, forging increasing links with industry in the hope that their pupils will have a greater range of skills transferable to business.

Finally, what employers will need to understand is that although schools will always own the responsibility of educating pupils for work, they do have an obligation to assist in the development of their potential workers, before they join the company.

References

KYSEL, F. (January, 1988), *Leaving School — A Survey of attitudes of fifth-year pupils in Tower Hamlets*, RS 1177/88, London, Inner London Education Authority, Research and Statistics.

PETERS, T. (1987), *Thriving on Chaos*, New York, The Chaucer Press.

SCOTT, G. and WEST, A. (September 1988), *Leaving School II — A follow up study of distinctions of fifth form pupils in Tower Hamlets*, RS 1205/88, London, Inner London Education Authority, Research and Statistics.

11
Responding to Change:
A Challenge to Further Education in Birmingham

Graham Clark, David Shepherdson and Roy Pinney

Introduction: A Historical Perspective

Birmingham, like anywhere else, has both distinctive and characteristic features which can be used to make generalizations, particularly about education and training in industrial Britain. The city was granted its Charter by Queen Victoria one hundred years ago, in 1889. At that time it was a thriving industrial city known throughout the British Empire, with a population approaching half a million. A century earlier, it did not even have a Borough Charter (this was granted in 1837). Poor Law Commissioners regulated parish affairs, the population was less than 20,000, and many people walked daily from surrounding villages to work in the developing and expanding factories.

Hutton's *History of Birmingham*, (1781) written at about this time, notes under 'Trade' the manufacture of buttons, buckles, swords, guns, leatherware, pens, brassware, pins, nails, bellows, iron, steel and brass, printing and brewing. People came to Birmingham to earn a lot of money, largely by converting metal into manufactured goods. Matthew Boulton originally made metal toys but was able to expand and diversify when the Scottish immigrant, James Watt, working through the new technology of steam, provided the power to enable thousands of workers to be employed in their Soho factories. Greater efficiency and a longer working day were possible when another Scot, William Murdoch, developed and installed gas lighting.

The nineteenth century was a time of great expansion for Birmingham. Fortunes were made and new names became significant locally and nationally. The Chamberlain family were able to devote themselves to politics because of the money they had made manufacturing nuts and bolts. The working class were more interested in earning a comfortable living than in espousing radical political ideology. When the Birmingham mob burned down Joseph Priestley's house in Moseley, where he was celebrating the second anniversary of the French Revolution, they chanted 'For King and Country', 'No Unitarians' and 'No Philosophers'. The Victorian philanthropic businessmen-politicians had a strong sense of civic pride and were committed to municipal enterprise to complement their own vigorous capitalism. Public utilities were established — gas, water, sewerage and even a municipal bank.

There was undoubtedly a philanthropic thrust in the development of education in the City during this century. However, there was also a desire to socialize the working class to accept the existing social order, and to train the workforce in the skills required to sustain industrial expansion. There was a continuing public debate on how the curriculum of the King Edward School could best serve the interests of commerce and industry, and adults could educate themselves at the Birmingham and Midland Institute (BMI) where there were separate classes for artisans and the middle class students. The city took over the technical establishment from the BMI in 1891 to found the Municipal Technical School. The contribution made by the industrialists is commemorated in today's names of many City educational institutions (for example, Matthew Boulton College, Cadbury College, Joseph Chamberlain College).

The twentieth century continued to enable the citizens of Birmingham to make a comfortable living from manufacturing, with a major significant change in emphasis. The motor trade became the major industry, such as Austin Cars at Longbridge and BSA Motorcycles at Small Heath. The city still had a thousand and one trades, but many of these were now directly or indirectly manufacturing motor vehicles or their component parts.

Politically, there has been substantial consensus as far as technical training is concerned. Quirky radical Tories, with a strong feeling of civic pride, and moderate Labour leaders, who were prepared to work with local industry, agreed that the city needed a system of further education to train the largely young, white, male workforce needed for the maintenance of the City's prosperity. In 1939, there were three technical colleges — at Suffolk Street in the City centre, Handsworth and Aston. There was a realization that this was inadequate and the desire to increase this number was widespread after the war. The government insisted that the city concentrate on implementing the 1944 Education Act and on upgrading primary provision. It was not until 1953 that a new college was founded and by 1965 there were nine further education colleges — most of them offering engineering as a major part of the curriculum.

The economic recession of the 1970s and early 80s had a particularly severe impact on the industry of Birmingham. Birmingham Small Arms Ltd. evolved out of the traditional local trade of gunsmithing (during the

Napoleonic Wars, two thirds of the arms used by British soldiers and sailors came from the city), but BSA abandoned small arms for motorcycles during this century. The recession came, and since the early 1970s, no motorcycles have been made at Armoury Road, Small Heath. Today a 'Brummie biker' would probably be riding a Japanese machine, and, if working at all, might be on an Employment Training Scheme showing foreign visitors around the National Motorcycle Museum at Meriden.

Unemployment rose faster in Birmingham during the early 1980s than anywhere else in the country. The levels reached approximately those of traditional high unemployment areas such as the north-east. Birmingham was no longer a place were high wages could be earned in the manufacturing industry. This had a very disturbing effect on many people in commerce and education.

The city council responded by establishing a powerful Economic Development Department. In 'Celebration of a Centenary' (1988) the council itself states that 'it is also directly involved in the economic regeneration of the City' and goes on to list examples such as the National Exhibition Centre, the International Convention Centre (for completion in 1991), Aston Science Park (for developing high-technology industries) and tourism and leisure, illustrated by the Halfords Birmingham Super-Prix. No mention is made of the traditional economic activities associated with Birmingham.

Responding to Changing Needs

It is arguable whether the people of Birmingham have adjusted to this shift in their required economic activities. One might also ask whether the further education colleges have substantially moved in attitudes. There are some symbols. In 1984, five of the nine colleges had the word 'technical' in their title. Today none of them has. One college now has a Department of Business and Leisure, rather than Business and Humanities. Short courses are offered for telephone sales people, taxi drivers and night-club doormen. The training needs of local industry have altered substantially.

Another major cultural change affecting Birmingham has been the origins of the more recent immigrants to the City; it has always prospered due to its new citizens. Originally they came from the surrounding villages in Warwickshire and Worcestershire, in the nineteenth century from other parts of the British Isles, some from Europe in the first half of this century, and more recently from the Caribbean and Asia. The newer immigrants, because of their appearance, language and culture are more easily identified and have been susceptible to individual, collective and institutional racism.

Industry needs to, and education must, serve all of the City's people. Forty per cent of the 1989 intake to primary schools were children from ethnic minority groups and these youngsters will obviously move inexorably through the system. At present black students are rather over-represented in Further Education (FE) Colleges (33 per cent in 1988 compared to 25 per cent in the secondary schools). There is an even higher relative proportion in general education courses (GCSE, A Level and BTEC) compared with high percentages of white students in vocational and professional courses. This may be because the school system has 'failed' black children and the colleges are fulfilling a traditional role of the 'second chance', or it may be because white pupils are more likely to stay in sixth forms (or go on to sixth form colleges) or to get jobs. Nevertheless, this is another dimension to the debate going on in the further education sector concerning the function of colleges.

Colleges have traditionally served industry. Many of them are now attempting to serve 'the community' although it appears that, for example, despite the unequal distribution of ethnic minority groups in the various districts of the city, most city colleges have an ethnic mix very close to that of the city as a whole. Two colleges have significantly lower proportions of black students than the mean, and only one (Handsworth) has a significantly higher proportion. This closely reflects the ethnic groups in its own locality.

Another important change taking place in the student population and in course provision arises from the increasing availability, and take-up rate, of places for women, particularly mature women. In 1988, 48 per cent of total enrolments were female students, a slightly lower figure than one would expect if it were a true reflection of the city's population, and the male/female ratio varies widely for different types of courses. For example, fourteen times more women than men enrolled for evening secretarial classes.

Women rightly demand education and training, and not just in the 'obvious' sectors such as caring and service industries. The city has an equal opportunities policy and colleges are attempting to respond to this by encouraging more female students and also providing courses such as 'Middle Management for Women' and 'Women into Technology'.

There has been a dramatic shift in the cultural and industrial base of the city. There are more black people in Birmingham, many speaking an Asian language at home, more women are demanding to attend colleges, and there has been a dramatic move away from manufacturing industry to leisure, service and high-technology industries. Nevertheless, the culture of many colleges is still close to that of their origins. There exists a cultural dissonance which, together with the many local and national new initiatives in education, has led to disaffection amongst many in the service.

The Role of the Further Education College

The socio-economic changes which occurred in Birmingham in the 1970s clearly illustrate the changes in the manufacturing sector generally, and engineering in particular, which have dramatically affected the environment within which FE institutions operate. One could argue that engineering formed the backbone of the typical 'tech' with an ethos and culture which revolved around the white, male, part-time student apprentice. The two published in-depth studies of individual FE colleges (Venables, 1967; Gleeson and Mardle, 1980), vividly describe organizations whose *raison d'être* is an instrumentalist view of knowledge and a function that trains and socializes young, white males for industry. Venable's study is indeed titled 'The Young Worker at College — A Study of a Local Tech', in which the students are described thus: 'Viewed sociologically as a male group, they were muscular, non-verbal, non-anxious and extrovert' (Venables, 1967, p.70). Whether or not this view remains valid is debatable, but it does illustrate the way in which FE students, and thus FE colleges, were perceived.

The dominance of engineering as an influence on the organization, ethos and culture within FE colleges has deep historical roots as explained earlier — traced back to the Mechanics' Institutes of the nineteenth century. One can still discern the remnants of this by observing the number of principals who have an engineering background. One could speculate that the typical senior manager in the recent past was someone who had an engineering background and had often progressed from an apprenticeship to non-graduate entry of a professional institute, possibly at a later stage undertaking part-time study for a Master's degree. Such a career progression involved a 'long, hard slog at night school' and through the step ladder of head of department, vice-principal and principal within the college. This reinforced the mechanistic, deferential and rigidly hierarchical perspective and contributes to certain peculiarities of FE. One aspect is the commitment to a certain form of teaching and learning in which didacticism is prominent, with the nine-to-five day of the day-release student to the fore.

Another aspect of FE was the slightly 'second-best' feel of an FE College, whereby one felt that the college was but an imitation of something better. One manifestation of this was the attempt to inculcate some 'culture' into the young clients. The Liberal Studies movement of the 1960s reflects this trend and, as Gleeson and Mardle (1980) point out in their study of 'Western College', there exist two cultures side-by-side: that of the technical teachers coming from a similar background to the students, and a mainly graduate Liberal Studies Department. This results in a slightly seedy, instrumental and pragmatic ethos within FE, or, as Gleeson and Mardle state, an atmosphere which reflects 'pragmatic training organizations which exude expediency'.

Such organizations often suffer from a sort of inferiority complex which reflects their ill-defined role in the educational world. This sense of inferiority, anxiety and insecurity is only rivalled by that of 'Adult Education Centres'. The inherent lack of a clear domain manifests itself in many ways in FE. One such is noted by David Terry in his book *Tertiary Colleges* (1987) where he described how he received letters from FE principals signed, for example: 'Dr J Smith BSc., PhD., C.Chem., FRCS, FRGS, AMBIM'. As Terry notes, 'you can see the anxiety and the desire to impress'.

Perhaps all of this is connected with social attitudes towards technology in our society and the historical roots of the social class system. But it also means that the traditional 'Tech', and the present FE college which inherited that tradition, still lacks a clear domain of its own. Anticipating the outcomes of this paper somewhat, one could propose that FE needs to define what is distinctive about the type of education it provides. A distinctive feature of FE colleges was, and often still is, the strength of departmental structures with foundations in broad subject areas or in vocationally related disciplines. Departmentalism manifests itself in 'empire-building', an emphasis on boundaries and concomitant insularity. The negative aspect of departmentalism has always been intricately related to the 'points' system which emphasized a narrow focus on student numbers (the 'bums on seats' syndrome), which itself is interconnected with rigid definitions of class contact for lecturers and archaic gradings related to levels of work. All underlie the strength of departmentalism.

The departmental structure co-exists with a strong role culture, with an emphasis on the authority vested in the role holder working within a clearly defined hierarchy and with clearly defined rules and procedures. The administrative system of colleges often resembles a local government bureaucracy in its form. The strength of departments often gives the appearance of fiefdoms, with Heads of Department as 'barons' operating in a political arena in which the relations between the senior managers influence the whole college. However, within this, there will be clear patterns of internal accountability related to the defined patterns of roles and procedures.

The increase in general education courses in the 1960s shifted the emphasis within some colleges to an extent, one result being the evolution of a strong 'second-chance' ethos. Again the financial system was such that it was in the interests of the college to maximize the number of full-time students, which along with departmental 'empires' meant that there was a burgeoning of GCE courses. This often enabled the Liberal Studies Department to become both respectable *and* powerful. The expansion of general education was but a precursor to more significant changes, particularly as a result of rising unemployment, the rapid demise of the traditional apprenticeship system and the advent of the new vocationalism in the guise of various youth training programmes.

The Impact of Change

The effects on colleges were primarily of two types, one being in terms of curriculum and the other in terms of funding. The change in the nature of the curriculum, and to some extent the client groups, entailed co-ordination and development which cut across the traditional departmental boundaries. The rise of the MSC as a funding agency, which is so closely related to the youth unemployment phenomenon, and significantly born of the Department of Employment rather than the Department of Education and Science, led directly to new forms of accountability. The traditional financial accountability to the LEA, coupled with a more diffuse accountability to students, employers and the wider community was changed considerably.

Two examples of changing accountabilities may be worth noting. The growth of YTS programmes within colleges often meant that the first shock of the 'new' accountability occurred when managers and teachers met the vocal (and, to many, surprisingly articulate and often pointed) comments of students and dealt with managing agents, employers and MSC representatives. A second development was that of the project based methodology adopted by the MSC which engendered both a certain expertise in 'duckspeak' and considerable scepticism (not to say confusion) from staff.

The impact of all these changes on FE teachers should not be underestimated (although the effect on students may have been less dramatic). Commentators and critics often do not appreciate that no other sector of the British education system has undergone, and continues to undergo, such a continuous series of changes. The continuing change, for example, in teaching Basic Office Practice has shifted from a Certificate in Office Studies to a BTEC General, which was then transformed into BTEC First Certificate with some deviations to CPVE along the way. Anyone working in this area, or any area affected by comparable curriculum changes, will recognize the imposed curriculum 'newspeak' of syllabus content, behavioural objectives, integration, skills based assignments — followed by NVQ style de-integrative processes and lengthy competency statements. If one couples this with changes in the type of students and the shifts in accountability, then one can sense the increasing and often conflicting pressures on FE. Thus, those in the system have had to cope with: new student groups including the often 'reluctant' new FE students; adult returners and disaffected merged classes; far reaching changes in the curriculum; changing financial structures and related shifting 'accountabilities'.

At the same time, the MSC as a major executive agency of government with a national overview led to a new emphasis on planning. Thus, managers in FE and LEA officers suddenly found that the previous historically evolved process of 'disjointed incrementalism', which was the basis of financial planning between LEAs and colleges, was irrevocably changed.

Although it is common for critics to highlight the rigidities, unresponsiveness, and what is often termed 'provider-led' approach of colleges, it is clear that FE has become one of the most adaptable and flexible areas of the whole education service. One only has to compare the breadth and variety of provision in a typical FE college with that of the sixth form or even tertiary institution. The lack of clear definition of just what FE is about, and its in-between, 'catch-all' status has led to a pragmatic, instrumental and 'muddling-through' response to planning and curriculum. Ideologically, the MSC and the government desired a growth in the private providers who appeared to be more flexible and responsive. But, many of those who work in FE suspect the quality of such provision compared to the depth and breadth of provision in the public sector.

A Strain on the System

The 'anti-education' bias of the old MSC could be interpreted as part of the desire of government to increase competition and reduce costs. The emphasis on value for money (VFM) which is exemplified in the various Audit Commission Reports from 1985 on, relates to the familiar litany of economy, efficiency and effectiveness. Apart from crude desires for cost cutting and a naive view of efficiency, the real debate is about effectiveness. Simply expressed, this is whether actual outcomes match planned outcomes. More pragmatically, this may be concerned with achieving *stated* aims — or of meeting client demand or community need — according to one's viewpoint. Even though the setting of national targets for efficiency was supposedly one of negotiation in the local context, the targets were to be negotiated between the LEA and colleges and should have been achievable taking into account all the socio-economic variables locally. But, put into practice by some LEAs and some college managers, the result was a new set of crude pressures which simply added to growing disaffection.

To the individual teacher, all of this meant teaching larger groups for longer hours, which, together with a different clientele, new curriculum, student-centred learning and changing organizational climate has not unnaturally led to low morale. Greater demands upon staff are underscored by a government that is unsympathetic to education and which consistently makes the case for efficiency rather than effectiveness. A teacher in FE may justifiably feel undervalued in relation to the higher profile of the teacher in higher education or schools.

The 'tyranny' of performance indicators places a great strain on the system to conform, which, coupled with demands for more information to prove that FE is actually performing satisfactorily, leads inevitably to a desire in colleges to generate the 'right' figures. The cost of this is very high, not only in resource terms, but upon the de-humanizing of an essentially people-focused activity. Apart from the pressures on teaching staff, these trends reveal weaknesses in the way colleges are managed. The adaptation of departmental structures to matrix style structures are one manifestation of the challenge to remove or reduce boundaries between curriculum areas, resources and people.

Stressful outcomes resulting from the new functional management roles are obvious: for example, the ex-head of department who finds it difficult to manage both an area of work and a cross-college responsibility. Conflict and confusion are manifestations of the process of change. An increased workload for the senior managers leads to increased delegation to unit heads or section leaders and pressure is placed upon the teacher to become the overworked teacher-manager. Peeke (1983) describes the phenomenon as 'role strain' which results from curriculum changes. One could say that role strain is almost endemic in FE.

One can sense in FE that a low morale and a desire to articulate fears, worries and stresses is constrained by 'fear of failure' both at a personal and an institutional level. The real need is to clearly express defined aims and objectives in relation to explicit roles and responsibilities within a cogent framework. This is related to the need to be accountable within a complex web of client demands and community needs. Often these are hinted at but not clearly stated. As Theodossin (1986) points out, 'there is little clear agreement about what FE should be responding to'.

The Education Reform Act (1988) continues to shift accountabilities in FE, with an underlying trend towards contractual relationships between clients and providers. The essential differences lie in the type of relationship that exists between the LEA and (its) colleges. The direct involvement in executive management by representatives of local business and commerce together with the local college, brings the issue of multiple accountabilities into clear focus. There is also an underlying tension between the need for planning, and the ideological concern for encouraging the free market system to operate in the education system. The role of the LEA is at the heart of this tension — on the one hand, promoting entrepreneurial activity and, on the other, seeking to plan and support a coherent and integrated provision.

Some envisage the abolition of LEAs to be replaced by 'regional executive agencies of central government', but others see the LEA as fulfilling a key role in articulating and meeting the needs of local communities. The LEA perhaps could, or should, have a pivotal role in ensuring that education does meet the needs of a wider community, rather than the sectional interests of a vociferous minority.

A Strategic Framework for Change

The Education Reform Act (1988) clearly represents a fundamental shift in the balance of power, authority and control by the devolution of responsibility to individual institutions within a framework of accountabilities. The main issue is how the quality of the service to clients can be enhanced within this framework, through more effective management of resources. In Birmingham, the LEA has addressed this through a strong commitment to quality development supported by a 'Quality Team'. In 1985, a Co-ordinator for monitoring and evaluation was appointed and her early work was concerned with the evaluation of YTS. The methodology was somewhat tortuous and involved large numbers of questionnaires. A radical re-think led to the current methodology, which stresses the role of the individual practitioner undertaking evaluation for the benefit of their own professional autonomy.

Initially, the 'Quality Control Project' was supported by Central Reserve funding (later by the Training Agency), but the work is now directly funded from the LEA. The role of the Quality Development Team is primarily concerned with staff development in colleges, enabling course teams, team leaders and managers to develop their own contextual approach to monitoring and evaluation, but within a broadly-based curriculum-led framework. This approach is somewhat unique amongst current projects and primarily relates to an awareness that such initiatives, however valuable and well-meaning, need a thorough commitment by all those involved to the basic integrity of the process, if results are to be of any use. The idea of 'supported self-evaluation' has been widely accepted by the FE colleges in Birmingham. Evidence suggests that practising teachers and managers who already engage in evaluative activity but in a relatively unsystematic and *ad hoc* fashion, would welcome the opportunity to 'firm-up' the process to fulfil accountability requirements.

Some time was spent examining the threats and opportunities that the process of evaluation presents to both individuals and institutions. The members of the central team have worked with all members of staff in the colleges, carefully preparing the ground for the implementation of a quality development programme. It was evident that the informal style evaluation, whilst adequate for the general day-to-day requirements of course teams, would not be enough for the new demands for accountability made by validating bodies, agencies of government and LEAs.

'External' evaluation by 'experts' poses a threat to individuals and institutions that is difficult to render more positive. Some feeling of resentment exists about the lack of negotiation, participation and ownership that this process involves. The key to avoiding this type of disaffection relates, therefore, to the empowerment of teams and individuals to undertake evaluation and to take primary responsibility for the design, development and implementation of appropriate instruments. Training and support mechanisms, funded through LEATGS and organized by management, would enable staff to devise strategies together with members of the central team.

The Education Reform Act (1988) sets out a strategic responsibility for the LEA to focus on the quality of provision across the service, where the college's ability to deliver agreed outcomes for students would be monitored and set against the allocation of resources. The 'strategic framework' for this in Birmingham would enable the colleges to:

1. Fulfil accountability requirements
2. Improve the quality of teaching and learning
3. Promote a commitment to research and development.

The success of the programme is based upon the individual's commitment to improvement of 'performance' through the identification of criteria they regard as significant. If staff are actively involved in the process of identifying 'issues' and setting criteria for judging how well those issues are resolved, the feeling of involvement provides a basis for improvement. In Birmingham the central team has progressed from the 'awareness raising' phase to the 'embedding' phase, where college groups with responsibility for evaluation have been identified and are undergoing training.

Whilst the responsibility for 'improvement' lies primarily with the individual, the support and guidance systems for staff development provide the framework within which they can operate. The reaction of staff was interesting. The team had perhaps expected a more outspoken criticism, in view of the proliferation of initiatives in FE with an attendant increase in workload for the individual. Changes in the college organizational structures had already led to an increased delegation of responsibilities for unit heads, section leaders and team leaders. They were already stretched by extensive teaching commitments, administration duties and various cross-college activities. We were in some danger of becoming the 'straw' for the camel's back.

What is more significant perhaps, is that staff welcomed an opportunity to discuss the issues of course design and delivery with members of the central support team, relatively unhindered by 'collegial' constraints. A deliberate policy was to distance our team from the 'inspection' function and to act primarily as moderators in the process of negotiation between the practitioners and the managers. This is clearly a difficult role, acting as 'honest brokers' in a field that is fraught with hidden meaning and agendas. After the initial difficulties encountered in providing a suitable framework for implementation, a more 'open' climate of discussion was used to promote the identification of priorities. The action plans of course teams formed the structure of a College Quality Development Action Plan which provides the focus for all evaluative activities within the institution.

Conclusion

Our experience of working with students, teachers and managers in the Birmingham colleges leads us to believe that the root causes of disaffection relate to a feeling of isolation, powerlessness and of being under-valued. The danger lies in an interpretation of the Education Reform Act that reinforces this for staff in colleges and schools. The temptation is to impose a bureaucratic superstructure for accountability that stresses inspection and appraisal at the expense of support and guidance. This would undoubtedly alienate further those members of the profession who are dedicated to the process of reform and improvement. It is only by talking and listening to *all* staff that some commonality of purpose can pervade institutions. There ought to be a belief in the efficacy of the educational process for bringing about change which involves consultation and participation. The factors that lead to commitment are empowerment and ownership, strengthened by the integrity of a support function. In this way, it is essential to recognize and support the relationship between personal, professional and organizational development.

Since the recession of the seventies and early eighties, the City of Birmingham has successfully diversified its economic base and future prospects look good. The mis-match between the current skills of the workforce and projected needs of industry suggest that the focus of education and training is on the colleges' ability to respond. The Education Reform Act (1988) provides a framework for improvement and an opportunity to make the service more 'user-friendly', in a way that is perhaps unprecedented. The dramatic fall in the number of young people available for work in the future provides a stimulus for rethinking the nature and delivery of provision. Without the support of all staff in colleges, this process will be more of a threat than an opportunity, and the survival of FE is jeopardized. The disaffection of staff in colleges must not be a contributory factor to the demise of further education as we know it.

References

BIRMINGHAM CITY COUNCIL (1988) *Celebration of a Centenary*, Birmingham, New Enterprise Publications.

GLEESON, D. and MARDLE, G. (1980) *Further Education or Training? A Case Study in the Theory and Practice of Day Release Education*, London, Routledge and Kegan Paul.

HUTTON, W. (1781) *A History of Birmingham*, Birmingham, Pearson and Rollason.

PEEKE, G. (1983) 'Role Strain in the Further Education College' in Boyd-Barrett,O. *et. al.* (Eds) *Approaches to Post-School Management: A Reader*, London, Harper and Row in Association with the Open University.

TERRY, D. (1987) *The Tertiary College*, Milton Keynes, Open University Press, pp. 57–64.

THEODOSSIN, E. (1986) *In Search of the Responsive College*, Blagdon, Further Education Staff College.

VENABLES, E. (1967) *The Young Worker at College: A Study of a Local Tech.*, London, Faber and Faber.

12
The Competence Race:
We Are All Qualified Now

Lorna Unwin

Introduction

The competence-based National Vocational Qualifications (NVQs), now being introduced in England and Wales, should carry a government health warning. This is not because NVQs are, necessarily, harmful, but because they should be handled with care, particularly by those responsible for the vocational education and training of school leavers. This paper will explore the inherent flaws in NVQs which cause them to be both liberating and confining as vehicles for helping teenagers in Youth Training (YT) achieve their true potential.

The history of vocational education and training in Britain is littered with the corpses of rhetorical statements which once exhorted educators, employers, parents and the government of the day to meet the nation's need for a skilled and adaptable workforce. Increasing unemployment and a decline in manufacturing industry during the 1970s gave greater prominence to the demands for a more accountable education and training system. The political and socio-economic debate surrounding those demands is not the particular concern of this chapter. Any discussion, however, of the design of NVQs and their employment-led foundations should take account of the context, albeit a muddled one, within which they have been developed.

At its most simple level, the goal of Britain's vocational education and training system has been and continues to be the production of employable people who are capable of gaining and developing the skills needed by industry and commerce. The problems begin when one realizes that to achieve this goal, a great deal of attention must be paid to the fact that a significant number of young people are not, for a variety of educational, social and psychological reasons automatically 'trainable' when they leave school. Interestingly, this fact, well known to teachers, trainers and workplace supervisors, is equally applicable to unemployed adults and is one of the reasons why the Employment Training (ET) programme is failing to deliver the pool of skilled labour it promised.

The Case for Personal Effectiveness

In 1981, an MSC report, the New Training Initiative (NTI), noted that there was a 'compelling need for a training system which enables all workers to acquire a basic range of skills and to develop and adapt them throughout their working lives' (NTI, 1981). Its stated objectives, which led to the development of YTS, urged this country to move beyond selective and restrictive apprenticeships to a system which created opportunties for all young people to be trained and educated beyond the school leaving age.

Three years before NTI, the A–Z Survey of employers revealed that the ability to adapt, willingness to work alone, taking responsibility, and other such attributes that have come to be categorized as 'personal effectiveness', formed their description of an ideal recruit to their businesses (ITRU, 1978). Moreover, employers were stressing that if a recruit demonstrated such attributes, his or her level of occupational competence was largely irrelevant for such skills that were needed could be acquired on-the-job or via off-the-job training programmes. The 1978 survey made no distinction between the post-school attainment levels of recruits, but it was recognized by the MSC that many school leavers could not easily meet the employers' requirements.

Turned off by years of academic failure at school, many young people lacked the confidence and motivation needed to made a smooth transition from school to work. A series of unsuccessful and much derided attempts to prepare young people better for that transition followed. Wholescale youth unemployment in the early 1980s, ironically, however, provided the MSC with enough funding to have another go at trying to meet employers' needs, and YTS was introduced.

The original YTS Design Framework created a fluid structure within which young people could grow accustomed to the skills, knowledge and attitudes required in different work settings without having to restrict themselves too early to an occupational specialism. The Further Education Unit at this time was also stressing the need for college courses to broaden their curriculum by introducing a 'common core' which all students would take alongside their vocational and job-specific studies (FEU, 1982 *Basis for Choice*). When YTS was re-launched as a two-year programme in 1986, the MSC translated the original eight curriculum design elements of the one-year scheme into four equally weighted outcomes:

Outcome one: competence in a range of job or occupational skills;

Outcome two: competence in a range of transferable core skills;
Outcome three: ability to transfer skills and knowledge to new situations;
Outcome four: personal effectiveness.

Yet despite giving the four outcomes equal weight, the two-year YTS Design Framework was less a reflection of any commitment to a broad-based vocational curriculum and far more the reflection of a shift away from foundation training towards becoming a much more definite vehicle for achieving vocational qualifications.

All school leavers and, it should be added, adults seeking employment, must, of course, have access to and be encouraged to aim for recognized qualifications. YT offers flexibility in the time allowed to complete a programme: it can be from 18 months to 3 years. Where originally YTS might have provided a breathing space from the certificate race, YT now demands that all trainees work towards a nationally recognized qualification. And, crucially, that qualification must be an NVQ. This means that YT trainees are unlikely to find room in their working or off-the-job training time for anything other than activities which fulfil NVQ Outcome One — competence in a range of job or occupational skills.

From Broad-based Vision to Narrow Focus

Achieving competence in job skills and having those competences recorded are, of course, essential goals for any teenager seeking paid employment. Traditional vocational qualifications with their emphasis on written tests, selective entry and classroom-based study largely ignored the potential of many young people who were capable of demonstrating practical competence but who under-achieved in an academic sense. Figures for trainees leaving YTS between April 1986 and January 1988 reveal that 76.8 per cent did so without gaining any qualification and those qualifications which were gained were mostly at the foundation and basic skills level (Jones, 1988, p. 65).

Now, through the work of the National Council for Vocational Qualifications (NCVQ), there is the chance that a more meaningful system of vocational qualifications can be created. By specifying and concentrating on learning outcomes or competences, that new system facilitates individualized learning by recognizing a person's prior achievements and allowing them to demonstrate further competence in the workplace at their own pace. At the same time, the Training Agency's work on occupational standards development has encouraged areas of British industry such as retailing and cleaning services to introduce vocational qualifications for the first time. Given the high numbers of YT trainees in the retail sector, the introduction of an NVQ for that industry at least offers those young people a chance to enter the qualification race.

Access to qualifications should be significantly broadened, however, through the central design feature of the NCVQ Framework. NCVQ have separated qualifications from the learning process by stating that NVQ awards:

> should be free from any barriers which restrict access to them and should be independent of the mode of learning. This is made possible by the form of an NVQ, which is independent of any education or training programme which may be provided to develop competence;

> upper and lower age limits, except where legal restraints make this necessary. Assessment for the award of NVQs should be open to people of all ages;

> a specified period of time to be spent in education, training or work before the award can be made. NVQs should not prescribe the time taken to acquire competence. This recognises the considerable variation in the time individuals take to learn, depending on their starting point, learning opportunities, aptitude and motivation.
>
> (NCVQ, 1989, p. 8)

In effect, any organization be it a college, company, private training centre or voluntary body can now register with an awarding body and begin assessing people for NVQ units of competence. Where once employers would have had to decide which employees it could afford to send out for further education and training, they can now develop their in-house arrangements and fit training much more closely to the needs of the company. For employees, this presents opportunities to gain credit for competence acquired on-the-job and less need to demonstrate ability in an academic setting.

There are, however, inherent problems with this new approach to vocational qualifications which could, if not monitored carefully, wipe out the very positive benefits that all learners stand to gain as the new system takes shape. Firstly, the emphasis at Level One on practical, routine tasks means that YT trainees could find their training severely restricted to a minimal amount of on-the-job instruction. This is compounded by 1989 changes to the YTS procedures which gave managing agents much greater flexibility in their interpretation of how on and off-the-job training time is to be allocated. Secondly, employers can now select from the lists of competences those which are immediately relevant to their company needs and so prevent employees from gaining a full NVQ. Thirdly, by encouraging private organizations to become deliverers of NVQs, the new system is forcing colleges to compete in the market-place. Colleges have, of course, much room for improvement, but in order to compete with private training centres and employers' in-house training arrangements, they have to demonstrate that their programmes are tightly vocationally orientated. Departments or individual lecturers who wish to provide space for activities whose vocational relevance may not appear immediately obvious, may find they have a tough battle on their hands.

This chapter is not advocating a return to the previously unstructured, often tokenistic attempts at promoting personal development found in some personal effectiveness programmes (alternatively labelled 'life and social skills'; 'world outside work') or the free-wheeling general studies lessons offered to day-release students. The content found in these attempts to bridge liberal education and vocational training was often well-meaning but ultimately patronizing to young people and relied too much on the personal interests of the teachers and trainers. YT trainees, of course, demonstrate their feelings by rejecting or suffering under protest any attempts to broaden their vocational curriculum and demand to be taught only that which is directly relevant to their current or future employment needs. Herein lies the paradox. The challenge is to find appropriate methods for encouraging young people to fulfil their potential both in and outside work, but not at the same time to be guilty of dishing out what is thought to be good for them.

During the first quarter of 1989, I spoke to a sample of YTS trainees and their tutors at a college of further education in the West Midlands. I also spoke to four local employers who provide work placements for trainees with poor school records or who have been rejected by other employers. It was clear from that sample that YT cannot afford to concentrate solely on Outcome One, but must take its other three outcomes more seriously in order to tackle the following issues:

- Many 16 year olds still have little knowledge or understanding of the world of work they are likely to find themselves in;
- Many 16 year olds have only a vague idea of the type of job they would like;
- Many still require help with basic skills;
- Some YT trainees experience disturbing social and domestic problems which affect their progress during their time on YT and this leads to changes of employer;

- Jobs which appeared to be glamorous and exciting often prove to be boring and routine;
- Trainees can be pressurized by their parents to choose a particular occupational route and lack the confidence or courage to change to the job of their choice;
- Despite many changes to the school curriculum, 16 year olds often find it difficult to work on their own and show the sort of initiative which employers demand;
- Years of failure at school results in a sense of personal worthlessness which encourages trainees to believe they are only capable of acquiring very basic skills at work.

The employers I spoke to reiterated the findings of the 1978 A–Z Survey and stressed the need to view YTS in its original broad-based format. They regarded any attempt by fellow employers to restrict training to specific on-the-job skills as short-sighted given the need for most businesses to diversify and make more use of technology.

If trainees are expected to concentrate purely on achieving a vocational qualification from the start of their period on YT, both trainees and employers stand to lose. Adequate space must be found within in any post-school training scheme to allow trainees to find a suitable occupational route, and, of equal importance, to develop self-confidence and the necessary maturity to make their own decisions. Such developments may require movement between employers in order to sample a range of occupations and types of company. Some trainees progress well in small work placements, working closely with one or two people, while others thrive in the less personal atmosphere of a large company where they can mix with employees of different ages and backgrounds. Adapting to working life brings trainees face-to-face with difficult issues such as discrimination, hierarchical structures and a sense of loss in being separated from school friends. If the space for personal growth is denied to trainees, they are likely to become quickly disenchanted. One trainee said to me:

> When I started YTS I wanted to work hard and get taken on full-time. I couldn't be bothered with the communication skills and that sort of stuff they gave us at college. I wanted to stay at work learning how to do my job better. Now I can do the job standing on my head but the boss won't let me try other jobs in the factory. I really miss just talking to other trainees and I miss my tutor because at least she listened.

For the employer, concentration on selected work-based competences may give them compliant drones but at the expense of a more confident group of employees able to demonstrate initiative and the ability to make well-founded decisions.

In their study of YTS in the clothing industry, Steedman and Wagner (1989) warn against the narrow focus which YT is now adopting. Although their comments relate specifically to the clothing industry, they are pertinent for most of manufacturing industry:

> On past trends there is every likelihood that some of those at present employed in the clothing industry will eventually need to seek work in a different occupational sector. Training which helps to raise general educational standards, and enables trainees to acquire broad technical knowledge and understanding, would provide the base for a more flexible and better informed vocational development; and it would ease the transition — should it be necessary — to other forms of skilled employment. In short: in an industry with contracting employment opportunities the limited years which a young person has available for training must be fully used to acquire broad competences, and it is a grave error of social policy for young people to be channelled towards training in an unduly narrow range of practical operations.
>
> (Steedman and Wagner, 1989, p. 48)

Steedman and Wagner compare youth training in the UK clothing industry with its German equivalent and find the former to be far more narrowly focused. This country has been compared unfavourably with its foreign competitors and EC partners for a long time, but those who are encouraging the current wholescale narrowing of the YTS Design Framework would do well to take another look at the German engineering industry.

In order to cope with the challenge of 1992 and adapt to an ever-changing industrial context, the Germans have rewritten the aims for their engineering apprentices and now expect trainees to be able to:

— use the acquired occupational competence in different enterprises and industries, as well as in generically related skilled work — if necessary after acquiring additional skills;
— position him/herself flexibly to work new structures, methods of production and technologies, with the aim of maintaining occupational competence;
— take part in continuing education and retraining in order to retain occupational competence and mobility (Fonda and Hayes, 1989, p. 116).

No doubt conscious of criticism about the narrow focus which its Framework has inspired, NCVQ is now encouraging 'the introduction of generic units to assist those with responsibility for national standards of performance to provide for breadth of application' (NCVQ, 1989, p. 4). NCVQ see these generic units falling into two categories:

1. fundamental aspects of competence, such as numeracy, communication, problem-solving and planning, required in many occupational activities;
2. common occupational activities, such as computing, supervision/management and foreign languages. (ibid)

Those readers familiar with the YTS Core, or indeed other cores included in pre-vocational certificates, will no doubt recognize much that is similar in the NCVQ's statements above. It is too early to tell how the Council will succeed in encouraging awarding bodies to broaden their qualifications to encompass generic units or how assessors will cope with the problems of assessing such competences as problem-solving and planning in the workplace.

We're All Qualified Now

Any change in the qualification system should be about empowerment for young people and adults alike. Access to vocational qualifications has been, and in some cases where an NVQ has yet to be introduced still is, restricted to people holding GCSEs or equivalents. The content, too, of traditional qualifications is restrictive and gives no recognition for basic skills acquired on-the-job. For those tutors and trainers working with YT trainees who previously fell outside the qualifications net, NVQs offer a lifeline to a world of certificates and awards which many of us take for granted. Trainees working in, for example, fast food shops, garages and on building sites carrying out routine tasks, can now gain credit for their ability by having each individual element of competence recorded. In time, having accumulated enough elements, they may acquire a complete qualification which will have national currency. For tutors and trainers, this facility to recognize each competence as it is achieved rather than having to pass or fail trainees on their performance in much larger chunks of skills and knowledge, provides the motivational tool they have been seeking. Instead of progress being simply recorded on a form, tutors and trainers can now see that progress translated into real credits towards, say, a City and Guilds, BTEC or RSA qualification

Collecting credits can, however, become an end in itself rather than a means to an end. There is a danger that in pushing young people on to a qualification treadmill, we force them to cling on regardless of how suitable to the chosen occupational route because falling off would mean a return to their previous unqualified status.

References

FONDA, N. and HAYES, C. (1988) 'Education, Training and Business Performance', *Oxford Review of Economic Policy*, 4, 3.

FURTHER EDUCATION UNIT, (1982) *A Basis for Choice.* 2nd edition, London, FEU.

INDUSTRIAL TRAINING RESEARCH UNIT (1978) *The A–Z Survey*, Cambridge, ITRU.

JONES, I. (1988) 'An Evaluation of YTS', *Oxford Review of Economic Policy*, 4, 3.

MANPOWER SERVICES COMMISSION (1981) *A New Training Initiative: An Agenda for Action*, Sheffield, MSC.

NCVQ (1989) *National Vocational Qualifications: Criteria and Procedures*, London.

STEEDMAN, H. and WAGNER, K. (1989) 'Productivity, Machinery and Skills: Clothing Manufacture in Britain and Germany', *National Institute Economic Review.*

Notes on Contributors

Colin Carnie is Manager of Burnside Day Centre in the London Borough of Redbridge. Since the early 1950s, he has worked with people with learning difficulties, as a nurse, in medical welfare and as a college lecturer. He is a member of the Assessment Panel for the Polytechnic of East London Certificate in Social Service Training.

Lynne Chapman is a Development Officer at Skill: the National Bureau for Students with Disabilities. She is also a trained personal counsellor and herself has a disability. Among her recent articles for *Educare*, the journal of the National Bureau for Students with Disabilities, are 'The provision of in-house disability awareness training for staff in colleges' (26, 1986) and 'Disabling Services' (31, 1988).

Graham Clark, Roy Pinney and David Shepherdson are all members of the Quality Development Team for Continuing Education in the City of Birmingham. The team have been working together with the Further Education colleges in the city, developing and implementing a positive approach to quality development which emphasizes self evaluation within an institutional context. They have all recently taught in further education colleges, as well as in schools, higher education and adult education. Research interests include management performance in colleges, personal and social development and organizational culture. All have a keen interest in the group processes and experiential learning, especially in the context of staff development and teacher training.

Jenny Corbett is a Senior Lecturer in Special Education at the Polytechnic of East London. She has a particular interest in further education and training. In 1989, she published 'Choices After 16' for the Open University Special Needs course, E241. Her doctoral research was a case study of 'Integration in Further Education'. Currently she is investigating curricular issues relating to independent living, school/college link courses and perceptions of people with special needs in training programmes.

Maggie Hollingsworth was the In-Service Co-ordinator for the London Borough of Haringey. She has worked with post–16 students and as an advisory teacher with the Inner London Education Authority Further Education Service. She has a special interest in educational disadvantage and experiential learning.

Alan Hurst is Principal Lecturer in Education Studies and Adviser for students with special educational needs at Lancashire Polytechnic, Preston. His particular areas of research interest are the sociology of disability and disability in higher education. His doctoral research is entitled 'Higher Education and Disabled Students: Individual and Institutional Perspectives'.

David Hutchinson is Director of Training and Staff Development at North Nottinghamshire College of Further Education. His areas of interest include psychology, special educational needs and staff development. His publications include 'Teaching Students with Special Needs in Further Education' (1979) and 'Transition to Adulthood' (1986), both of which were co-authored, 'Work Preparation for the Handicapped' (1982) and 'Supporting Transitions to Adulthood' (1990).

Paul Jeffcutt is a Lecturer in Organisational Behaviour at the University of Stirling. Whilst a Lecturer in Post-Compulsory Education at Southampton University, he was editor of the Post Compulsory Education Papers series. He publishes regularly on matters relating to management and organization. His doctoral research is called 'Persistence and Change in an Organisational Culture: A Longitudinal Study of a Retraining Scheme for the Female Adult Unemployed'.

Brendan Major is a Lecturer at Haringey Community College, North London. He initially trained and worked as a carpenter and joiner before taking qualifications in music and sociology. He is a member of the Institute of Carpenters and, currently, Assistant Regional Secretary (Outer London) for the National Association of Teachers in Further and Higher Education (NATFHE). He has a particular interest in students with special educational needs.

Lorna Unwin is a Lecturer in Post-Compulsory Education at the Open University and has previously taught in further and adult education. She has extensive experience of staff development in industry and has been a consultant for training programmes. She has a special research interest in the assessment of work-based learning and employer involvement. She is co-author of a staff training pack 'Delivering NVQs' (Open University, 1989).

Derek Wheeler is a store manager for Marks and Spencer. He is currently seconded as Director of the West London Compact, an educational initiative which brings employers and schools together. He has managed several Marks and Spencer stores in the London area and was responsible for the training and development of management and supervisory staff in the south-eastern division of the company.

Anne Wilkinson is an Assistant Education Officer in Further Education, in Hertfordshire. She was formerly a lecturer in further education, where she worked with students experiencing a wide range of needs in a multi-cultural, inner-city area.

Index